Interviews from the Edge

Interviews from the Edge

50 Years of Conversations about Writing and Resistance

Edited by
Mark Yakich and John Biguenet

BLOOMSBURY ACADEMIC
NEW YORK • LONDON • OXFORD • NEW DELHI • SYDNEY

BLOOMSBURY ACADEMIC
Bloomsbury Publishing Inc
1385 Broadway, New York, NY 10018, USA
50 Bedford Square, London, WC1B 3DP, UK

BLOOMSBURY, BLOOMSBURY ACADEMIC and the Diana logo are
trademarks of Bloomsbury Publishing Plc

First published in the United States of America 2019

Cover design by Alice Marwick
Photograph © Shutterstock/Roman Sigaev

A catalog record for this book is available from the Library of Congress.

ISBN: HB: 978-1-5013-4747-4
PB: 978-1-5013-4745-0
ePDF: 978-1-5013-4748-1
eBook: 978-1-5013-4746-7

Typeset by Deanta Global Publishing Services, Chennai, India
Printed and bound in the United States of America

To find out more about our authors and books visit www.bloomsbury.com
and sign up for our newsletters.

CONTENTS

Introduction

Mark Yakich is the Gregory F. Curtin, S. J., Distinguished Professor of English at Loyola University New Orleans, where he has been editor of *New Orleans Review* since 2012.

John Biguenet is the Robert Hunter Distinguished University Professor at Loyola University New Orleans. He worked as a student intern on the first issue of *New Orleans Review* in 1968 and edited the magazine from 1980 to 1992.

MARK YAKICH: The interviews in this book are selected from fifty years of *New Orleans Review* (*NOR*), the literary magazine published by the English department at Loyola University. You were there at the very beginning—1968. What was it like to be a student at Loyola and to be working on the magazine?

JOHN BIGUENET: The hiring of novelist John William Corrington as chair of English and poet Miller Williams as the founding editor of *NOR* established a new emphasis on creative writing at Loyola. The journal signaled a new direction, as well, both for the English department and the university with its focus on the interdisciplinary and the international, thanks in part to Miller's academic training as a biologist and his interest in literary translation. Interviews of Ernest Gaines and Joseph Heller appeared beside early work by Joyce Carol Oates and Annie Dillard as well as translations of César Vallejo and José Augustín Goytisolo—but also beside a scientific article on "The Nature of Light." The sense of excitement about the new magazine mirrored, of course, the social and artistic tumult of the late 1960s. With its commitment to social justice, Loyola attracted students who were deeply committed to the civil rights and the anti-war movements. The journal did not ignore the issues rending the nation, even soliciting an essay on "The American Challenge" from Hubert Humphrey, who had lost the 1968 presidential election to Richard Nixon. *New Orleans Review* began at a moment of great anxiety and great vitality but most importantly at a moment of great change.

YAKICH: As I went digging into the back issues, I was struck by the internationalism you just highlighted. There are volumes devoted to specific countries and regions—"New British Writing," "Latin American Issue," "Czech Writing After the Velvet Revolution." Aside from a few relatively recent venues, like *Words Without Borders* and *Guernica*, such appreciation of non-U.S. writing rarely makes it into the pages of literary journals. Do you think *NOR*'s history here is due to various editors' predilections or is there something else going on?

BIGUENET: Literary translation, especially by poets, was another expression of the changes roiling traditions and institutions in the 1960s. *Modern Poetry in Translation* was founded by Ted Hughes and Daniel Weissbort in 1965, for example, and in 1967 Rainer Schulte started *Mundus Artium*, a journal dedicated to the publication of translated literature. When *NOR* began publishing in 1968, it was part of this movement to explore foreign literatures. So widespread was this impulse that by the end of the decade Jean Garrigue edited a book in 1970 entitled *Translations by American Poets* that included translations by more than forty major American poets. But if *NOR* was part of a larger movement in publishing translations, it was one of the first literary journals to include coverage of film, such as our early interviews of Lina Wertmüller and Bertrand Tavernier. Even today, half a century later, how many literary magazines engage contemporary cinema with the same focus they bring to literature?

YAKICH: From its inception, *NOR* seemed interested in offering its readers a broader conversation than traditional journals had up to that point.

BIGUENET: Yes, we described ourselves as a magazine of discovery, both in introducing new writers and also in introducing new areas of coverage for a literary magazine. This sense of discovery extended to art and even to the design of the magazine, which has undergone radical transformation over the last fifty years, especially under your editorship.

YAKICH: Design has always fascinated me—especially the interplay between text and image, which is what all book and magazine covers must negotiate. Diving into our past issues, I found fabulous covers, as well as interior art portfolios, by José-Maria

Cundin, Rufino Tamayo, Martin Chambi, Franco Alessandrini, Helen Escobedo, Lila Katzen, Athena Tacha, and Lee Crum, among many others. This was all quite something to live up to, I felt, when I became editor in 2012.

I quickly realized, however, two things. First, the depth and breadth of the writing and art in *NOR*'s archive deserved a wider readership; and so we began making back issues available as free pdfs on our website. The second was that, on the whole, literary print magazine publishing was evolving. In the late 1990s, I had been assistant to Andrei Codrescu working on his infamous *Exquisite Corpse*, a journal that largely defied prevailing trends. *The Corpse*, as it was affectionately called, had a trim size of six inches by fifteen inches so that it not only could be read easily, with one hand while standing on the NYC subway (Andrei's notion), but that it also made a striking literary object even if it was printed solely in black and white on cheap bright white paper. In heading up *NOR*, I envisioned the print issue to be a similarly valued object— one that no reader or contributor would toss in the recycling bin a few months after its printing. We changed the print issue to a smaller, stocky, nearly square trim size, used a single designer adept at collaging word and image, and began reimagining what a literary magazine could offer. My first issue was a set of five chapbooks devoted to long-form prose and brief poetry collections. Later issues included another set of chapbooks—this time housed in a glossy slipcase—and themed issues on science fiction, Shakespeare, and contemporary writing from Africa.

BIGUENET: But despite the evolution of the journal over the decades, one of the surprisingly consistent elements from the start has been interviews, at first with novelists, poets, and film directors but then with critics and activists as well.

YAKICH: Even amid the literary and cultural stand-out works— from local legends like John Kennedy Toole to international icons like Pablo Neruda—I kept returning to the interviews. They are full of fascinating takes by creators on their creations, whether it's Jorge Luis Borges genuinely asking, "Who would make a living out of my literature? Nobody can," or it's Sheila Heti commenting, "I just think there's something so strange about the idea that a person writes alone. You don't raise yourself, you don't kill the food you eat, you don't educate yourself." But what I found both surprising and invigorating were the insights interviewees had on social and political issues, relevant not just to the past but to today. For instance, James Baldwin: "It didn't occur to me to be audacious. It occurred to me, first of all, to be very frightening. Rather than audacity, it involved a great deal of humility to use myself as a witness, which is different from an example, to the condition of others who are in your condition but cannot speak—or cannot be heard."

BIGUENET: Yes, the interview is a surprisingly flexible form. Some are basically backstage tours of the creative process—for instance, when Baldwin recounts the researching and writing of *The Evidence of Things Not Seen*. But others are about the moral backdrop of a writer's work; it's still shocking to read why, in 1969, Ernest Gaines felt he could live in San Francisco but not back home in Louisiana or why, in 1971, Joseph Heller might condone acts of violence in protesting the war in Vietnam. And still others are master classes. There's much to learn from John Ashbery's consideration of the sestina as a liberating form versus the sonnet as "too loose to have this liberating effect" or Susan Bernofsky's explanation of how to avoid footnotes in a literary translation. Among the most engaging are those that shift between anecdote and argument—when Jack Gilbert, for example, argues for the primacy of love over literature by using the time he spent on a pleasure barge in Kashmir as evidence of his assertion. Then there are the personal and professional autobiographies that emerge in conversation—Eudora Welty's and Luisa Valenzuela's come to mind. But the interview is also a form that inspires moments of charming insight, such as when Borges reviews Anglo-Saxon, Greek, French, German, and Spanish terms for the moon and the sun and the sky and concludes that the English word for each is actually the best.

YAKICH: Each interview has an idiosyncratic arc that is both delightful and unpredictable. This may have to do with the form itself—the question and answer, the call and response—that goes back to the origins of literature as well as politics. It's not only that dialogue is crucial to inquiry and fleshing out issues, but that it's improvisational in its back and forth movement, often yielding a collaborative unexpectedness that is uncommon in other literary genres such fiction, poetry, or essays.

BIGUENET: The interview is our only literary form that by definition is composed collaboratively—except, in a sense, for translation. Translators, though, are more likely to describe their work as a performance of a score than as a collaboration: just as Glenn Gould's recordings of *The Goldberg Variations* do not alter a single note of Bach's composition, neither does Arthur Golding's translation of *Metamorphoses* revise a word of Ovid's Latin text. So a translation can be understood as a reading of a work of literature, which is why we admit the possibility of retranslation. But the idea of recomposition—we don't even have a word for it, really—strikes us as ridiculous.

YAKICH: Borges makes that clear in his witty story "Pierre Menard, Author of the Quixote."

BIGUENET: Yes, we can't actually describe what Menard has done to the two chapters by Cervantes in repeating them word for word. The story does remind us that a translator shares with the interviewer a kind of modesty that we might describe as transparency; both serve merely as a lens through which another's words are focused. The difference, of course, is that the interviewer teases out, perhaps inspires, those words through questions. The interviewer conducts, as you say, an improvisation even while deferring to the subject of the interview. But those deferential questions often push past clever evasions to the very edge of belief. This joint composition can prompt a statement stripped of the artifice that distinguishes a work of literature from ordinary speech and brings us to a naked admission of intent. The interviewer and the interviewee engage in a conversation that is as much duel as duet, one that often takes place on the border between art and life.

YAKICH: That border—that edge—is precisely what I find vital in our media-driven times. When so much is, or appears to be, fraught at the national and international level, it is encouraging to read how these writers and activists are able to navigate their interior lives in the wider world. Toward the end of my interview with Sister Helen Prejean, we talk about "presence" and "the moment"—the moment of our interview itself as well as any moment shared between two people in honest interaction. Sister Helen says, "We give ourselves over to it [the moment], and see what flowers from it." Then she alludes to the fact that our in-person conversation will later be recounted, or translated, into a text: "To write something good that's going to refer to something bigger than both of us." It occurs to me now that the interviewer and interviewee share a potentiality that is not unlike that of the reader and writer. In the following pages, both readers and writers will find much to commiserate with, to enjoy, and to be inspired by.

Ernest J. Gaines

Interviewed by Gregory Fitz Gerald
and Peter Marchant
(1969)

Ernest J. Gaines, child of a Louisiana plantation, won a Wallace Stegner Creative Writing Fellowship to Stanford in 1958 and the following year received the Joseph Henry Jackson Literary Award. Atheneum published *Catherine Cormier,* his first novel, in 1964; his second, *Of Love and Dust*, was published in 1967 by Dial Press, who brought out in 1968 to considerable acclaim his collection of stories, *Bloodline*. Mr. Gaines now lives in San Francisco, where he is at work on his third novel, once more utilizing the Louisiana plantation setting he knows so well.

This conversation results from Mr. Gaines's appearance in February 1969 on the Writers Forum program at the State University of New York, College at Brockport. With Mr. Gaines are Gregory Fitz Gerald, Director of the Forum, and Peter Marchant, author of *Give Me Your Answer Do.*

NEW ORLEANS REVIEW: I have been reading your remarkable novel *Of Love and Dust*. Can you tell us what inspires a book such as this?

ERNEST J. GAINES: I don't know when the idea of *Of Love and Dust* came into my mind; I really don't know. But here are a couple of things which led up to my writing it: my hobby is collecting records—when I have the money to do so; I collect jazz records, the spiritual, folk music, and blues, especially the rural blues of the Negro. I was listening to one of Lightnin' Hopkins records one day entitled "Mr. Tim Moore's Farm." Lightnin'

Hopkins is one of the great blues singers of this country and someone I consider a worthwhile poet. As I was listening to his "Mr. Tim Moore's Farm," one of the verses of the song struck me. It went something like this: "The worst thing this black man ever done, when I moved my wife and family to Mr. Tim Moore's Farm. Mr. Tim Moore's man never stand and grin, say if you keep out the graveyard, nigger, I'll keep you out the pen." Now, a period of about ten years passed between the time I first heard that record and the time I started writing my novel *Of Love and Dust*, but I remember that verse.

NOR: You said there were "a couple of things" that led to the novel?

GAINES: Yes. Hearing "Mr. Tim Moore's Farm" was one. The other was something that happened to me a couple of years later. I was visiting some of my people in Baton Rouge, Louisiana, in 1958, and a friend of mine and I went to a bar out in the country. This is the same parish in Louisiana that Rap Brown comes from; this is the same parish in Louisiana from which James Farmer in 1963 escaped a lynch mob by riding in the back of a hearse disguised as a dead man. My friend and I went to this bar, and in this bar I saw a fight between two young men. This bar is surrounded by fields— cane, corn, cotton—and most of the people who come here are from the country or from small towns not very far away. They come to drink; they come to dance; they come to gamble; they come to fight; they come to steal your woman; they come to steal your man; they come knowing they might end up in jail that night, but still they come. They come to forget the hard work in the fields all week; they come to forget, to forget, and to forget, and they're ready to accept whatever fate is awaiting them. If nothing terrible happens, then the night has been somewhat of a success; if something bad does happen, then these things are expected in a bar such as this one. So it was here that I saw the knife-fight between the two young men. Fortunately for both, the fight was stopped before either was fatally wounded. Now, when I saw this fight, just as when I heard the record by Lightnin' Hopkins, I had no idea that either event would eventually lead into writing *Of Love and Dust*, or writing anything else. There was a period of eight or ten years between those events and the time I wrote one word of the book.

NOR: It took this long for your first novel to get under way?

GAINES: It took that time—but it was not my first novel. Hardly, during that time I wrote at least four other novels. Only one, *Catherine Cormier,* was published. I wrote at least two dozen short stories, of which only six were published. I had been writing all the time. But now it was early spring of '66. I had very little money; I had practically no money at all; I had been sponging off my friends and my brothers for drinks, and I had not bought one drink for them in over a year. I had not given my poor mother a birthday present, a Christmas present, or a Mother's Day present in over two years. My girl had dropped me quite a while ago—a normal thing, I feel, when a man is unable to buy a hamburger in a place like McDonald's. I needed the money; I needed money badly. But I didn't want to go out on an eight-hour-day job that would take me from my writing.

I wanted the money, but I wanted to earn it by my writing and by writing only. Now, if that was the case, I had to get something done. There had to be another novel in me somewhere that a publisher would accept. I don't know how the tune "Mr. Tim Moore's Farm" got back into my mind; maybe I heard it played again; I really don't know. Or maybe when I went back to Baton Rouge in 1965 and visited that same bar in the country that I had visited in '58, I saw something there that began to stir my imagination. Anyhow, in early spring of 1966 I got started on the novel. I started with these two ideas: "Tim Moore's man never stand and grin, say if you keep out the graveyard, nigger, I'll keep you out the pen"—that, and with the fight between the two young men in the bar. So all right, I had two ideas, but where did I go from there?

NOR: To construct your plot? Did that come quickly?

GAINES: The plot—the story anyway. I kept asking myself, where do I go? Where, where, where: I kept asking myself. Then things began to fall into place. I was born on a Louisiana plantation in 1933, and I left from there in 1948. The novel takes place in the summer of '48. But during those fifteen years, I had learned a lot about plantation life and about the people who lived in that part of Louisiana. I knew that Mr. Tim Moore's man, whom Lightnin' Hopkins sang about, didn't necessarily have to be an overseer on a farm in Texas; he could be a Cajun overseer on a plantation in Louisiana. I knew that my young man in the bar could have landed on that plantation if he had killed that other boy in the knife-fight.

So I had him kill the boy, and I had the owner of the plantation bond him out of jail.

In this way, I brought my young killer to the plantation. But where would things go from there? I had a good starting point, but was that enough? What am I going to do with my young killer? He's no plantation worker; he's not even a country boy; he's from the city, Baton Rouge. He's a playboy. He's a lover. And he hates authority, especially when this authority is given out by a Cajun whom he considers white trash. So what am I going to do with these two people? I have two people on my hands who will never— can't ever—get along with each other. What am I going to do with them? Let me see now. Let me see. My young killer is going to be here five, seven, maybe ten years of his life. He will need a woman. Yes, yes, he will need a woman, and she will be my third character. Now he must start looking for that woman, but he doesn't want just any woman, no, not a lover as himself; he wants the most beautiful woman on that plantation. But when he finds her, he finds that he can't have her. And why not? Because she is the overseer's mistress.

My imagination really starts moving when I start writing!

NOR: May I ask you a question? Your material dealing with the brutal white overseer and the black man is very hot political stuff. At the same time, you're writing about blacks and whites who are people first, who only happen to be black and white. One feels sorry for them, and at the same time one laughs at them. Do you possibly get this from the Russians?

GAINES: Maybe I do. My first heroes, I suppose, were the Russian writers. I think they have influenced many writers.

NOR: What attracts you to the Russian writers? Is it their sense of the soil, of being close to the earth, to the people?

GAINES: I think so. I think the thing I recognize in Russian writers, especially when they're writing about the peasant, is some of the same sort of thing that I've experienced in the southern part of the United States. I've gotten this from Tolstoy, Chekhov, and Turgenev much more than I've gotten it out of the white American writers who deal with the same sort of thing. When the white writers are writing about the blacks of the fields, they seem to make them caricatures rather than real people, but the Russian writers made their peasants real. I felt that they did. I suppose this is why I've studied them and loved them so much.

NOR: I'd like to know how you happened to discover the Russians.

GAINES: Once I started reading, I used to read everything, and I suppose I just stumbled on them. Turgenev's *Fathers and Children* was first. This was in the library at Vallejo, California (when I first came to California I was living in Vallejo) and I read it. What I read I liked, and from then on I went for the Russians.

NOR: You mentioned Vallejo, and also the fact that you were born in Louisiana. What about those early years? Were you a plantation worker?

GAINES: I went into the fields when I was about the age of eight, or maybe nine. I think my first job was picking up potatoes—white potatoes—we called them Irish potatoes. I worked for about 50 cents a day, and stayed there until I was fifteen. So, by the time I left for California, I knew a lot about the work and life on a plantation. For instance, in the novel, I mentioned having the plantation owner bond my young killer out of jail and putting him to work in his field. This was a normal thing in the 1940s. Some of our best Southern gentlemen did it; this was still going on in the 1950s. And as late as 1963, when I was in Louisiana, a friend of mine pointed out a black youth who had killed another black youth and had been bonded out and put to work only a few days later. The only catch here— when the prisoner, the convict, found himself bonded out of jail— was that he usually spent twice as much time on the plantation than he would have spent in the penitentiary. Many times he found himself working just as hard, and maybe even harder, and there was nothing he could do about it, because the day he decided to run, the white man was going to put the sheriff on his trail again. So when I brought my young killer to the plantation, I knew the kind of house he would have to live in; I had lived there fifteen years myself. I knew the kind of food he would eat; the same kind that I had eaten. I knew the kind of clothes he would wear, because I had worn the khaki and denim clothes myself. I knew the work he would have to do. I knew the people he would come into contact with day in and day out.

I had many other experiences, of course, I went to the one-room schoolhouse . . .

NOR: That's the background, isn't it, for much of your fiction? Is it not the same schoolhouse that we see in your story "A Long Day in November"?

GAINES: Yes, it's the same school I went to, yes.

NOR: How did you make the transition from plantation worker to fiction writer? When did you begin to write?

GAINES: When I went to California—I hadn't tried to write until then. But I was terribly lonely for my friends and relatives. And as I said, I went into the libraries to read. And I read and read, but I did not see myself and my friends and family and relatives in the stuff that I did read. I didn't see us in the Southern writers. I didn't even see myself in the Russian writers, although the Russians came close. So I began to try to do it myself and, of course, I went back to my childhood to write about. I suppose that most writers, when they first start out, try to write about their childhood, and this is what I did. And I'm still sticking to it. On and off, it's been about twenty years, I suppose, that I've been trying to write now. Professionally, I think that I've been writing since about '57. By "professionally" I mean writing every day—four or five hours a day. Every day, since '57.

NOR: Do you see yourself as a humorist at all?

GAINES: I don't tell jokes. Whenever I do tell a joke, no one laughs. So I'm not a joke-teller. My brother is, but not myself. I think I am more of a listener, really. I listen. I like to listen to the way that people talk, and I like to listen to their stories. Then when I get into a little room some place, I try to write them down. Just like a man hearing a song some place, and he's afraid to sing out on the street or someplace else, but when he gets into a bathroom, he starts singing, and he thinks that he's the greatest in the world. But this is what I do in writing, I go to a little room; I go to my little desk, and try to write something down. But I'm no storyteller, I'm only a listener.

NOR: But your work is not without humor. It seems very difficult now for a black writer to write about whites and blacks in a way that's funny, provoking an easy laughter. Yet you manage to do it.

GAINES: No, I don't think it is so difficult. As I said, my brother tells jokes about whites and blacks all the time, and he can make them very funny. A story can be tragic, and he can make it very funny. You see, where I came from, my people were sharecroppers. After the land was turned over from the plantation system, it was turned into a sharecropping system, so my uncles and my father were sharecroppers. Their competitors were the Cajuns, the white people there. The people you make fun of more are the people who are closer to you. So when my people had to make fun of something, when they had to laugh, they made fun of the whites. You always make fun of your competitors. They are the people very close to you. And we had this relationship all the time. I saw these people, the Cajuns, every day; we went to the same store, but we could not drink in the same room. They didn't allow that. But we bought our food at the same place, and we talked to each other going to and from the fields. All this was going on. And the Cajuns have this distinct way of speaking, with this French accent, it's a broken accent. Of course, we could not speak English any better than they could speak French, but we thought they sounded very funny. And I suppose when my own people would speak French using the Creole accent, we sounded as foolish and funny to the Cajuns as they did to us. But still we laughed, and I'm sure they laughed at us also.

NOR: Mr. Gaines, do you feel alienated in any way from your people in Louisiana—the people you grew up with—now that you are living in San Francisco?

GAINES: No, I don't. I keep going back to Louisiana to see the people all the time. Some I cannot communicate with, others I can. In a bar over a drink, you can talk to almost anybody. We could talk about old times.

NOR: These are the people who appear in your fiction. I recognize them. What strikes me as being rather remarkable about them is that in an age when contemporary characters in fiction are so anti-heroic, your characters are sympathetic or empathic. How do you account for your mode of writing outside the vein of what seems to be so popular with many contemporary writers?

GAINES: Well, as I've said before, I've never read about my people in fiction, and before I can make them anti-heroes, I have to try to give them some good qualities. I don't read too much contemporary fiction. I don't follow these writers' ideas too much, I suppose.

NOR: Then you feel that contemporary fiction has had relatively little effect on your own work?

GAINES: Oh, yes, I suppose. I haven't stopped reading contemporary fiction altogether, but I don't read it daily, or weekly, or anything like that. I still read Hemingway. I'll pick up a Hemingway book anytime to read a story or a novel. I'll pick up Faulkner, too. Someone like this I'll read all the time.

NOR: I'm wondering about another element of your background. You have suggested that you're interested in jazz music. Do you think that it has been an influence on the development of your work?

GAINES: I think jazz is basically folk music. Originally it was, though I'm not sure what they're doing with it now. And folk music is a very simple thing. All folk music is very, very simple. Listening to jazz, I find simple rhythms, simple repetitions. In order to communicate jazz to the layman it has to be simple and, of course, these musicians were playing to people just like themselves, uneducated people. I wish to reach the same sort of thing in my fiction, to use the simplest terms in the world, you know, terms like *Jesus wept*; I think that's the simplest statement you can make. It's probably the most beautiful two-word sentence that has ever been written. It has all the meanings in the world in it. Another thing about jazz is that to be impressive, it has to be repetitive. You get hooked upon a phrase and you stay with that phrase until you have really convinced the people.

NOR: In some of the stories in your new collection, *Bloodline*, I notice that you tell the story not only in the first person, but from the point-of-view of a child. This poses, of course, certain problems for the writer. Could you tell us how you came to write so convincingly from the point-of-view of a five-year-old in "A Long Day in November," and from that of an eight-year-old in "The Sky Is Gray?"

GAINES: I suppose we have all been children once, and the knowledge of the child's viewpoint is perhaps something that was buried down in my subconscious since that time. In each story, I've myself gone through much of the same experience as these kids have, not all but much of it. This was in me all the time, but I had to find a way to bring it out. Both Joyce and Faulkner helped me to do it. In the first part of Faulkner's *The Sound and the Fury*, the Benjy part, Benjy uses the simplest terms to express his feelings: "the gate is cold," "the fire is good," "I stamped my shoes on," all this sort of thing. This childlike section is so convincing that I really fell in love with it. I really did. At the same time that I was reading Faulkner I was also reading Joyce. I had, personally, the experience of the little school the child goes to in my story, the house he lived in, the quarters he walked in, the heater in the little school, the bench that he had to sit on because he had no desk. I had all this experience. So I got Faulkner's rhythm and I got Joyce's "day" thing; you know, as in *Ulysses*, the "Let's do it all in one day" sort of thing. So I had this kid to start with and I said, "O.K., I'm going to take Mr. Faulkner's rhythm and Mr. Joyce's idea of day, and go kid." And I did that. This is how I did it. But I don't know if it's anything so different—I suppose we've all done it. Twain did it late in life when he wrote the Huck Finn and Tom Sawyer books. Hemingway did it. They all have done it; Steinbeck, Chekhov, they all have done it. The child stuff, yes. They were much older than I when they did it, too.

NOR: A few minutes back, you talked of watching a fight between two boys in the same parish which begat Rap Brown. But yet you manage to avoid being politically didactic. You obviously resist being a political writer, but do you hope to do something in that vein with your writing?

GAINES: Oh yes, definitely so. To me, literature expresses man's feelings and relationships much better than politics ever can. I think there are many Rap Browns who can tell you in a political way what's going on. What Rap Brown would say is: look what the whites are doing here! What Ernie Gaines is trying to say is: I see and I agree with you; but we also laugh and we laugh as much or more than other Americans, we dance as much, and sometimes better, and we sing as much, and we have dishes like gumbo and jambalaya and Southern fried chicken and shrimp and all this sort of thing. And we love these things also. Besides the conflict between the white and black, we also carry on a full life: we love, women have children, men gamble, shoot at people, have fights, everything.

NOR: One of the interesting things to me is that your book is really the first one I've ever read that really revealed the innate gentility and nobility of your people. This struck me as an outstanding quality of it.

GAINES: I just try to capture what I see of people and what I hear.

NOR: I'm thinking specifically of the characters in "The Sky Is Gray." Here's a mother with such a really wonderful strength, a strength that comes from the earth, a strength that goes beyond the strength of Faulkner's Dilsey to a kind of independent, proud spirit. She is rearing a son in the same tradition, and she succeeds very well indeed. That toothache that the little boy, James, has—it sounds as if it has to be one of your own personal experiences.

GAINES: Yes, I had a toothache when I was a child at that age, and I had to ride the bus, just as he rides. At that time, on a bus in the South, you had a little sign hanging over the aisle and it said "White" on one side and it said "Colored" on the other side, and you had to sit behind that little sign. I also went to a Catholic school in this little town, which I call Bayonne in the story. I also could not eat uptown. There was no place for me to eat; whether it was cold or sleet or rain; and there was no place to eat. There was no place to warm a child eight-years-old. To do it, a mother had to take him back of town, which was about a mile, three-fourths of a mile, something like that, and there was no transportation unless someone picked you up when they saw you walking by. You have that in the story. I also knew about the dentist's waiting room, the cluttered little place that might be full of people waiting to have dental help. Of course, there were all black people in here; the whites were sitting someplace else. So I had gone through all that. This is why I knew what a child would experience. As a writer, I was interpreting the feeling of this child at the time I myself was thirty years old, but I did know the experiences that he would have gone through. I knew the things that he was going through, yes.

NOR: While Mr. Marchant was talking about the political aspects of your writing, I couldn't help but think that the scene in the dentist's office in "The Sky Is Gray" could easily be seen as a marvelous presentation of black militancy, on the one hand, and tradition, on the other. The people gathered in that room seem to be from all walks of life, as if you were deliberately creating a kind of microcosm of the South. Would you agree with this reading?

GAINES: I would hate to say yes because no matter what I do, no matter how much I write, I feel I will never fully represent the South, really. Just little bitty pieces. I would hate to say that any story or book is "really" representative. You can catch a little touch of it maybe, sometimes.

NOR: To what extent do you feel that you have come under the influence of contemporary writers? Do you feel that Mr. Ellison's work has influenced you in any way or that of other black writers?

GAINES: No, it hasn't. I didn't read anything at all by Ralph Ellison until I had formed my own style of writing. My early influences were Faulkner, Hemingway, the Russian writers such as Tolstoy, Turgenev and Chekhov. I think I've also been influenced by Greek tragedy, but not by Ellison or any black writers. I knew very early what it was I wanted to write about. I just had to find out a way to do it, and the white writers whom I've mentioned showed me this way better. I looked at Hemingway as a man who can really construct paragraphs; when I want to construct a good paragraph, I read a little Hemingway. You can look at Turgenev's structure of his *Fathers and Children* for a perfectly constructed little novel, or at F. Scott Fitzgerald's construction of *The Great Gatsby*. You look at everything in Tolstoy, who I think is the greatest of them all, the greatest man to write a novel. So you learn from all these people; I've learned from all of them. I learned how to get what was in me onto the paper. As I said about the story "A Long Day in November," I had to get it from Faulkner and from Joyce, but not from Richard Wright or Ellison or Baldwin or anybody like that. They showed me how to get it much better than the black writers had done because so many of them really dealt with style, whereas I think the black writers are much more interested in content—you know, putting it down like it is—and the style is sort of secondary.

NOR: Do you find that it helps you to live in San Francisco and write about Louisiana from that distance?

GAINES: Well, in San Francisco if someone's against you, they know how to vote you out of an area. If someone's against you in Louisiana, or if I wrote a book and they did not like it or me in Louisiana, they might shoot me anytime. It's much safer to live in San Francisco than it is in Louisiana. I think I could write in Louisiana just as well, but I know that saying some of the things I say, I cannot live in Louisiana and say these things; I mean I can't say them daily and still go through my life every day. And I don't feel that I want to write about something and not have guts enough to live it. What I mean is that, if I were to live in Louisiana and write about an interracial love affair, I should be brave enough, myself, to love; and brave enough to stand beside anyone else who tried. In San Francisco, I could do these things. In Louisiana it might be a little problem to do the same things. So, as you know, I live in San Francisco.

NOR: Are the old social patterns breaking up in Louisiana? Are they changing?

GAINES: Yes—in some cases. In the cities they're changing much more. In the countryside you have much of the same sort of thing as years ago. The physical makeup of the country is changing. People are chopping down more trees and plowing up more land, but the people themselves are pretty much the same. In the cities, I noticed this last time that more people are eating at the same counters, blacks and whites together. There are more black people working as clerks. I went to one of the biggest, newest buildings in Baton Rouge, the Louisiana National Bank, only a week or so ago, and I saw two black clerks working as tellers in the bank. This was unheard of two years ago. But things have changed. Now take this little drugstore on the corner of Third Street and North Blvd. in Baton Rouge; in here all the people are eating together, blacks and whites eating at the same counter, a black boy behind the counter is serving and ringing up the cash register. Once this black boy could come in and clean the dishes off the place, but he could never serve anybody. At a later time, he could serve and he could collect the money, but he could not ring up the cash register; he had to pass the money from the customer to the white clerk. Now he can do both. But just across the street—well, that's another story.

NOR: How long will it take those across the street to catch up?

GAINES: Only God knows.

Joseph Heller

Interviewed by Alexis Gonzalez and John Mosier
(1971)

Literary history is written in the first paragraph of this interview. Joseph Heller states bluntly who the contemporary thinkers are who influence his writing. When *Catch-22* appeared in the 1950s, no one thought to ask who influenced Heller's writing; his whole approach appeared totally fresh. For those who got a romantic bang out of World War II novels, Heller's almost naturalistic bent jolted. For those who liked realism, his existential sense of the absurdity of the real jolted. For those who enjoyed wallowing in black humor, the crack of the dawn of hope jolted. For those who just liked to escape into a great tale, his insistence on meaning jolted. No one thought to ask whom Heller read or whom he was like. He wasn't really like anyone. He still isn't. If you expect the ordinary reflections by an author on his novel-made-flick, you won't understand Joseph Heller.

NEW ORLEANS REVIEW: Are there any novelists who influence your writing?

JOSEPH HELLER: Kafka and Samuel Beckett are two of my most important novelists. Kafka did influence *Catch-22* and is influencing *Something Happened*. I was not familiar with Beckett when I wrote *Catch-22*, but I have since been amazed by certain very striking similarities in view and language-use in *Catch-22* and Beckett's early novels *Murphy* and *Watt*. This past summer, I read Beckett's trilogy, *Molloy*, *Malone Dies*, and *The Unnameable*, and found to my astonishment that very, very much of Beckett's view and technique in these are present in *Something Happened*. And from here on in, the resemblances in *Something Happened* will be conscious and deliberate. And Kafka's view of the world, too, is present in *Something Happened*. The difference is that I try to present the same dilemmas and all the horror in situations that are not in any way abnormal or out of the ordinary.

NOR: What about the contemporaries?

HELLER: I think that compared to my present admiration for Beckett as dramatist and novelist, any admiration I might express for any of the contemporaries would be small by comparison. I think I would choose Philip Roth, John Barth, and J. D. Salinger as those whose works hold the greatest amount of interest for me at this time.

NOR: Have you seen the film version of your book, *Catch-22*?

HELLER: Yes, I have, and I think it's one of the best movies I've ever seen. It isn't a photographed version of the novel. If it were, it would be a very dreary motion picture as most film adaptations taken from plays and novels usually are. Many characters are left out, many episodes are omitted, as they would have to be. It is, after all, a very long novel with too many characters to make a successful movie. Things are compressed; characters are combined. The effect is to create in cinematic terms pretty much what I would have created had I set out to write a screenplay rather than a literary work. The spirit is there; the episodes are there. The formula or relationships of humor to the morbid has a sort of grotesque effect. The use of time, rather than sequential flow, exists. It exists as a unity. The fragmentation of episodes as in the movie in place of those values which only fiction has reflects the interior monologue, depth, pace, turgidity—these are really critical to a fiction writer. Mike [Nichols] has used the camera, the color in a very strange way; I have never seen anything like it. The use of light and composition in some scenes becomes works of art, works like one can see in some of the best museums in the world. The visual elements are the best I have seen because they're not visual in their visual prettiness alone: they are organic. They fit not only with the book, but they seem to stem from it and serve to constitute an organic whole. I've never seen a movie, I think, that was so much of one piece as *Catch-22*.

Alan Arkin as Yossarian is superb. He gives the best performance of his career, and the best performance I can remember, and yet he does not dominate the movie but fits into the totality. These are things you don't often find in a movie and which I regard as the only way to get a faithful representation of a novel, which is really to exploit a novel form or to forget the sequence of the book, forget the prose, but to take the intention of the author, and the content of it, almost as if to decompose it and put it back together in a new formula or structure, using the same materials, working within a different medium.

Scenes in the movie which I thought Mike might have eliminated from the beginning are included. These are very tough scenes, scenes which I thought might be too strong for a movie. A scene, for example, of Milo blowing up his own squadron. I would have suggested that he leave that out, because in the novel it's almost an allegorical scene rather than a literal one, and I would have said that the audience would not have believed it. In the film, however, it is vivid, frightening, and totally credible. Mike has chosen those scenes which are very strong in the book, and it's a good movie. Mike has done a good job . . . he has done a much better job than I thought was possible.

He is a humorous man. If you had to work in this movie, you'd have two things you don't often get: a director who is an extremely literate person, and a leading man who is also extremely literate, an intelligent person. These are two people, Mike and Alan [Arkin]—I don't want to suggest that the others aren't, but I know these two fairly well—who have highly developed sensibilities. They've read everything, just about; and they are very serious people. It's a pleasure to sit with them. You can get into a discussion of Bach's music or Marcel Proust; there's no allusion, no subject that we can come up with that they won't know about.

NOR: Did you go on location?

HELLER: No. I had nothing to do with the movie.

NOR: Did the film's scriptwriter, Buck Henry, consult with you?

HELLER: We had a meeting which at the time I thought was a kind of courtesy meeting. Mike Nichols called me and said that he'd like me to read the script. I read it and met him at dinner. I told him all I liked about the script and a few things that troubled me. I came away with the feeling that it was really a courtesy session. But when

I met Mike a couple of weeks later in California, he made reference to some of my remarks, so apparently he did remember.

And also a quality of that version of the script that had troubled me had been edited out of it, as I felt it should have. And Nichols, once I got to know him better, I realized how sensitive he was, how much of a perfectionist also. I felt that some of the lines of dialogue were kind of joke lines and superfluous. That troubled me. Anyway, they're all out of the movie. I don't think there's a superfluous moment. There's no searching for an easy laugh anywhere in the movie. Anyway, he did remember some of the things I said.

NOR: What was the budget? Did they go over?

HELLER: It depends on what date they pick. I think what they tend to do is to take the starting date of shooting as the budget date—that is the day they send the first technician down to an area. By that time, which was January, I think the budget was up to $13 million. Mike says $14.7 million. Other people say $18 million. I don't know who's right. I hope Mike is right. He's annoyed at the $18 million. I think originally, when they were at the talking stage, before they realized how good a movie Nichols wanted to make, they were speaking of about six to eight million dollars. Mike has said in other interviews that he would not have made a cheap picture out of *Catch-22*. In one meeting with people at Paramount, he said it should either be done right or not at all, that they were going to have to spend at least ten to twelve million dollars for it. And he's done it right. People don't understand that in order to do something, one has to hold fast. It's difficult to understand why one minute on the screen can cost $300,000, because it might take five days to shoot that one minute perfectly.

NOR: Did you see the completed version, the one that will be released?

HELLER: I saw the version that will be released apart from some improvement in the sound and perhaps some minute changes Mike might still want to make. I saw it on a Sunday, two Sundays ago. That Friday or Thursday, the movie was sneak-previewed in Boston, and editors of the college newspapers in the area were invited. Word had leaked out that *Catch-22* was to be shown at 8:00 p.m., and people began lining up at the theatre from 10:30 a.m. on and sat through whatever the feature was four or five times, and so many remained outside that they ran a second showing. The audience reaction there was everything that Nichols and the executives at Paramount and a number of movie owners in the area could've hoped for. They laughed at all the funny parts, were stunned, stone still at the serious parts, and there was considerable weeping. A person at Paramount who's in charge of campus publicity was there, and he said that he had never before been part of a movie audience where college kids began to cry. It is possibly one of the most powerful movies I've ever seen.

NOR: The Board of Censors has given *Catch-22* an "R" rating. What did they object to?

HELLER: Well, an R rating is better than an X rating. I think it barely escaped an X. I think they objected to a bit of bad language. There are a couple of sex scenes, but they're very tame. Alan Arkin is in bed naked with a girl, naked, but they are covered and they don't make love. Thank God! There is also one quick scene of an act of love, and it's no more than a tenth-of-a-second long. As Alan walks through the streets of Rome, the camera hits an alleyway, and there's a soldier and a girl there, and it's so quick that many people will miss it. It could have been that. There is some language, but I don't recall. I really don't know. I didn't know it was R-rated.

NOR: Have you seen Robert Altman's *M*A*S*H*?

HELLER: No. Not yet. In New York you have to stand in line for hours to see a good movie. Ring Lardner, Jr., who did the screenplay for *M*A*S*H* I know very well. He knows *Catch-22* very well. He was one of those who went to jail with the Hollywood Ten during the black list days of Senator Joseph McCarthy. These were men who could have pleaded the Fifth Amendment and suffered no penalty. I think Dalton Trumbo, Ring Lardner, Jr., I don't know about Abraham Polonsky, went to jail. They were ten, and they refused to plead the Fifth Amendment and decided to defy the investigation on the basis of the First Amendment, freedom of the press and speech, and they were found guilty and sentenced. I think, since then, there were some Supreme Court decisions which would have allowed that sentence to be reversed.

NOR: Mr. Heller, could you comment on the present student protests?

HELLER: I am in total sympathy with the students. I think indifferences and stupidities of the government administration have made it necessary to move from peaceful dissent to acts of violence. I hold the administration guilty. Nixon and Agnew are particularly guilty for the shooting at Kent State. Agnew has been inciting to riot in every speech he makes; they are almost paraphrases of the Nazi speeches in Germany . . . the "rotten apples" that have to be separated from our society. It's almost a license to the local policemen or National Guardsmen to treat these students as they do. I think Nixon and Agnew are as guilty of the deaths of those four pupils as the men who did the shooting. I think that any other course than this at this time would result in a loss of freedom in this society. The war is illegal. Nixon has not signed a declaration of war. There's an absence of a declaration of war. Nixon is a liar. He's a habitual liar, as Johnson was before him on this Vietnam war. Nothing he says has any right to be believed, but whether the troops will or won't be withdrawn by the first of July, I think it's a mistake he made, and he knows it, because they're apparently accomplishing nothing there anyway. But even apart from that, he's never sought a declaration of war for the Vietnam War, and so consequently it's an illegal war. It's a moot point as to whether the Selective Service Act can be enforced, and the government has carefully avoided any court case which would bring the legality of the war into question. I think the students are the most hopefully refreshing thing in the country. I think they're doing the dirty work for a lot of middle-class respectable people like myself.

NOR: Do you think these kids are the Yossarians that have sprung up and are doing what he would do today?

HELLER: When I wrote *Catch-22*, things were relatively calm in this country. They are doing what he would do and what he should have done in *Catch-22*. The possibility of such collective action, of such widespread dissent was not really something to be considered in the 1950s. It just didn't take place, and there didn't seem to be any immediate need for it. This is an alternative that he doesn't consider in the book. It's touched on very sparely in *Catch-22*. The idea of collective action, when the character Dobbs wants him to become his accomplice in an effort to kill the colonel and Yossarian declines. Later Yossarian decides he must kill the colonel, that his salvation depends on it. Then Dobbs won't do it. By the end of the book, there is no one left for Yossarian to join with. I think undoubtedly that what Yossarian is reacting against has come to be a reality in the past four or five years and intensifies. He would be reacting to that, and he would be out with them, and I am all for it. I mean, there has been no act of violence yet. I can't recall any except for the incident in New York where the building blew up. I can't recall when somebody has been killed except by the police or the National Guardsmen. And anytime I read about these firebombs going off in mysterious explosions all over the country, I am delighted, because I think that the enemies of this country are in Washington, and it's nonsense. The argument that all these protests encourage the enemy is nonsense because the enemy is first Lyndon Johnson, then Agnew, Nixon and Kissinger. They are the ones, I think, that are the danger to this country, and they must be opposed in the only way left for us to oppose them.

When Martin Luther King turned back from the bridge at Selma, he lost the support of so many, particularly Eldridge Cleaver and the ones who later became the Black Panthers because they had come down there for violent confrontation, as Cleaver writes. This was an opportunity to expose publicly the real nature of the opposition to the blacks in Alabama who had been turned back from the bridge. There was a great lessening of enthusiasm and a feeling of defeat. It is a fact that violence and the terrorism that it suggests is and always has been an effective weapon. And since the government is deaf, dumb and blind to the poor attempts of persuasion—there is nothing left but violence or protest. The protest has been met with indifference and contempt and insult, and an enticement to more violence, particularly by Agnew's suggestions that these people should be mistreated the way that the local authorities want them to be.

NOR: Have you been involved in any peace marches or protests?

HELLER: I have a daughter of 18, and she's been on peace marches and civil rights marches, but these have tended to decrease as they've been ignored. I've not been asked to, to any extent. Yes, I think I was asked to go to Washington, to go in the parade. I couldn't come to Austin to make a five-minute speech on the moratorium—it's a long way from New York—but in New York I would. I was on the last Washington march. I'm not considered a first stringer. They generally go for Norman Mailer first.

NOR: Do you think *Catch-22* influenced today's college youth?

HELLER: I don't think a writer's work of literature really influences people. It shapes them. It does confirm what they themselves might suspect. I think *Catch-22* is attractive to people today because the people themselves are attractive. They themselves have certain thoughts, certain ideas, certain attitudes, and they find them expressed in *Catch-22*. The same with Bob Dylan's songs, the Beatles' songs have an appeal for them because they themselves can respond to it now, in a way that many people could not respond to *Catch-22* when it first came out but do respond to it now. Many, many people said they couldn't read it, or were not interested in reading it past the first two pages, when it first came out, then tried again a few years later. There was a girl at Our Lady of the Lake, yesterday, I suppose she was about twenty, she said she couldn't read the book when she tried it about four or five years ago, then went back a year or two later and couldn't understand why she had trouble the first time. It's the prose style; hundreds and hundreds of people have called me and told me they started reading it and stopped because it was too confusing in the beginning. So many people have told me that that I think it's a valid criticism.

If I were doing the novel over again, I would try to make the early chapters a little more coherent. I wanted to suggest confusion by being confusing, but not so confusing as to chase readers away. But I hear that less and less among people, for two reasons: now the novel has a reputation, and people will have patience with a novel that has a reputation. Most good works of literature are not all pleasure—if you've ever read Thomas Mann or James Joyce or Marcel Proust. The novel isn't intended to be easy the way movies are. Movies are easy forms of apprehension. Plays are. If they aren't, then audiences don't enjoy them. Plays and movies go at their own pace. You can't re-read them. I think cinema is close to being a sybaritic kind of entertainment, and I suspect that many people go to see many inferior movies only because they're too lazy to read a book.

NOR: Do you go to movies or the theatre much?

HELLER: I almost never go to the theatre. I go only if someone I know is connected with the production. And I go to the movies seldom. The kinds of plays I like are not produced anymore, and if they are produced, they're off-Broadway in uncomfortable theatres and close before I get tickets. I did make it a point to see *Mahagonny* in New York because it's the first time it's been in this country, and I would go to see Samuel Beckett's plays, even though I'm not sure it's a pleasure to watch Samuel Beckett. Like fiction, the theatre is not supposed to be pure pleasure. Movies are almost always pleasure.

Most movies I find, even the good ones, are somewhat shallow and thin. Even what passes for a serious movie is very thin compared to what passes for a serious play, and I think both are pretty thin and shallow in contrast to what can be said about a work of fiction. Movies I distrust very much because there's a kind of pandering that goes on to the popular taste and very often it's subtle enough so that the public is taken in by it. I think there's a considerable amount of pandering going on toward the young audience. They're not good movies. They are movies that deal with things the young people want. And they are movies which have a viewpoint which I know young people have. And the uncritical spectator will rate and appraise film only for those reasons, not because the film is particularly good, not because the screenplay is good, not because it's authentic, but simply because it has a scene with a hippie smoking pot and a lovemaking scene which they identify with.

NOR: What is the book you're working on presently?

HELLER: It's titled *Something Happened*. It's about this executive who is 43-years-old, married, with children, unhappy with his marriage, his children, his job, the condition of the world. But he finds that at this point of his life what means more to him than anything else is to be allowed to make a three-minute speech at the next company convention in Bermuda.

That's pretty much the plot of the novel. It's going to be very long, unfortunately, because it's going to take me a long time to finish it. The title is ironic because nothing happens in the novel. There is no plot, no action. So far it's very successful; the two people with whom I checked *Catch-22* out as I wrote in sections are rather astounded at how effective it is so far. If I can sustain this another four or five hundred pages, I'm hoping to finish it this year, but I may be two or three months late. I worked on *Catch-22* seven years. This will be hard to measure in time because the play, *We Bombed in New Haven*, took me away from the novel for two full years. I don't know where the time went. I wasn't working that hard on it. The thing I don't like about the play is that even though there isn't work to be done, the process of production commands one's whole attention anyway. And I would sit around for weeks or months at a time just raising a question or giving answers to a question and yet being unable to concentrate on any other kind of work. Working with so many people, it does really become a collaborative effort, one in which the playwright and the script are not the most important elements.

Christopher Isherwood

Interviewed by Sarah Smith
and Marcus Smith
(1975)

Christopher Isherwood was born in England, is now an American citizen, and resides in Santa Monica, California. He is the author of many novels, plays, translations, and autobiographical books.

NEW ORLEANS REVIEW: There seems to be a general fascination today with the Weimar Republic. Not only are scholars studying its collapse, but one also encounters a rather widespread popular fascination with that period of German history. Could you reflect, in terms of your own experiences, on the state of society and politics of that time and the United States as you see it today?

CHRISTOPHER ISHERWOOD: To tell you the truth, I don't see very much relation between the two. I never have. I'm constantly asked, "Do I think the Nazis are coming?" The answer is no, not in any way which could be compared to the ending of the Weimar Republic. Perhaps this is due in part to a sort of irritation I feel toward doomsayers. My experience in life has always been that while you're watching one mouse hole, the mouse comes out of another. Since I'm not in any sense a political observer, and wasn't in those days, I only go on a kind of instinct. But I find the capacity of this country to remain more or less afloat almost infinite considering the things that have happened.

NOR: Is this merely economic luxury, the fact that we can afford stability, or is it because of some cultural or spiritual quality?

ISHERWOOD: It must always be something psychological. It must be something in the inhabitants. I remember so well, for example, in Colombia, when I was there in 1947, several Colombian intellectuals said to me, "Our respect for the Constitution and for the principles of democracy is the only thing that makes us superior to Paraguay." Barely four months later there was the most appalling civil war in Colombia. General Marshall was visiting and had to get out of Bogotá, along with other American representatives. A very popular politician named Gaitán had been murdered, and as a result, there was a tremendous slaughter in the streets. I always felt in South America this could happen to any of the countries that we were in. I don't say that North Americans are necessarily more law-abiding. It may be partly a sort of saving streak of apathy. I don't know.

NOR: What about the young people today who have such a deep hunger to believe? It seems that anything can be packaged and sold to them.

ISHERWOOD: I have been appearing on campuses for many years, and something has developed in the last fifteen years or so. The young are constantly asking about religion. They want to know. And I never try to push it. I never try to say more than I dare. I never try to seem holy or pretend to have knowledge beyond the absolute basic thing about which I can say, "Well this—I really promise you—I believe this much." If you try to fake anything, they see through it instantly. Stalin was in a theological seminary when he was young, and needless to say, he left. Gerald Heard used to say what an awful tragedy it was that there hadn't been anybody really spiritual at that seminary. Obviously Stalin had seen right through the whole lot of them and had therefore decided that religion was indeed just the opium of the people. I think it's frightfully important, and this is really much more difficult than it sounds, *only* to say what you *absolutely* believe. I mean, never to kind of skate around difficulties; if you feel that there's a difficulty, you say honestly, "I don't know—I would like to believe that or think that, but I'm really not sure myself."

NOR: How does one communicate to others a sense of mystery without specifically saying this is the mystery that one ought to believe in?

ISHERWOOD: Well, I'm absolutely sure that everybody has a natural sense of the numinous, of something mysterious, something that awes you, beneath the appearances of things.

NOR: How does this relate to your interests in Vedantic studies?

ISHERWOOD: I cannot say too often that I am not in any sense a guru, anything of this kind. I never set out to be. I am simply somebody who is able to write the English language a little better than a lot of people, and as such, put my know-how at the service of this monk, Prabhavananda, who is also my guru. This is a very, very different thing. I mean I never did anything except just put into rather more readable language what *he* said, what he taught me, and everything that I ever wrote about it was very carefully passed on by him and indeed by the head of the Order, and all sorts of people in India (in the case of the book about Ramakrishna). So that you can hardly call that independent writing in the sense of making something up or even thinking something out.

NOR: Do you then regard yourself as simply an editor?

ISHERWOOD: Well, really, yes—not much more than that. I mean, the only Vedanta book to which I contributed anything of my own (other than in a purely stylistic way, such as in the choice of words) was *How to Know God*, the commentaries on the Yoga aphorisms of Patanjali. In that book from time to time, I would think of illustrations, examples, things that would appeal to Western readers, or make comparisons with things said in other literatures on the same subject. That was about the extent of my contribution, really. You see, Prabhavananda speaks very good English. And he's also spent almost all of his adult life in the United States. He came to the United States when he was just thirty, has been here ever since, and he's now over eighty. So naturally, he has quite a way with the English language. He has very little opportunity even to speak Bengali except to his two assistants; most of the time he's speaking English.

NOR: You mentioned that you did not regard yourself as a guru, and even suggested that you disliked being cast in that role. Do you see yourself as a seeker? Are you pursuing mysticism? Have you achieved what you think is a . . . ?

ISHERWOOD: What I've achieved is open to question, but there's no doubt in my mind whatsoever that I am a believer and a disciple, and that's only strengthened with the years. The degree of my involvement is apparent when I try to imagine myself without it. That would be like taking away the whole frame of reference from my life.

NOR: Do you practice yoga, and if so, what type?

ISHERWOOD: Oh, just a very simple form of meditation. I don't practice *hatha yoga*, the exercises, although I have done them in my time—I took some lessons. The general attitude of our particular group toward the *hatha yoga* physical poses is that they are okay—many of them are like the exercises you are given in a gym. But we very much frown on the breathing exercises, because if you really practice them hard—that means *hard*—you may very well bring on hallucinations and psychic, as opposed to spiritual, visions, and this may lead in its turn to your becoming mentally unbalanced.

NOR: You mentioned a particular group. Which group is this?

ISHERWOOD: It's the Ramakrishna Order, one of the largest orders of monks in India. The Hindu monks I'm associated with are members of the Order who have come to teach here, not as missionaries but simply in an informative capacity. You see, as a matter of fact you could quite well be a devotee of Jesus of Nazareth and be a Vedantist at the same time, just as it's entirely possible to be a Quaker and not be a Christian, because this belief that the Quakers have about the "inner life" is really nondescriptive. The enormous majority will say, "Yes, it's something to do with Jesus," but, if you really get down to it, it isn't, necessarily. So this is a situation where it's not necessary to make these kinds of choices, and there's no question of being a missionary if you don't have to "save" people from something. That was what always upset the Christian missionaries in India so much, because they would come to India and they would preach, and they were listened to by Hindus who said, "Yes, we see that Jesus of Nazareth was a divine incarnation, an avatar, and we shall worship him." But what upset the missionaries so much was that the Hindus went right on worshipping other divine incarnations as well. The missionaries said you can only do it through Jesus. They replied that that's perfectly all right, that Krishna in the *Bhagavad Gita* said, "Nobody comes to the truth except through me." But of course, when an avatar says "I," he really means that he's a part of the eternal—it's quite a non-personal statement. And so you go back and forth and sideways and upside down, and some people find this a terrible sticking place, and that's why you find people who feel that the Hindu thing is unacceptable. But the Hindus are more than ready to accept the Christians, if by Christianity you mean the special cult of Jesus of Nazareth rather than of somebody else. Because for the people who are inclined toward devotion, a cult is of course necessary. I mean, this is in itself a way of knowledge. The word *yoga* is also used without any reference to physical exercises to mean different approaches to religion. This devotional approach is what's called *Bhakti yoga*. Then again, there's what they call *Karma yoga*, which is what we call "social service"—it's what the Quakers are doing all the time. This is to say you see the eternal in your fellow men, and therefore you serve them, not because you're helping your fellow men—that's a terrible egotism: if anybody is being helped it's yourself, for having the privilege of serving God in these people. Then again there's another path, which is much more rarified, called *Jnana yoga*. This is a path of intellectual discrimination where you don't actually worship anything but maintain a state of rigorous discrimination—always asking yourself, "What is the reality?"; "What is unreal?"; "What is real?"—to arrive at a state of enlightenment. I suppose this is true, for instance, of people like Krishnamurti, if you're familiar with his lectures, because he's always analyzing. All these different attitudes you can find in Christianity, in a way; you have the three yogas represented: the intensely devotional attitude of somebody like St. John of the Cross, and the intensely intellectual attitude of the Jesuits, and the "serving" orders such as the Franciscans . . .

NOR: It's a question of choosing what's right for you?

ISHERWOOD: Exactly. As a matter of fact, Vivikananda, who is one of Ramakrishna's chief disciples, always said he wished there was a different religion for every single being on this earth. In other words, he felt that you shouldn't try to force yourself into joining something; you should evolve your own attitude toward the unseen. And he said that everyone's attitude should be just a tiny degree different from everybody else's.

NOR: How are you supposed to work this out? Do you have to have somebody who helps you—somebody to follow?

ISHERWOOD: Well, of course I'm very much in favor of a guru, that's to say somebody to help you along the line. I personally can't imagine I could get involved in anything without meeting somebody because I'm that sort of person—I understand things through people. I used to infuriate my intellectual friends by saying, "I should have understood Marxism if I'd met Marx." Or Hegel, or anybody you'd like to name. The British philosopher Freddy Ayres was telling me that he'd been down to lecture at Washington. And I said, "What on earth did you say to them?" And he said, "You come around for lunch tomorrow, and I'll tell you." And before lunch he sat me down in a chair, and he gave me a lecture. For almost the whole lunch afterwards, I understood his philosophy perfectly . . . But then gradually it all faded away. I even had a friend once who met Einstein and that happened. He was mad with excitement—he rushed to the phone, called his wife and said, "I understand relativity!" Einstein did it very simply: he took out some matches and laid them end on end, smoked his pipe and explained— and it was almost within my friend's grasp.

NOR: In your lecture last night, you were discussing *Cabaret* and said you were unhappy with the bisexual play that Michael York involved himself in. You didn't like that. You seemed to be saying that there are certain absolute categories: one is either heterosexual or homosexual, and there should be no casual crossing over.

ISHERWOOD: When I was discussing *Cabaret*, I was criticizing much more the way that something was done, not what it was that was done. I'll tell you what I do dislike, and this of course is admittedly a slanted thing. I dislike people who find it cute to make little sallies from the well-guarded fortress of heterosexual respectability and who then come back and say, "What are the homosexual tribesmen out there fussing about? What are they complaining about? Sure, I've had my little flings, and I've done this or that. Why are they so serious about it?" What these people don't understand is that they are being sheltered by the public heterosexual side of their lives; they are protected from anything horrid ever happening to them, from ever coming under any kind of stigma, and by insisting to everybody else, to other heterosexuals, that that's of course the important thing and the other is just a kind of game. They even get a certain approval. People think, "Well, he's really a devil, he goes in for anything, he's marvelous, he's a swinger." But what they mean is a swinger swinging very heavily to one side rather than both. Now all of this will be absolutely, utterly unimportant in the Kingdom of Heaven, or even in a genuine democracy, but it's just a little bit distasteful to those of us who are actually suffering from this persecution, which is very real.

NOR: The young boy in *A Single Man* is to some extent playing that game.

ISHERWOOD: Yes, and I deplore this, too, very often because it's an attempt to pass. Of course, when I say "deplore" and all these angry, superior words, I have the greatest sympathy for anybody who tries to wriggle out from under an intolerable situation, if he finds it intolerable. I have the greatest sympathy for a Black who tries to pass. Passing exists in one way or another in every minority. It is not confined to the homosexual by any means. And of course with Jews, too, you'll find it again and again—they assume those Scots names. All right, good luck to them. You see, when there was a question of making the film *Cabaret*, first of all there was another company doing it, and they asked me and my friend Don Bachardy to do a treatment. And after great deliberation we made Chris a heterosexual, for that very reason. We thought, let's not have any "chi-chi" about this. There are only two tolerable positions: either Chris is one thing or the other. If Chris is a homosexual, this of course alters the whole story and is indeed an absolute fountain of dramatic situations which don't occur in the book because I was sort of fudging. I was fudging for a rather different reason; I wasn't trying to conceal the facts. I just didn't want Chris to be an important character; I wanted him simply to be the narrator. And a character who is a homosexual becomes from a fictional point of view too interesting, too important, too way-out. Especially at the time when I was writing. What I wanted to say to the audience was, "Don't mind me, I'm just telling you the story." What I don't like is teasing the audience—equivocating and trying to make something a little bit naughty. People always say about Berlin in the 1920s, "Oh, it must have been so decadent!" All they mean is homosexual.

NOR: Do you regard your fiction as outstanding from the point of view of the technical evolution of fiction? Do you think that you tried to push forward the form of the novel?

ISHERWOOD: It never occurred to me. Anything that I might have done in that way, if I did indeed do anything, was purely a side effect. What I was concerned with was just trying to say what I thought was interesting about my life. A fan letter that I like almost better than any I've ever received was oddly enough from a war hero who had become some kind of big wheel in British aviation in later life. He said, "You try to describe what it's like to be alive." Of course, that was a thing that Hemingway was constantly doing—it was his whole stock in trade.

NOR: But didn't Hemingway always get his sense of being alive by juxtaposing something that was dead, or in the act of killing?

ISHERWOOD: Well, because he was intensely interested in danger and courage. I enormously admire some books by Jack Kerouac. In a sense I find Kerouac more interesting than Hemingway because Kerouac tells you about the physical thing but also goes into fantasies and philosophical speculations, mysticism and everything. I very much like *The Dharma Bums* and *The Desolation Angels* and *Big Sur*. Fiction or nonfiction is not a very important distinction to me, and Kerouac could have said the same. Kerouac was practically nonfiction, and Hemingway was frequently very close to nonfiction.

NOR: What about your own work? Has there been a shift toward or away from nonfiction?

ISHERWOOD: I find the difference between my fiction and nonfiction slighter and slighter. The difference is diminishing. Because what I'm really interested in is commenting on experience.

NOR: Would this hold for, say, a novel like *A Single Man*?

ISHERWOOD: Well, it's almost entirely a comment on my own experience. But I've hardly ever in my life written about anything that I hadn't done.

NOR: And yet at the end you try to go beyond your own experience—even into the mystery of death.

ISHERWOOD: Yes, well, I mean, since it's a mystery, everyone has the right to have an attitude to mystery. That's all it amounts to. The actual scene of the coronary occlusion is lifted out of a splendid book called *Man's Presumptuous Brain* by Dr. A. T. W. Simeons.

NOR: Isn't there also an echo of Auden's poem on Yeats? You talk about the various parts of the body deserting . . .

ISHERWOOD: Oh, yes, "the provinces of his body revolted." Well, you see, not only were we very close friends, but Auden as you know was the son of a doctor, and I was a medical student for a short time. One of the many, many connections we had was that we were both very interested in medicine and therefore rather looked at things in the same way. As a matter of fact, you'll find similar images in a passage in *Man's Presumptuous Brain*. So I just rewrote that, and I asked some heart specialists about it. In fact, one was so pleased with the result that he always reads the ending of *A Single Man* aloud to his students when he's lecturing on coronary occlusions.

NOR: But you go beyond a heart attack and have George's soul or spirit or his unconscious that's gone out to sea come back and find the dead body, his own dead body there, and presumably then have to confront eternity.

ISHERWOOD: Well, that's my guess at it. But what I was going to say was that after all, what does it all amount to? If you write about your own experiences, you turn them into fiction I guess for two or three reasons: one is that experience is so messy; there are far too many people around; things don't fit together very well; and you very often tidy things up by simplifying them in order to tell a narrative. And this involves eliminating characters, and you gradually pass at least in a negative way into fiction. So that's one way, which is the only difference as far as I'm concerned. Secondly, of course, there's the question of discretion. It's only recently, for instance, that I could write with the extreme frankness that I do now on the subject of homosexuality.

NOR: Why is that? Is that a personal decision, or is it because of changes in society that allow you to be frank in that respect?

ISHERWOOD: I suppose in a way I was sort of moving toward it, and I'm very much a child of my time in that way. I mean I go at the same pace as other people. But quite aside from that, what I have to say now wouldn't be nearly as good if I'd said it in fiction. Because what I'm interested in is not revelations either about physical acts or about specific lovers, but really studying the psychology of my whole outlook on life, which I realize is far more influenced by my homosexuality than I'd ever supposed. And I begin to see that every word, in a way, that I wrote about Berlin and everything, is all very slightly off. It's not absolutely focused.

NOR: Because of its accommodation?

ISHERWOOD: Yes. To give you just one very simple example, it immediately branches out into sociology and politics much more than anything else. You take the whole of my relationship with the working-class movement, or let us say, Communism. Now, on the one hand, you get a situation where for sociological/sexual reasons—that's to say because I was a kind of upper-class boy brought up in a nicey-nice home—I was drawn to another class. And in order to be drawn to another class of course, you tend to accept the politics which represent the cause of this class. So you tend toward socialistic or Communistic attitudes. But when you look toward actual Communist states, or toward the labor movement in many countries, you find the deplorable fact that they are exceedingly puritanical, and that they want to impose a heterosexual dictatorship just like the capitalist dictatorship. And so you see this is a very intricate pattern, and it causes a lot of bounce back and forth between two attitudes. The question is, are you going to say "my dictatorship right or wrong," or are you going to say "my tribe before everything else"? Also, of course, it's acutely embarrassing to recognize the dimensions of your tribe, because some of the people in it you'll find deplorable, just as Jews suffer embarrassment over some Jews, and as I'm sure is the case with Blacks, and, well, with any minority one could name. But, to return to the question of fiction and nonfiction, nothing is more fascinating than the enormous complexity, the subtlety, of certain kinds of fiction. You couldn't have a nonfiction Henry James; it wouldn't be the same thing at all. His sensibility, of course, when he's writing the book about coming back to America, *The American Scene*, is terrific, but there's an element in James that you couldn't possibly have except as fiction, because it's necessary to have a lot of invention and a sort of crystallization of the situation. And that applies to a great many writers.

NOR: You're working, I understand, on a new autobiography?

ISHERWOOD: Yes, you see *Lions and Shadows* ends when I went for the first time to Berlin in 1929. And this new book starts on that day and goes through a period of about ten years, to when I embarked for the United States in 1939.

NOR: Do you have a title?

ISHERWOOD: No, I haven't got a title yet. I don't know what to call it. My working title is *Wanderings*, but that's just simply because you have to call a book something when you're thinking about it yourself. Either this will be a complete volume in itself, or it will be connected up with a second volume which is about my first three or four years in the United States. Now that's much easier for me to write because I have extensive diaries which I kept at the time. This first section is very difficult because I've forgotten an enormous amount, and I'm reconstructing it out of letters and bits of my diaries, of other people's memories, which are wildly unreliable—I'm always checking up. Auden didn't even know the year he married Erica Mann—he got it quite wrong! But of course there are always people who love to check these things out, and by degrees I'm zeroing in on most of it.

NOR: Is there anything you'd care to say in conclusion?

ISHERWOOD: Did I tell you my exit line? I was speaking a few days ago, and I was trying to figure out how to leave the podium. I suddenly paused, and I said, "I had this great friend, the actress Gladys Cooper, whom I loved dearly (she's dead now), and she was being asked about acting because they were talking about method acting and she was very scornful. And she said, 'It's ridiculous, there's nothing to it. You just know your lines, and speak up, and then get off the stage as quickly as possible.'" As I said this, I walked off!

Anaïs Nin

Interviewed by Jeffrey Bailey
(1976)

Anaïs Nin has attained a long-delayed place of honor in contemporary letters through the impetus of her renowned diary and five-volume *roman-fleuve*, *Cities of the Interior*. Born and reared in France, of Spanish and French-Danish parentage, her lyrical insight into the human condition has touched the emotional and intellectual lives of people around the world, people who are linked to her (and to each other) by an abiding belief in the reality of imagination and the possibility of a benevolent and evolving self.

The following are excerpts from a conversation between Anaïs Nin and Jeffrey Bailey, recorded at her home in the Silver-Lake area of Los Angeles.

NEW ORLEANS REVIEW: There is an interesting quote from Volume One of your *Diary*, in which you say, "I only regret that everyone wants to deprive me of the journal, which is the only steadfast friend I have, the only one that makes my life bearable, because my happiness with human beings is so precarious, my confining moods rare, and the least sign of non-interest is enough to silence me. In the journal, I am at ease." I think you were referring to Henry Miller and to certain other friends who didn't understand your obsession with the diary. You also say, "This diary is my kief, hashish, and opium pipe. This is my drug and my vice. Instead of writing a novel, I lie back with this book and a pen, and dream . . . I must relive my life in the dream. The dream is my only life." How much of a conflict was there for you in expanding from the privacy of the diary into the novels which, unlike the diary, were meant for immediate public consumption?

ANAÏS NIN: At one moment, it seemed like a conflict. The feeling that Henry Miller had and that Otto Rank had was that the diary was a refuge and a shell, an oyster shell, and that I was going inward instead of coming out to face the world with my fiction, since I concentrated on writing something which couldn't be shown to people. The conflict doesn't exist for me anymore. I see them as being interrelated, the novels and the diary. I see that the fiction helped me to write better for the diary; it helped me to develop the diary in a more interesting way, to approach it more vibrantly than one sometimes does when you're simply making a portrait or communicating a whole series of events. I feel now that they were really nourishing each other. At one time, I seemed to be trapped in the sense that I couldn't do the outside writing; I was more comfortable not facing the world, not publishing, not facing criticism; I was hypersensitive about those things. I was more willing to incite others to write.

NOR: Was it intuition that attracted you to your famous friendship with Henry Miller?

NIN: Yes, it really was. Intuition, and the fact that Henry had, and has, a great presence, a sense of himself that is quite overpowering. Essentially, I just enjoyed his company and although his work and his style differed a good deal from mine, I respected his efforts and admired his goals. But I never discount the importance of intuition. It was intuition, for example, that made me recognize Antonin Artaud as the great talent he was; much more than an eccentric, a true poet and mystic.

NOR: Would you say that most of your friendships with other artists came about as a result of their exposure to your work?

NIN: Well, it works both ways, of course, but a good number of them probably did. My work made it very easy for me, and I'll tell you exactly why; I'll make a confession: when I was sixteen, seventeen, really up until the time I was past twenty, I was horribly shy. I didn't talk. Henry Miller said recently that I was the best listener he'd ever had—and it's because I simply didn't talk. And that, of course, is partly why I went to the diary. I wasn't open myself, but I like others to be, and they were with me. Eventually, the shyness disappeared because other people made the first gesture. That's the wonderful privilege about being an artist, because once you've said something that means something to others, they come towards you and the shyness is no longer a problem. For instance, last year I was able to lecture extemporaneously in front of a large audience, which is something I never would have done when I was younger. I never could have even imagined it. Henry said he couldn't believe it, having known me. Sometimes it doesn't turn out so well, but you do have the feeling that you're talking directly to the people.

NOR: What are your daily writing habits? Is maintaining a regular routine important to the accomplishment of your writing goals?

NIN: Routine and discipline—that is, writing every day, and never erasing or crossing out—have been very important. I always write in the morning, usually between 7:30 and noon, and the afternoon I devote to correspondence and miscellaneous things. I type when I work in the mornings, and only write longhand in the diary.

NOR: So much of your style reflects a belief in spontaneity and continuous "flow." What is your attitude toward revision and re-writing?

NIN: Re-writing is a special problem because it means that something about your book is basically flawed and has to be corrected. If that's the case, there's no escaping it. My attitude about revision has never been enthusiastic, probably because I dislike obsessive perfectionism. I would always prefer to start another book than to concentrate on revising something I'd already done; I think when you go on to something new, you learn new things and you tend to become better. I just think that you benefit more by going forward than by backtracking.

NOR: I believe that you first began writing in English when your mother brought you as a girl to New York City. Did you keep writing in English after your return to France? How do you compare the two languages?

NIN: I wrote the diary in French from the age of eleven to about seventeen. After that, everything was in English. I think that whatever language you master, you love; you can't avoid being involved with it in a very intense sort of way. I fell in love with English as a second language when I studied in New York public schools, and my mother was very helpful. She had learned beautiful English at a New England convent. I think you've got to appreciate each language for its unique qualities, its particular resonance. I thought the word "you" was the most beautiful thing I had ever heard.

NOR: We seem now to be swept by a tide of nostalgia, a series of tides, really. How do you react to this? Are you nostalgic?

NIN: No, I'm really not. I love my present life, I love the people who visit me now. I'm much more interested in experiencing new cycles than in looking back. I tend to feel negatively about nostalgia; I think we go back when we feel stunted in the present life. People who are nostalgic have known something good in the past and want to pick it up again; say, for example, the houseboat period in my own life. When I'm in Paris, I look at those boats gently tossing on the water and I recall many good things, but I really don't have that nostalgic craving. Each cycle of my life interested me equally, but I have no desire to go back to any of them.

NOR: Your published diary begins with a beautiful description of Louveciennes. Is your house there still standing?

NIN: It's still there, but it's crumbling. It's in the guidebooks and everyone who goes there sees that it's falling down.

NOR: Does anyone live there?

NIN: People live there in summer. The French landlords are like Balzac's miser; they don't want to fix anything so they let it go and rent it during the summer when it doesn't matter if the furnace isn't working. The place is 200-years-old, you know, and when I had it I had to fix everything myself. But Louveciennes is lovely. It's got a wonderful atmosphere, very rustic, although it's only twenty minutes from Paris by car. The Americans built a modern village next to it for the army, but they fortunately didn't touch the old village so that it's just the way it was, with the church in the middle and the shops around it, a typical French village. It's quite historic, too; Renoir lived there, although I didn't discover that until after I had left. You know, I went back there under rather strange circumstances which should show you that I'm really not nostalgic. German television wanted to do a documentary, and we did a whole day's work at Louveciennes and had many complications. For one thing, they wouldn't let us into the house, but this was good in a way, because it allowed new things to happen; it forced us to create something out of the immediate present, out of what we are experiencing. It wasn't any longer focusing upon the past.

NOR: Paris in the 1930s was the place to be. What did you think of Fitzgerald and Gertrude Stein and that group?

NIN: The younger writers thought that they were passé, too 1920s. We were trying to be our own writers, and we didn't have much respect for Hemingway or Fitzgerald. We weren't thinking about them so much as about ourselves.

I went to Gertrude Stein's place once and found her very tyrannical. As we know now from the biographies, she didn't like women. She thought that they were frivolous, even stupid. She much preferred the company of men and tended to isolate the women. I felt myself that that was true. It's very clear, from those biographies, just how poorly she regarded members of her own sex.

NOR: Did you have much contact with writers in New York in the 1940s?

NIN: In the 1940s, when I came to New York, I could have met a great many of these people; in fact, however, I only met a few. There was Richard Wright, and Theodore Dreiser, who was quite an old man then. I didn't meet a lot of these people because I had a rather severe problem with them: they all drank so much. I liked several of those who drank: James Agee, for example, and Kerouac. They were both great talents. I remember being very keen on meeting Kerouac, but I just didn't have that capacity for drink. So often someone would come to meet you already drunk, and I found that frustrating. I think it reflected an inner frustration on their part. I can see two people who already know each other going out and drinking together, and having a good time, but only after something has been established. It works well with some, of course. One hears, for example, about how Tennessee Williams and Carson McCullers drank and wrote together, sometimes consuming tremendous amounts and yet producing marvelous work. But this business of going off and being dead drunk is something else.

NOR: This is a common stereotype of the writer: someone who re-orders reality through his work and escapes from the outside world through drink or drugs. Do you think that having some sort of pervasive neurosis is simply part of the artistic personality?

NIN: No, I don't think so. But I do think that, as Americans, we have a collective neurosis. My belief is that we create better without it. There are a great many romantic notions that neuroses are necessary; that pain and sorrows are necessary for the writer. I reject this as a false romanticism. We all have problems, of course, and some of them turn into neuroses, but the object is to get rid of them. As I shed mine, you see me entering into new cycles. The minute I would shed one neurosis—I had many of them—I would then be able to go on to another cycle. There was the cycle of obsession with the father, and I dropped that; and then there was the obsession with the mother, and I dropped that, which is the way it should be. We're none of us ever just one thing, and we shouldn't allow our growth and development to be blocked.

NOR: Your *Diary* is famous for its massive size as well as for its style. How do you handle the problem of editing, of deciding what to publish and what to delete?

NIN: There are several problems determining what can go into the published diary, and people are sometimes hostile about what I've left out. They don't understand that you have to consider two things very carefully: one is your own ethical standard which concerns protecting the privacy of people who have confided in you, and the other deals with the publisher who demands that I receive permission before the portraits can be published. So, of course, I'm inhibited that way. The editing is really dominated by my own ethics because sometimes you can write something which doesn't seem to be destructive but which can, in fact, be harmful. For instance, we had a charming storyteller friend in the Village days. He was an alcoholic and a homosexual; we didn't think anything of that, and in the diary I just described his storytelling. And when I sent it to him he said, "Please! I'm working for the State Department!" Had I published the piece, I would have hurt him without intending to, which is why I'm glad about the permission requirement. I have to send these portraits to the people who are concerned, and sometimes they tell me to change something or it would have a bad effect upon them. I don't want to be destructive.

NOR: When you send these portraits to close friends or associates and they ask you to make certain changes which you'd prefer not to make, does this cause special problems?

NIN: No, because we talk about them. For instance, with James Herlihy, he read everything I had referring to him and corrected one factual error, a date concerning his play, I think, and that was all.

NOR: A number of expatriate writers who have settled in Los Angeles have been attracted to various religious cults found here, particularly to Eastern sects. Have you ever been drawn in that direction?

NIN: No, I was never attracted to Eastern religions and I'm not attracted now, even though I have great admiration for Asian culture. Nor was I ever attracted to Eastern philosophy. I love the East, but I was trapped once, and I am determined never to be trapped again.

NOR: How was that?

NIN: In Catholicism. They say, "Once a Communist, always a Communist; once a Catholic, always a Catholic." It's very hard to come out of a dogma, to transcend it. Although I finally did, I'm very wary of dogma, and of any organized religion. I am religious; I can accept the metaphysical, but not the dogmatic. That's why I didn't have the same intimacy with writers who veered toward religion here, the closeness that I had with my friends who were primarily concerned with art. The kind of metaphysics I found here simply didn't attract me. Of course, I know that many of the young are attracted to it.

NOR: Why do you suppose that is?

NIN: It makes for a balance in American life. It gives a space for meditation, for repose, to a way of life which doesn't have repose. If you go to Japan and sit in a restaurant, everything is so quiet, people are taking stock of themselves. Everything is done so quietly, and there is a natural meditation. You don't need to make an area of quietness; just having tea takes on that kind of quietness.

NOR: Can you come to some sort of "religious" realization through art?

NIN: Yes. I once read a description of satori by a Spanish author, and for the first time it was a very simple description. He said that it was a feeling of oneness with nature, a oneness with other human beings. I said, "Is that all it is? I feel that; I always have." It's not such a complex thing that you have to go through such a discipline.

NOR: You are known for your use of the *roman-fleuve* concept. It seems to me that the *roman-fleuve* requires a special way of looking at all the elements of good writing: character, motivation, personality, timing, construction. It really rejects the conventional idea of storytelling.

NIN: You're quite right. I think that that comes out of a philosophy, or an attitude. My attitude was one of free association. I saw things as a chain, and felt that everything is continuous and never really ends. I had a sense of continuity and relatedness; relatedness between the past and the present and the future, between races and between the sexes, between everything. That's an attitude that sustains me as a writer.

NOR: For a long time, American publishers resisted this conception. Why do you think that was?

NIN: I think that when you are uneasy, when you are not at one with things that you tend to lose yourself in technique. Publishers are very big on technique. The technique of the novel and the short story was that it had a beginning, a middle, and an end, and they taught you that. They taught you to make plots, to plot the novel before you wrote it. The technical part of writing became the reality, but in fact this isn't at all true to life. The people who did this claimed to be realists and that I, supposedly, was not. Actually, I know now that I was nearer the truth than they were, because we don't live our lives like a novel. We don't have these convenient denouements, these neat finishes; it just isn't so. Life goes on and on in circles; perhaps the past will tie up the future for you, but who knows? One can only guess.

NOR: Do you think that the *roman-fleuve* concept will affect the future development of the American novel? Will we grow further away from the ideas of definitive plot and tight construction?

NIN: Yes, I think so, but for the moment I can't really tell; for the moment, there is this great interest in diary writing. But then,

American society is set in such a way that this interest in the diary is quite natural; it tends to reassure people about their own individuality.

It's important to let your imagination go, especially at a young age. I let mine run free when I was young. I loved to make a drama out of everything, even the weather, and I allowed this to come through in the diary. If you do see things through the eyes of imagination, you should relate it. Obviously, as far as the dramatization of experience or feelings is concerned, I was doing that when I was eighteen. Very little happened to me at that age; I blew it up and let myself go. Maybe I did that because I considered it a work that no one would see and I therefore felt free. And I have everything in there: quotations from other writers, notes on things that I hoped to do someday, ideas for stories. The storytelling element in a diary is good; it's what distinguishes it from a boring journal. A number of women send me their diaries, and many of these diaries aren't interesting because of the way they are told. But it's only the way they're telling it that's not interesting; the things themselves are always interesting. They don't know how to bring it out, mostly because the imagination is stifled.

NOR: Does it ever bother you when critics say, or insinuate, that your diaries are more fiction than fact?

NIN: No, that doesn't bother me. After all, I know the facts, and I know that the facts are true. I also know that I see events in a lyrical or dramatic way and I feel that this is valid. I know that the way I see Bali, for example, is not the way the travel writer for the *L.A. Times* sees Bali; he will write about the hotel prices, and the shops, and all that, which is important. But my point of view is valid, too.

NOR: How do you react to the criticism—which is voiced by people who apparently have had only a cursory exposure to your work—that you are self-obsessed; they seem fond of using the term "narcissistic"?

NIN: I try to laugh that sort of thing away, because I think they are terribly wrong. I think the reason we have felt burdened or constricted in America, why we have felt so alienated, is that we didn't have any Self, we didn't have an "I." The cultural atmosphere of France did affect me in the sense that all the writers there kept diaries, and you knew it was Gide, and you knew it was Mauriac;

they were entities. That's where I got my tradition, and there is no diary without an "I." So I laugh at this criticism because I think it comes from Puritanism. I think it comes from the Puritan conception that looking inward is neurotic, that subjectivity is neurotic, that writing about yourself is immodest. I think it's terribly funny. Every now and then the narcissism charge comes up; they apparently don't know what it means. One French woman said, "If that's narcissism, it's a pretty exigent one. She's demanding an awful lot of herself." Quite obviously, to anyone who is very sensitive, the diary reflects a *lack* of confidence, a *lack* of certainty about myself, and the reason why I wrote down the compliments was because I needed to.

Anyone who can read through a psychological character knows that I wasn't very pleased with myself. I was always in a struggle to achieve more in my own character. I was always involved in a confrontation with myself, which is painful. I think that's our heritage from Puritanism. It's a lack of self-understanding. Most people have an illusion about their being objective. They feel that by not talking about themselves, they are doing an honorable or virtuous thing. Again, this is from Puritanism. And I must tell you this, because I think it's interesting: the women, the ones who really went into the diary, took it very differently. They said just the opposite, that this was not my diary, but theirs. They bypassed this business of narcissism and the "I" and said, "that 'I' is me." What they wrote to me was, "I feel that way about the father. Your father was not quite like mine, but I felt the same way." They wrote that about many things, that they felt the same. My feeling was not that I was at all a special being, or an eccentric, but I was voicing things for other women, and for some men, too, because there are men who understand the diary very well. It's a falsity to say that because you have a sense of yourself it means that you are also speaking for others, but the result of the diary, for those who are really into it, is that they feel that I have helped make them aware of who they are, and where they are going, and how they want to get there.

NOR: And this couldn't have been an intentional effort on your part?

NIN: No. I thought I was telling my own story, and that I was exposing my neuroses so that I could be rid of them. Simply telling the story was more important to me than any other consideration. I needed to tell it.

NOR: I'd like to turn to the question of the persona, which is a subject that you've pursued in both the fiction and the diaries. Would it be accurate to describe the persona as a necessary but transitory state, a condition which we should try to outgrow?

NIN: I think that the persona is something we create defensively. It's what we present to the world, what we think the world will accept. We all do this to a certain extent, but I don't think that we can ever really communicate on the basis of persona to persona. Thus, we become lonely within the persona. I experienced a great deal of this loneliness in the early diary, when I was playing roles, pretending to be a wife, pretending to be this or that, but never fully bringing myself into anything. Only in the diary did I really exist; only in the diary could I open myself to others. When you realize something like that, you become angry at the persona because it's keeping you from contact with others. If I sit here trying to create a persona for you, everything would be ruined. And only when you outgrow that compulsion to conform to a mere image—and I think you do outgrow it, as one truly matures—it's what Jung called the "second birth"—will you really dare to be yourself and to speak out about your own experiences. In the beginning, I couldn't do that face to face with people; I could only do it through the diary. There again, you see that I was really a scared person. But I was willing to go back to the diary when I saw that it could help me destroy the persona.

NOR: Then, in a healthy person, the persona always dissipates entirely?

NIN: I think it's one of our goals that it should dissipate because it's a defensive thing, it can imprison you. We've all known personalities—celebrities—who are imprisoned by their own public patterns. With me, recognition came too late for me to be caught by the public image. I was already mature and rid of my persona, and I wasn't going to take up one for the lectures or TV. Fame came so late that I could really be myself, on TV or anywhere else. I wasn't constrained by all these things which create artificiality. But if it had happened to me at twenty, I don't know if I could have done it.

NOR: I was wondering about the female characters—Lillian, Djuna, and Sabina—who appear in *Cities of the Interior*. Oliver Evans described them as "archetypes," and I wondered how valid you felt that description was. Also, to what extent would you say these women were conscious extensions of your own personality?

NIN: I wouldn't say that they are archetypes, except in the very broad sense that each of us is an archetype of our predominant character traits. I certainly didn't conceive of them in a rigid way that would make them literary archetypes. As far as their being conscious extensions of my own personality, I wouldn't say that at all. One can argue, of course, that every character comes out of an author's perception, and that since perception is a major part of a writer's psyche—of his personality if you prefer—it may be said that fictional characters are therefore, in some way, representative of the author. But that argument is a bit convoluted.

NOR: We talked before about the mutual affinity which seems to exist among many artists. Is there also an inherent antagonism?

NIN: Oh, yes, I suppose. But that's from envy and jealousy, don't you think? In France, it was less so because the stakes were not material, the writers didn't really make any money. There was none of that rivalry that I found when I came to this country where there was a great deal of envy and jealousy. Here, there is a struggle for material status among writers. I found that they were not as collective, or communal, or fraternal, not as willing to help each other, as we were. But then, we didn't have the temptation. We weren't expecting to make $20,000, or anything like that, so I'm aware that not having these temptations made being fraternal much easier. The American experience, to me, became obviously tied up with commercialism, with making rivalries and competitions. In France, the young writers didn't think they were going to make it; that's the truth. I can remember going with Henry Miller to the Balzac Museum and he said to me jokingly, "Do you think our manuscripts will ever be shown this way?" We really didn't think they would be. We weren't aiming at that. So it was easy enough to be fraternal and devoted, whereas the American has a terrible financial temptation.

NOR: We've all heard stories about famous writers who were once friends but who have come to a parting of the ways. As an extension of these rather personal antagonisms which arise between individuals, have you ever seen Man, the social entity, as being a natural antagonist, either to women as a group, or to you personally?

NIN: Oh, yes. I think we have all suffered from that. We don't know the origins, but I certainly think that there are wars between men and women. I think that certain active Feminists are currently trying to make a war.

NOR: Is it a justified war?

NIN: No, I don't believe in war, in any kind of war. War isn't going to solve the problems of our relationships, or affect our psychological independence, or our freedom to act, or our standard of living.

NOR: Historically—and psychologically, I suppose—the sexes have tended to circumvent each other, and have thereby thwarted understanding and mutual acceptance. Much of this is due to role-playing. Do you see this as inevitable? Is it bound to continue?

NIN: No, I don't think so. I think it only happens when something's gone wrong. We all have causes for hostility which aren't necessarily related to sexual matters—we all get injured or get betrayed—but in proportion to how we can transcend those things, we become a different sort of human being. I didn't have any bitter feelings, for instance, after being ignored for twenty years, when the same publishers who turned me down began sending me books to comment on. I don't feel bitter about that; it's something I understand. But some people accumulate bitterness or hostility, mostly when they blame others for where they are. I think women tend to blame men for where they are when they should be spending at least an equal amount of energy looking inward to see how they got there.

NOR: One can't argue very much with the economic points made by the Liberation Movement, but somehow I feel that many women underestimate the more pervasive psychological power or influence which they have always had, and I don't mean merely the sexual power over men. It's something more nebulous than that.

NIN: That's the kind of power women had in Europe, but women here never seemed to have that power; it's really a kind of spiritual power. Somehow the Frenchman considers the woman's opinion rather automatically when making decisions. The Frenchwoman may not have had many legal rights or the power to earn a living, but she did have this other power. She was not simply a sexual object; she had an influence. But I think that the whole thing will mellow, it's mellowing already. You know, Americans essentially love to foster hostility. They encourage it; they love to fight. The media encourage it also. They don't encourage reconciliation, and understanding, and compassion. They never try to reconcile, they love the hostilities and the prize fights. That's one thing I find much less in Europe. Perhaps they've already worked out their aggressions through the wars, I don't know.

NOR: Of the younger women writers being noticed today—Joyce Carol Oates, Erica Jong, Susan Sontag, Germaine Greer, the late Sylvia Plath—are there any about whom you're very enthusiastic? Also, when you were beginning your career, were there any writers to whom you looked for guidance or inspiration?

NIN: My inspiration writers were always Lawrence and Proust. About the younger writers, I'm afraid I'm not very enthusiastic, although I do very much admire Germaine Greer. I think her efforts have been very worthwhile.

NOR: Many people feel that the official recognition that you are now enjoying is long overdue. How do you react to this sort of "establishment" approval?

NIN: I react in different ways. My first impulse is to back away from organizations and official honors; but I'm also aware that recognition has an important psychological impact which affects a number of people, not just the person being recognized or honored. I'm often reminded of that by my young women friends, whom I call my "spiritual daughters." They remind me that being given a public forum also gives one an opportunity to exert a positive and constructive influence.

NOR: After your long involvement in the composition of your continuous novel, *Cities of the Interior*, *Collages* seemed to mark a new phase in your approach to fiction. Do you have plans for anything similar?

NIN: *Collages* was a flight, really. I was so disillusioned by the reception of the novels, it seemed like I had reached a dead-end. And then I suddenly began to think that maybe my major work was the diary. So now, of course, I'm involved in finishing Volume 7. When I do finish it, I plan to go through some of the childhood diaries; then, who knows? But I had the feeling that fiction, for me, was disastrous. Even though now people write quite beautifully about it and seem to understand the fiction, somehow I have become detached from it.

NOR: It's hard to imagine that you could feel that way.

NIN: It could just be because the fiction led me to a wall. It led me to a sort of troubled silence, and it could be that that influenced me. But it could also be that I realized I had put much more into the diaries. And, as I said before, there are imaginative elements in the diaries, too.

NOR: On the whole, would you say that your life as an artist has been as rewarding as you could have wished it to be?

NIN: Definitely, yes. There is a special kind of reward which is wonderful, and it's something which, I think, only artists enjoy. It has nothing to do with material rewards. It's the reward of finding your people, the chance to make a world, a population of your own, and that's wonderful because you find yourself as a connecting link between people who think as you do and feel as you do. And suddenly you're not alone; there is a constant exchange which you enjoy yourself and which you help to promote among others.

NOR: Are you optimistic about what you see happening around us all today?

NIN: I'm optimistic only about the new consciousness of the young, that's all. I'm not optimistic about the country or about the tyranny of business all over the world. Now it's too late for revolution. We couldn't make revolution against the corporate establishment no matter how much we wanted to because it's simply too big. But I am optimistic about people's ability to develop themselves in a more meaningful and more lasting way than we've experienced in the past. I believe that the change of consciousness will have an impact for the good.

Lina Wertmüller

Interviewed by Ernest Ferlita, S. J. and John Navone, S. J. (1976)

Lina Wertmüller's films include the recent international hits *Swept Away* and *Seven Beauties*. This interview took place on October 25, 1976, at Lina Wertmüller's apartment in Rome. It appears in *The Parables of Lina Wertmüller* by Ernest Ferlita and John R. May, a recent release of the Paulist Press. The interviewers were Ernest Ferlita, S. J., and John Navone, S. J.

NEW ORLEANS REVIEW: I was sorry to hear that your film on Caligula would not be made. I became very interested when you told John Simon that it would be about "the great trap that is God." Would you be willing to say more about that idea?

LINA WERTMÜLLER: You are turning the knife in my wound.

NOR: I realize that must have been a great disappointment.

WERTMÜLLER: I like very much the idea of my Caligula. I've been trying to get it done for ten years! When Guccione—the producer of Gore Vidal's *Caligula*—came to me, I told him I didn't see how I could do it. For two years we went on about it. Finally, I had to tell him it was impossible. I know Gore Vidal is a good writer, but I had my own ideas.[1] If you wait, I think you will see my *Caligula*.

NOR: I surely hope so.

WERTMÜLLER: It is necessary to be patient. I love my idea about this man Caligula. The historical Caligula was a very young man, very strange, very centralized. His situation was so special it is difficult for us to understand. He became emperor probably as the result of a series of crimes, which were nevertheless quite in accord with the times. They would be evaluated in a way very different from the way we'd evaluate them today. Certainly, he achieved absolute power. The power of a Roman emperor—that is not easy for us to grasp. It would be as if he were the ruler of America *and* Russia and every other power—all summed up in one man. The greatest known power in the world. Then, at the moment of his ascendancy, he was struck by a cerebral fever. I am speaking now of his true-life story. He went into a spiral of madness. It's his madness that is interesting. Think of the great tyrants, like Hitler. Hitler tended to absolute power. He was convinced he was working for his people. He never suspected that he himself was a monster. That's the irony. All the documents on Caligula are very fascinating. Caligula thought that he was God, and he imagined he was always being betrayed by men. Therefore, he put himself in a very particular position vis-à-vis humanity. For rather base reasons he needed money: to put on his big spectaculars and to run his armies. And so, inspired by the aristocratic concept of the Roman citizen, he was always thinking of traps for men to fall into. The Roman citizen had a great tradition of justice, and Caligula used it to set his traps. We find something like this in the behavior of the Nazis toward the Jews. In Poland, for example, they would ask the rabbis for the names of thirty men to save 300. Usually the rabbis were so desperate they would rather die themselves than make this decision. But sometimes they gave them the names, and the Nazis would give great publicity to what they did in order to discredit them (as well as the concept of spiritual father) in the eyes of the Jews. Now this is similar to what Caligula did. It's a use that power often makes in its administration of justice when it wants to accomplish something unjust, namely, the besmirching of the very concept of justice as represented by certain men. The fathers of the Roman Senate were symbols of justice. Caligula spent his life trying to show that they were men unworthy of the people's esteem. He would lay traps for them, get them into compromising situations, make them do abominable things, and in that way discredit them before the people. He did it to get money but mainly to disassociate himself from the concept of the Roman citizen, to put himself above it, to transcend its responsibilities and obligations, in order to exalt himself into the position of God. In effect, he pushed everything toward corruption and then turned and denounced the perpetrators of it. It is a very interesting mechanism, a mechanism that has operated throughout the history of man, with respect to power.

NOR: And this grasping for power is "the great trap that is God?"

WERTMÜLLER: Very often power outdoes itself in this way. Another variation of it is what happens in the Soviet Union. Russia is a country where people do not count for much. They have very little news there. For ages the same idea has operated in the Church—through the "dark" ages! *(Laughter.)* But now the Church has other problems.

NOR: This idea is linked to another one of yours, is it not, to your concept of "man in disorder?"

WERTMÜLLER: Yes. I think we are living in very interesting but dangerous times. When I speak of "man in disorder," I realize I am using a dangerous phrase. Because disorder is more fascinating than order. And that is terrifying. We see all around us mortal signs of disorder. But there is also a terrifying moment in the concept of order. I believe very profoundly in the concept of the growth of man. Only when this condition of growth exists for man, for every single human being, can there be any possibility for that harmony which we seek in place of order. Order is understood here as something imposed from above, and therefore it has all the risks of concepts or structures imposed from above. Harmony is certainly utopian. But when a man has achieved awareness, he can hope for utopia. The ways in which man has gone in pursuit of harmony throughout his history are many, the first of these being religion, in its original inspiration. All religions, in a certain sense, are the same with respect to the concept of man, i.e., of the man who achieves harmony with all that surrounds him, with life, with others, with himself. When I speak of man in disorder, I am talking about a man who even though he now and then makes mistakes is nevertheless growing in harmony with himself and the world. In the original script of *Seven Beauties* that little phrase "man in disorder" was part of a monologue written for the anarchist that went on for fifty pages. Cited in those pages was that stupendous scene by Thomas Mann from his book *The Magic Mountain* in which he recounts the conversation between the Jesuit and the socialist.[2] Mann presents the concept of faith and of rationalism in a new relationship. He presents them in a way remarkable for his time. What we are given is the concept of the new man, of harmonious man, and he shows how this man can be born through faith, through intelligence, through humanism, through the maturation of society. The whole presentation may strike one as theoretical, but it is so relevant for a world that seems to be rushing headlong towards destruction, lacking all good sense and reason. Yes, man seems to be rushing towards destruction; and yet there are all those other resources, whether religion or reason or culture, that are positive forces for man's harmony.

NOR: When you talk about disorder or anarchy, you tend to oppose it to those things that stifle man's growth. You bring to mind what St. Paul said about the tension between law and spirit. Your notion of anarchy seems to correspond to his notion of spirit. And your notion of imposed structures to a very formalistic application of law. Because what counts for both you and St. Paul is the growth and development of the human spirit.

WERTMÜLLER: Definitely.

NOR: I've always felt that Italy operates on the jazz principle, on the principle of perpetual improvisation. The laws and structures in Italy are something like a beanpole. Your anarchy, and Paul's spirit, are the vine that grows around the pole.

WERTMÜLLER: Just so. An imposed order is stifling. We have some terrible proof of this. I've always been a person of the left, but the history of art in the Soviet Union has been dreadful. There were many great artists and intellectuals who helped bring about the revolution, but then they were alienated because insofar as they were individuals who could quarrel with the revolution they were considered harmful. An imposed order is dangerous in every area of life, even in the Church, when we remember how it retarded important historical developments. One must try to understand at what historical moment a certain form of order came to be.

NOR: In fact, for Jesus himself, it was from organized religion that his principle enemies came.

WERTMÜLLER: Certainly.

NOR: Jesus, then, was "man in disorder" relative to the pharisaical order of the day.

WERTMÜLLER: Exactly. Jesus always tried to show in extraordinary ways what man was all about. Like St. Francis of Assisi. That's why Dostoevsky is so remarkable in his portrayal of the Grand Inquisitor. This was the very problem he was dealing with—the problem of political order and power. It's a very great human theme. One of the greatest. Always under discussion. But beyond words there is always the truth that is difficult. In our age we must make ourselves go beyond them, because we are faced with a series of unarrestable social misdeeds, such as overpopulation. Already we number four billion people. What's going to happen in fifteen or twenty years? And then there's science, with its perilous research projects—the mysterious bomb whose consequences it does not know. And this fact has its impact on human nature. I have my days of pessimism when I fear we are just not going to make it.

NOR: In *Seven Beauties* Pasqualino's salvation is "to survive."

WERTMÜLLER: But of course that kind of salvation is a death.

NOR: Where does the vision come for a man like this?

WERTMÜLLER: It comes from the other character, from the anarchist, the one who says that man must achieve his harmony as quickly as possible. But it's not a vision so much as an intuition of the times. With respect, for instance, to massacre. In all those pages I cut out there was a link with all the great massacres of history—the massacre by the Spaniards of the Indians, of the Aztecs, the Incas; the massacre by the Inquisition; so many others. When we read about the figures of these massacres, including that of the Jews, we get some idea of the massacres that could occur under the pressure of overpopulation. All the scientific tests on the relationship of aggression to overpopulation are nightmarish. The man who has a certain harmony with his own space reacts very differently from the man in disharmony. In experiments with rats, aggression rises in proportion to overpopulation. This is a major problem, like the problem of pollution. Of very immediate concern.

NOR: There is still the question of woman as it relates to man's predicament, as you describe it. In *Love and Anarchy*, love was represented by one woman, anarchy by another. In *The Seduction of Mimi*, I have the impression that love and anarchy coexist in the character of Fiore. Do you see her as a kind of ideal that shows man what he should aim for?

WERTMÜLLER: I'm going to confess something to you. I don't make a distinction between man and woman in this sense. My characters are symbols for me of certain things having to do with human beings, quite independently of their sex. I don't believe in the distinction of the sexes. *(Laughing.)* The Council of Trieste spent three centuries trying to establish that woman had a soul.[3] You can understand how they came to this conclusion, since the Roman matron had even more than a soul, she had tremendous power. Latium (the region of Rome) was a matriarchal society. However, I want to say that I reject every distinction between man and woman. This is so true that in my film *Swept Away* I have the woman representing industrial society and the man representing the Third World. For example, the most obscure proletariat, when he comes home, gives vent to all the frustration and humiliation he has endured during the day by making his subject (his wife) the "Third World," by making her the butt of his rage. This presents a great problem for future societies regarding feminism. The day that man loses this woman upon whom he relies for so many services, he will become even more fragile than he is now. This imports a great change in the family structure. In this case, as in so many others, if you look with attention, the Church has given some very important directions, because the monastic or conventual concept is a great one. I believe that only the creation of communities will enable man to survive this blasting of the atom that was the family. Once the atom or the molecule of the family is broken up, society loses a great element of its equilibrium. Especially if you don't put an end to overpopulation. It's indispensable to arrive at a concept of group, of commune. This has nothing to do with any silly sexual idea. Today we're bombarded with sex. I am obviously against any type of censorship. But the identification of pornography with liberty is something that I reject outright. I am constantly called upon to support causes that I have to support for conformity's sake. You cannot but support causes for total freedom of expression. *(Chuckling.)* On the other hand, I am continually faced with the absurdity of identifying pornography with liberty. I have a great respect for human sensitivities and sentiments. And so I don't think there's any relationship between the concept of pornography and the fostering of authentic human development. Assuredly, pornography is more easily a loss than a gain, just as the concept of sin is a loss. But if we get rid of the concept of sin, everything seems to lose its fascination. This construction, which has been erected for so many centuries, is a delicate one. It has brought man to a sense of mystery, of fear, of vitality, of his own desires, of the possibility of sublimating them or of expressing them through his own body and intelligence. The breakdown, historical and therefore inexorable, of so many delicate equilibriums leaves man with all his values destroyed, bombarded, without putting in their place anything that conduces to his harmony. You're a Jesuit, aren't you?

NOR: Yes, the both of us.

WERTMÜLLER: You Jesuits have always been great workers in this field. Wonderful interpreters of the human soul. Great historians of the human spirit. St. Ignatius especially. A great genius. And all your schools!

NOR: Do you know Father Arrupe, the general of the Jesuits?

WERTMÜLLER: I don't know him personally.

NOR: I think you would find him very similar in temperament to you. He has a profound rapport with the contemporary world and a genius for addressing it.

WERTMÜLLER: That is the way of the Jesuits. They are great experimenters. Do you know the drama called *Sur la terre comme au ciel*? It's about the anarchical, socialist experiment that the Jesuits made in South America.

NOR: Oh, yes, in English it's called *The Strong Are Lonely*. It's all about the reductions in Paraguay.

WERTMÜLLER: And the necessity of having to work out that very difficult equation between faith and knowledge.

NOR: The same improvisation was made by Father Ricci in China, adapting the faith to its culture.[4]

WERTMÜLLER: Exactly. It's in this way that a true salvation can come about for the Church. The Church has never in a thousand years been in such a perilous state as it is today. What's needed is more than just having the priest turn around and say the Mass in Italian. I mix a lot with people in southern Italy, with the poor, with women; I've talked to them a lot. And they're very opposed to all these changes in the liturgy. They wouldn't go as far as the French in their insubordination in regard to Vatican II, like LeFevbre, I mean. But it was an elitist decision rather than the kind of grassroots decision that the Church has always made in the past. The Church is wise. *(Laughing.)* It has usually waited for fashions to pass before making crucial decisions. And this business of putting a cement altar in the middle of the church! *(Laughing.)* It does violence to the beauty of the church; the churches just weren't built for that. I remember when I was a child listening to the women saying the Ave Maria, even though they didn't know the Latin. There were these sounds apparently devoid of meaning; what they conveyed was an overall meaning rather than the meaning of any particular word; the words *represented* prayer.

NOR: It was a kind of self-transcendence.

WERTMÜLLER: Yes, because in the subconscious there is a very profound sense of mystery. Mystery has always been the great support for all the comforts of religion. Even for fear. The comfort of fear must be as mysterious as fear itself. It can't be rationalized in a catechism. I had a conflict with the Church when I was young, a great conflict, which may sound rather silly if I try to explain how it came about in me. I was thirteen years old when I reflected on the first principles of the catechism. I reasoned on this equation that was proposed to me: God is omniscient, omnipresent, omnipotent. Therefore, he knows all, he wills all. Then he decided to create humanity *the way it is*, with free will, knowing (because he is omniscient) all that would happen, with man placed within the confines of good and evil and with his great facility for slipping into evil. And so if at the end of all this you propose to me a heaven and a hell, I have to think that this omniscient God knows from the beginning that he will construct a series of eternal miseries. He has himself constructed the whole mechanism, and therefore he is bad![5] You laugh, but this is what brought about a revolution in me. I refuted every concept of faith, didn't I? This was no way to teach me catechism; you ought to tell me rather that God is a mystery. *(Laughing.)* On this point I fought with everybody, with all the priests and all the nuns, and I broke my links with the Church.

NOR: I have a feeling that the Church betrays itself when it is too literal in conceptualizing its beliefs.

WERTMÜLLER: That's exactly what I was saying when I spoke of all those changes in the ritual. The ritual was full of mystery.

NOR: You need the image to preserve mystery.

WERTMÜLLER: Definitely.

NOR: This has always been the strength of the great myths—the myths of Paradise, of Adam and Eve, of Moses—because the myths are not doctrine.

WERTMÜLLER: I agree.

NOR: Myths are always open, and you can reflect upon them for further insight into the mystery they attempt to convey. Once, when I was studying the Old Testament, a classmate of mine asked the professor: "Wouldn't it have been better if Von Ranke had written Genesis instead of that mythmaker? With Von Ranke we would have known right off what was true or false." The professor answered: "No. When you speak of mystery, myth is far more appropriate."

WERTMÜLLER: Bravo.

NOR: You can't imprison mystery in a phrase.

WERTMÜLLER: The Jesuit in *The Magic Mountain* says the same thing. It's quite extraordinary because he comes to the conclusion that a great mystery, if it becomes the object of faith, thereby becomes the truth. Magnificent. You should reread this passage.[6]

NOR: Would you say that your films are attempts to construct new myths for modern man?

WERTMÜLLER: What I hope to express in my films is my great faith in the possibility of man becoming human. I have to set man up against society because I believe that the concept of the masses is a dangerous thing. It frightens me. The masses live according to the law of the anthill. I believe the greatest danger for man lies in this kind of anthill existence. Therefore, the greatest defense for man, with all his intelligence, is to understand that *he* is society. Therefore, if I have children, I am one and all. I am one become five. It's my end, and everybody's end. There's no more harmony. When the Bible says, "Increase and multiply, as the grains of sands in the desert," you should interpret that ironically. If you increase and multiply like the grains of sands in the desert, you will *have* a desert. *Un de-ser-TO*. *(Laughter.)*

NOR: Now for a final question of fact. You mentioned Thomas Mann, Dostoevsky, the Bible. Are there other major intellectual influences in your life?

WERTMÜLLER: I really wouldn't know how to answer that because there are many and none. I believe that we are all the other. We are everything that has been: we are cellular, which is more than being culturally united. Cellular. I am not a very learned person, but I am very much alive. I love people very much. I believe in life. I enjoy it. I believe in my work. I believe in action, and my way is not to create living beings but to create culture in life. I do whatever I can to contribute to harmony. Many people were influences on my life—certainly there are many people that I have loved, many who have enlightened me. I can speak of my most recent passion, "my last love." My last love is Ceronetti. Do you know Ceronetti? *(She takes a book down from one of the shelves.) La carta è stanca* (*Paper Is Tired*) by Guido Ceronetti. He is an intellectual, an Italian essayist, a young man of thirty-five living in Rome. I can read a little of him to show you something of his thought. Here's something he wrote at the end of 1975, a message for the New Year. Something stupendous. May I read you part of it?

NOR: By all means.

WERTMÜLLER: *(Reading.)* "If only people would understand that above all they need to get their breath again! They need a rest from history! A generous letting go, a pulling back, a slowing down, economic, demographic, industrial, scientific! Less industry, less money, fewer universities, fewer shows, fewer newspapers, less smoke! Silence. Truce. Little occupations. A few books. Not to have to go to the bathroom so badly. To die on time. Not to go around clawing in a sewer for a gigantic, imposed idea pulled up by black rats out of an intellectual language towards the clogged foundations to a dead end . . . for an excess of civilization we are losing it."[7]

Notes

1   As it turned out, Gore Vidal's *Caligula* did not, according to him, follow his original script anyway. In a conversation with the interviewers he said that his Caligula was a man obsessed with death.

His Caligula would watch people die as if to discover what secrets death might hold.

2   The Jesuit in *The Magic Mountain* is an ambiguous character, to say the least. Naphta is a Jew turned Jesuit but not quite. He is not, as the young hero of the book (Hans Castorp) puts it, a "proper" Jesuit, never having been ordained or having taken final vows. What Castorp (and apparently Thomas Mann) imagines a Jesuit to be is only a little less strange than Naphta's own misapprehension. The conversation between Naphta and Settembrini (Castorp's Virgil on the Magic Mountain) to which Wertmüller refers is probably that section of Chapter VI entitled "The City of God, and Deliverance by Evil" in which Naphta speaks of the proletariat taking up the task of Pope Gregory the Great "to strike terror into the world for the healing of the world, that man may finally achieve salvation and deliverance, and win back at length to freedom from law and destruction of classes, to his original status as child of God." (H. T. Lowe-Porter's translation of *The Magic Mountain*, Penguin Books, 1960, p. 404.)

3   No doubt Ms. Wertmüller intends this remark with a certain irony. Actually, we were unable to find any such council on record, and while certain theologians have questioned the quality of a woman's soul, the official teaching of the Church—much to our relief—has always been that at least she had one.

4   In Paraguay, the State stepped in and undid all the work of the Jesuits among the Indians; in China, the Church stepped in and undid their work among the Chinese. Both chapters in the history of cultural interaction make highly instructive reading.

5   It is interesting to note that Wertmüller rejects this concept of God because, like Caligula, he sets traps for men.

6   Wertmüller is probably referring to the passage in Chapter VI: "Whatever profits man," Naphta begins, "that is the truth." (Ibid., p. 404.)

7   Guido Ceronetti, *La carta è stanca* (Milano: Adelphi Edizioni, 1976), pp. 386, 387.

Bertrand Tavernier

Interviewed by John Mosier
(1978)

Born in Lyon, France, in 1941, Bertrand Tavernier established himself while still in his twenties as a film critic and historian by writing three books on American film. He was employed by a film promotion company, and as a press attaché, he worked with Claude Chabrol, Jean-Luc Godard, and Pierre Schoendoerffer. During this period, he founded the Nickel-Odeon, which screened films rarely seen in France or the United States.

His latest film, *Des Enfants Gates (The Spoiled Children)*, was completed in 1977 and opened the Semaines Universitaires, Loyola University's tenth annual festival of new French film. John Mosier, assisted by Sarah Elizabeth Spain, conversed with Tavernier in New Orleans on March 15, 1978, when the director attended the premiere of *Enfants*.

NEW ORLEANS REVIEW: One minute no one had ever heard of your work, and then it was one bombshell after the other: *The Clockmaker, Let Joy Reign Supreme*, and now *The Spoiled Children*.

BERTRAND TAVERNIER: Yes, it was an accident. None of the films I made were for the U.S. They were all made for French audiences. I think—and this is my greatest belief—that film should be rooted in a national culture, a national context. I think that the worst thing about film now is when films do not seem to belong to any culture, to any country, to any society. *The Clockmaker* took me a year to make, and during that time one of the arguments against it was that it would never sell in the U.S.

And I kept saying to them that I'd studied the U.S., that I wrote a book on American cinema, that I had been to the States several times. The films that work in the U.S.—at least they work in a few cities and in the universities—are not the films that French producers and directors make for the American public, which are imitations of American thrillers. The films that are successful are those like Jean Renoir's *Grand Illusion*, like the films of Truffaut, Rohmer, Chabrol. Those films that are very French are successful in the U.S., and if you look into it you see that films like Tachella's *Cousin Cousine* are like *The Clockmaker* in this respect. The Americans, the few Americans who are interested in foreign films, don't want to see imitations of what they already have.

NOR: But you've taken that principle further than almost anyone because two of your films, *The Judge and the Assassin* and *Let Joy Reign Supreme*, are embedded in French history.

TAVERNIER: It's true. I adore history. Someone asked me—you always wanted to make a political film, a social film, why did you choose an historical film? Why didn't you make a film about today? And that puzzles me. Looking back at history, trying to understand what happened, is part of our culture, part of our education. Those actions in the past are closely related to the present.

When people think they are making a modern film, a more personal film when they make a film about life today, they're crazy. Because what about the historian? What about, after all, Marx, Engels, Lenin? They wrote about the past. They tried to think what had happened. I believe that if you can look at the past in a certain way, that past is always related to the moment when the audience is on jury duty in front of the film.

Of course, that makes things difficult sometimes for foreigners, although in such cases it seems to me the critics should play an important part in explaining the film. But people, even in the colleges, do too little work in seeing a film. First, forget it if you don't know one date, one little historical detail. Forget it. Try to see the film as though it were a film about today. Try to see the emotions, because the emotions which are inside the people in that film are still modern. *Let Joy Reign Supreme* is the story of a man who is refusing power, the fight for freedom, for justice, the relationship between corruption and power, the moment, I mean. It's the story of a man who is against the church and wants to speak with the devil. The man wants to experience sexual freedom and at the same time he's killing himself. It's modern. I think that people should work from there and forget the history because I don't think that any French audience knew much more about the history than any foreign one. The regency is a period no one knows.

NOR: It's a fascinating period.

TAVERNIER: Yes, fascinating. It was like an explosion. People were researching in many ways. It was after twenty years of Puritanism, and the end of Louis XIV. It was terrible then, so there was a kind of explosion, which went too far, but at least they tried. It's a pity. It's where the word "inflation" was invented, along with those notions about paper money and gold. But I think that people should forget history. They have to think with a feeling and later to work on the historical level. I hope that the film makes them want to read a book, or at least to ask questions. I hope it provokes curiosity. So I think even if you don't know the history very well, you should at least be able to get the sense of the film as though it were a contemporary film, to feel the emotions, because the emotions that are inside are still modern. Then of course if you know the history, it will help you.

I don't think it's necessary to be very educated to understand the film. The problem is not in the film; it's in the people, in all of those people who when they suddenly see some dates, some costumes, some names, immediately have an inferiority complex. I discovered history through Dumas and Hugo as well as through classes and the cinema, too, through Westerns even. To see *Broken Arrow* was a shock for me when I was very young, and I wanted to know more about the Indians and what happened in the West. And then I discovered genocide and all of that.

NOR: So the Westerns began to stimulate your interest?

TAVERNIER: Yes, and you know why? It's because the Western is the historical film which is not filmed by anyone in the world as an historical film. When people go to see one, they never have the feeling that they're watching history.

NOR: The Western is timeless?

TAVERNIER: Yes, because the people, even if they don't know who Wyatt Earp is, or if they don't know the meaning of the cattle barons, can work on their feelings. They don't know that the hero of *Broken Arrow* is a real person who actually existed, and they don't feel inferior about the fact that they don't know. The problem with historical films is that some people, critics, teachers, despise them because of the distance, as though they're childish. Most of the time when you say historical film, people say, "Okay, it's Cecil B. DeMille." It's very difficult to work within that range and do a film that will not make an audience feel inferior, and at the same time will not be despised by the critics.

NOR: Obviously, you've been able to do that. I can't think of anyone else in France, or in Europe for that matter, who's attempted what you've done here. It's as though there are no previous models.

TAVERNIER: It's not fashionable. There's Rene Allio, but I think he's too cold. He wants to be too analytical. Sometimes he forgets that history is made of flesh and blood and people who behave accordingly. He wants to be Brechtian, but he forgets that Brecht used comedy—in *Galileo*, for instance. It has a lot of humor, it has guts, it's funny, it's wild even, and it's moving. So I think that notion of distance doesn't work too well for filmmakers.

And there were people who tried to do this before the war. Jean Renoir's *La Marseilleise* is an incredibly good film. And in theatre there were people who worked on plays by Molière and Marivaux and suddenly those plays, which we had studied in class. . . . They put servants in and the people staging the play suddenly made Marivaux like a play of today.

NOR: And filming history as flesh and blood has really become one of your aims?

TAVERNIER: Yes, and Italian directors do it—people like Comencini, whose *Youth and Adolescence of Casanova* is a brilliant film.

NOR: But now after two films, you've moved away from history and made a contemporary film, like your first one, *The Clockmaker*.

TAVERNIER: Yes, but I think every film should be a challenge. The most terrible thing for me is routine, and the most terrible danger for a director is to be self-conscious about what he can do: then he will follow the old paths to be safe. I want every film I make to be a new challenge, not only because I think that it's the only way to keep learning things, to keep learning my job, but because it's the only way my vision can become wider. I love to work on projects where after I've made the film, I think I've learned something. What I would like to get on the screen in two hours is something that would enable the audience to share the knowledge I gained, the anger I had, the fun I had during those nine months or a year or eighteen months when I was making the film. Not the same experience, but at least I concentrate in two hours what I have experienced during those months.

And for me it's always a kind of joke that I could stop making films and either do some lectures about the eighteenth century or the nineteenth century or about the problem of tenants. I'm an expert on rent control, and I was very good at knowing about all of the crime stories in Lyons in 1968. I think we work in a medium that allows us to see fascinating people, to learn interesting facts, to discuss problems with specialists—judges, lawyers, clockmakers, specialists on urbanization.

And now I'm working on a sociological science fiction film and I've already met people who are specialists in futuristics. I'm learning, and I want to learn, and I want to share with the audience the joy I had because I think that's the only way for me to show them that I treat them as equals. I'm not despising them, sending them some fast food on a tray and saying eat it—it's garbage, but you'll love it. I'm very happy when they laugh.

NOR: Your next film will put you in competition with some world class directors?

TAVERNIER: No, because I don't think it will look like Lucas or Spielberg. It will be without any special effects, and it will be shot in the streets, perhaps more like the style of Louis Malle in *Black Moon*, but certainly not like Kubrick's *Clockwork Orange*.

NOR: Because of Kubrick's distance from his characters?

TAVERNIER: Kubrick is cold. He's cynical. I like people more than he does. It's not a difference of quality, of someone being better.

NOR: No, but it's an attitude that certainly comes through with you: your characters feel like people I would like to have sitting in the room with me.

TAVERNIER: Yes, but I think that watching the death of Hal in *2001* is a moving experience, although it's ironic that the moment when Kubrick is really warm and moving and desperate is the death of a computer. *(Laughter.)*

NOR: One thing that interests me is that you've mentioned Molière as someone who seriously impressed you, but I always associate a diamond-like quality with him; his characters seem to glitter; they're very hard and precise, and your vision of human beings is much more sympathetic.

TAVERNIER: Yes, although I think that *Tartuffe* or *Don Juan* can be very moving, even tragic. But I like to put the audience close to the character. I mean intimate, which doesn't mean that I want everything in the film to be explained by a character, by the psychology of characters. I think that what I'm trying to do is to relate the social and historical background, to explain how it sometimes motivates or gives a kind of reality to what characters do. But I want the audience to be intimate. I would love it if I were successful in giving the impression that the film had been filmed the year that it actually happened. I made *Let Joy Reign Supreme* as though the camera were invented in 1720.

Many historical films are made by people who made them with their cultural education of the present, which means that they shoot an actor near furniture, near a chair, and you feel that in that shot, there is the knowledge that the chair, the costume, is beautiful because it's part of history. It's rather a question of showing a chair in such a way that the director feels "Well look at that beautiful regency chair," but for the character it was not, it was only a chair.

NOR: But how did you accomplish that with the actors?

TAVERNIER: I took a long time with them. We read the screenplay, and then we talked. I said I hope you will not only be very comfortable, but very close to the decor that is around you. I want you to feel at ease and to do exactly what you would do in a room in a Hilton—because you can do anything in a Hilton room, as we all know. When we went to try on wigs, Phillip said that they were heavy and hot. So I'm sure that as soon as a character was alone in a room he would take off his wig. I tried to do that. I tried to imagine that it was very cold, so where would they go near the fire.

NOR: You tried to give the feeling that this is where the people really live, it's not a set.

TAVERNIER: I tried to go even further. In *The Judge and the Assassin,* I asked Noiret to pick all of his costumes, and the glasses he has in the movie are now his glasses in life. And I told Brialy that I wanted him to feel at ease in his flat. I didn't want an art director's flat. He had two days to work, to pick up everything and to put it where he wanted it.

NOR: When you got through, were you surprised by the acting?

TAVERNIER: I'm always surprised by the actors. I love them. But I want them to be relaxed, to be happy. I want them to bring me thousands of things and I will choose maybe 100 only, to be as open minded as I am when I'm trying to discover something with the light.

In *The Judge and the Assassin,* I was not happy with the light, so I said to my cameraman cut off all the light. I want the room lit by candles. We realized immediately a change: when Brialy was reading a paper by candlelight, he spoke less loudly because it was darker. Jacques Tourneur told me that. He was fascinated by the fact that people were always speaking too loudly in film, and he always tried to capture the natural sounds of the voice, as if the actor were speaking to me. And immediately it's more subtle.

NOR: You've been talking about attention to detail, and also about how you simply enjoy making films and dealing with people. Your films have very clear views about man dealing with society; they seem to be extremely political.

TAVERNIER: I feel they are, but I don't want them to be political in the way a politician speaks; I want them to be political in the way that Balzac is political or Dos Passos is political. They are political because they try to relate the life of the people, the experience of the people, to what's around them, the underlying reality. I try to build my film with a slow camera movement—a crane movement that starts on one fact, on one detail, and then goes backwards and you begin to see a pyramid, a view of society. *The Judge and the Assassin* was made like that. It was made starting out with a little cry, what Feiffer would call "Little Murders." Somebody shoots a girl whom he wanted to marry and could not. Then from that point which we see—three lines in a paper—we try to see how the action of the character of the assassin is related to his time. Slowly we get a wider view, but slowly, which is why I always have problems with endings because I'm trying not to end the camera movement on two or three characters, but on everything. That's why people sometimes feel that the end of *Let Joy Reign Supreme* is suddenly too political. They call it propaganda, but it's an attempt for me not to reduce a film to the main characters.

NOR: *The Judge and the Assassin* is political in the broadest sense, isn't it? It tells us what the dialectic of French society is.

TAVERNIER: I was very pleased by the reaction of the director Fernando Solanas, a political director whom I respect very much. I thought his film, *The Hour of the Furnaces*, was an analytical, but very passionate, moving, exciting film, and when he saw my film, he told me that he was moved, that he felt he had seen a moment of reality, of history, and that he understood that moment.

NOR: Isn't that the moment that he was trying to capture for Argentina in *The Hour of the Furnaces*?

TAVERNIER: Yes, and that film made me think, but at the same time it was didactic, it was lyrical. Now it's true that a lot of people want so much to tell things, but sometimes they forget to be lyrical and moving and funny, and that's a danger when you deal with a subject. Dealing with it is to become rather too self-conscious or too pompous.

NOR: Yes, but you let your own characters do that. Solanas put slogans on the screen.

TAVERNIER: Yes, but it was different, I mean it was a different time. It's a different country. He had things which were really important to say at that time. You have to relate the director's work to the time and the audience it was trying to catch. And that film was very important for Argentina at that time. I read the screenplay he has done recently, and I think it's not at all the same. (*The Sons of Martin Fierro*, first shown in the Director's Fortnight at Cannes in 1978.)

NOR: *The Hour of the Furnaces* is very much a national film, a film that's firmly rooted in Argentina. The city of Buenos Aires is almost the main character.

TAVERNIER: Yes, we talked about that with Solanas. Maybe it was more important in this case in a South American country that has to deal with true American imperialism. But when you get to Brazil or Cuba you see there are so many difficulties for those directors working there, and at the same time, television is full of American serials. The theatres are full of American films. And you begin to understand the people's anger, their fears. They feel that they are oppressed so that the only way is to fight, and at the same time I think it goes beyond that. I think there is a need now for everybody to look for what I would call his cultural identity, and in the films I made, the historical films that I made, I was trying to do that.

In the same way that Americans made a lot of films such as *Harlan County*, *Jeremiah Johnson*, or *They Shoot Horses, Don't They?* or those films shot in the Midwest, in the provinces, like *I Walk the Line* and *The Rain People*—all of these things are not an accident. You can see these kinds of films being made all over the world, Canada, Brazil, France, Switzerland.

NOR: But many people, many film theorists, would argue that film has to be, is, a universal language, one that instantly communicates, and here we are talking about the national origins, which you say gives cinema its strength.

TAVERNIER: Yes, but one doesn't prevent the other, I think. It's like *The Grand Illusion*. It's one of the most French pictures ever made, and it's international. Look at literature, at music. What's the most national music? Jazz. There's nothing more national than "Black and Tan Fantasy" by Ellington, or Miles Davis, or Charlie Parker, but they become international. Everyone perceives them. I don't see why something, I mean a film, a play, or a piece of music, should not be national and international at the same time. What prevents us from seeing that is not the films, but the way they are released. What prevents a film from becoming international is television. It's almost impossible to see a foreign film on American television except on public television.

NOR: Yes, but it's more than that, even, because television is destroying national consciousness faster than filmmakers can create it. Certain directors—Solanas, whom we've mentioned, Glauber Rocha, Rui Guerra—are all trying to find this national consciousness you've spoken of. But I get the feeling that much of the new French cinema is trying so hard to be international that we really can't identify with anything in it or any of the people.

TAVERNIER: Also, two things: First, it is difficult to speak about the whole French cinema in general because I think it now has a very wide range. There are many talents going in many different directions. In a way, it's wider than at the time of the New Wave.

NOR: Yes, in speaking about this before someone said it's as though we had a *new* New Wave.

TAVERNIER: Yes, it's true—but try not to. I hope there will not be any label on it. You have people of different talents. Even though some of them are not my cup of tea, I respect their work: Duras, Bertuccelli, the man who did *The Red Poster*, Frank Cassenti, to Belmont to Girod. You have people like Chris Marker, who made a good, a very impressive four-hour documentary, a moving film. It's about the part of the world that Marker knew after the Vietnam War, and it's about the deception with Castro, about Allende, about 1968 in France. It's full of questions. It's desperate. You leave the theatre and you feel like fighting, but I think it's very courageous. It's a film that tried to ask all of the right questions about the left wing in certain parts of the world, from Cuba to Czechoslovakia. He tries to see why things didn't work.

So, the second thing, I think it's true sometimes the films are too general. The answer to this is given to us filmmakers when we make films about precise things. Everybody told me that the rent problem would not be understood in the United States. I mean, it's a very precise problem. Many people said, "You are making a film about something too small, too precise." I think a filmmaker should do the thing he wants to do and forget about making a film for the American market, although it's true that we live in a world where the pressure of money and the pressure of the American system is very big. I mean we live with television contaminated by American programs, which in France doesn't buy one minute of French film. And that creates a problem, and we have to hope that we will be able to sell film because for us sometimes it's a question of recouping the money. Not for me, maybe, but for certain directors it's a matter of life and death. It's true, but normally I would say . . .

NOR: To make the film that is in you . . .

TAVERNIER: Yes, and forget everything else.

NOR: And there seem to be many films in you. You're interested in almost everything—rent control, the Regency, crime, the eighteenth century . . .

TAVERNIER: All of those things are related I think politically. They all make me angry. I read that someone asked John Ford in 1931, "Is it true that you make films when you are angry at certain things?" and he said, "Do you know a better reason?" I like that answer.

NOR: But your films are also very objective.

TAVERNIER: I think they're a bit polemical sometimes, but I think these things are all related because they all deal with justice, the feel of justice. It was not conscious, but a lawyer told me that in each of my four films there is a trial that we never see—and it's an unfair trial. I don't know, it's unconscious, but it's true that I'm dealing with that, all of the time with the subject of people who make a desperate struggle to communicate, to try to contact, to touch, to express, who succeed sometimes or who are destroyed in trying to.

The Judge and the Assassin is about a cry for help. The man is crying, "Cure me, cure me. I'm sick. Help me!" and they kill him. It's a paradox. It's why I think that in all of the films I've made, the words, the lines, the language are very important because it's difficult, this communication. And another thing, I think sometimes the scenes that are not shot are as important as the scenes that are shown. I want to leave the audience with some work to do. It's up to them to finish the film.

NOR: "The epilogue starts when the lights go on," as Silvio Back would say.

TAVERNIER: Yes, that's right. I never put the end on my films, never. I mean I refuse, because I don't think there should be an ending.

NOR: There should be a dialogue.

TAVERNIER: And the dialogue belongs to the film itself. It is part of the film.

NOR: If you're in Europe, maybe, but the disturbing thing here—and maybe the reason is television—is that the lights go on and the shutters go down on their eyes and they get up and walk out.

TAVERNIER: That's not completely true. I had a very good discussion in Los Angeles, and I had a very good discussion in San Francisco, and in Austin, too.

NOR: Mostly student audiences?

TAVERNIER: Mostly students. They were less aggressive than in France. Maybe sometimes they react better in France, but they are so aggressive that they won't think. The first thing they have to do is to be superior to the film that they are seeing. They are so frightened to look unintelligent that they become completely aggressive and completely stupid. For example, someone asked Elia Kazan why did he sign his work. The questioner said that you have a kind of power. They see your name and they relate the film to your previous films. If you wanted to do really political films you should not sign them. I mean it's crazy. That's the bad thing of '68.

NOR: You talk about the failures of the left. That's one of them?

TAVERNIER: That's one of the failures. It succeeded in some ways, but that's one of the failures.

NOR: You keep going back to things that make you angry, to analyses of failures, such as Marker's films, Solanas's work, Guzman's *The Battle of Chile*, but your own work has a sort of lucid compassion that's missing from all of these things you're so interested in.

TAVERNIER: I think that a director should be interested not only in what he tries to do. I mean sometimes I leave certain films, and I feel desperate, especially after certain documentaries. I would love to do documentaries. Maybe I will never do them. Maybe it's only a dream that I have. I know that there would be a moment where I would suffer. I would need to put in a little more irony or humor. But *The Sorrow and the Pity*, for instance, is a very warm film, don't you think?

NOR: You and Ophuls seem to share a sense of respect for the individual's integrity, even if you don't like him.

TAVERNIER: Yes, why despise your enemy? First, I think it's a practical mistake. I've just read *Rumor of War*, and it shows clearly and honestly that the first people in Vietnam thought they would win the war in three weeks . . . because they were right, because they were fighting poor peasants, and had helicopters, John Kennedy, we had everything, the spirit, and were going to free the world. It's not only bad for artistic reasons, this non-knowledge of the enemy, it's a political failure. I even try to give people lines . . . in *The Judge and the Assassin* where the judge says to the girl, "But the people he killed, didn't they yell?" And he's right, he's right. It's not him that I'm criticizing. I'm criticizing beyond him to what he represents. It's too easy to deal with these things superficially.

Several months ago, someone asked me why I chose to have the action of *Des Enfants Gates* set in the middle class and not the working class? I say, okay, if you have a rent strike in the working-class buildings, everyone will be for them, but the middle-class people are not politically minded, do not relate to politics at all. If they begin to be political, something has happened. If it were the working-class people, they would be more political. It's easier for them. But these people in the film are teachers, shopkeepers, *petite bourgeoisie*; they have shops and things like that. If they begin to question the system . . .

NOR: Yes, but that's like Pudovkin's *Mother* . . .

TAVERNIER: Yes, I like that. One of the men whose influence I respect the most is George Orwell. He was always honest, as in his tribute *Homage to Catalonia*, and when he says the beginning of freedom and democracy starts with letting two and two equal four. Let two and two equal four, and the rest will follow. I always say, I'm trying to make films about people who go from A to B, while in most films they go from A to Z. But I think that going from A to B is sometimes the most difficult, and you have to appreciate that, to respect that goal. And it's a subject. Orwell was deeply into the period of Stalinism. He was attacked. He had to be pessimistic. I'm less pessimistic. I think people can move, and I think you have to appreciate that move.

NOR: The hero?

TAVERNIER: The peasant, the people who build the carriage in *Let Joy Reign Supreme*, the unknown people, the clockmaker himself.

Eudora Welty

Interviewed by Jeanne Rolfe Nostrandt
(1978)

Eudora Welty was born and has lived most of her life in Jackson, Mississippi. Her last novel, *The Optimist's Daughter*, won the Pulitzer Prize for fiction in 1972, and her latest book, *The Eye of the Story*, is a collection of her criticism. Her work includes four collections of short stories, two novellas, three novels, a children's book, a book of photographs taken during the 1930s Depression, and one collection of criticism.

This interview took place during our visit to Williamsburg, Virginia, in my room at the Williamsburg Inn on May 13, 1978. We had driven with a friend across the state from the western part to the eastern. It was Miss Welty's first visit to Williamsburg, and we had just returned from sightseeing, somewhat tired and ready to relax. The tone of the interview, therefore, took on more of a relaxed conversation than question/answer format. Perhaps this is inevitable when two Southerners get together to talk about a common love, in this case—writing.

Eudora Welty is a tall, greying woman whose charm and warmth become apparent with her first words—softly spoken with the musical drawl that characterizes her as Southern. She is eager to talk about her work and more than tolerant of hasty questions put to her by students and interviewers. She is confident in her art and in her presence, but never patronizing or cold. Her knowledge of the human being and his condition so prevalent in her fiction becomes equally as obvious in her speaking or reading aloud. Her sense of humor is ever at hand, as the following interview will show.

NEW ORLEANS REVIEW: As a child, did you hear stories from older people, especially black people?

EUDORA WELTY: Not from black people, mostly because I never saw black people then except in a white household as a servant or something, and though I would hear bits of superstition or remarks that I later remembered, I never heard black people talking among themselves. I heard many white people. I used to hear family stories and also in my neighborhood there were a lot of grand talkers that I used to sit at the feet of and listen to, telling not only family stories but just what went on in their own lives and interpreted in a dramatic way.

NOR: Like people who talk about their operations, or some event?

WELTY: Yes, exactly, and dramatizing things, too, which gave me several ideas in writing. Then I heard my family stories, stories I used to hear when I would go up to West Virginia with my mother to her family. She had five brothers and they had families and they would sort of have a steady reunion while we were up there. I was still a very little girl when I began hearing these stories and it went on as long as they lived, most of them, and I heard many stories *as* stories well-told by good storytellers, things that were in the good sense of, of what you and I mean. That is, everybody knew these stories, but they just loved telling them and laughing at them and the more because it wasn't 365 days a year, but just in the summers, and I would look forward to it. They could also play all musical instruments—just by ear. They were all musical except for my mother, and they played the banjo and horns and things like that. They lived way up on a mountain. I could just listen enchanted to the old songs and ballads they were singing to the banjos and things—things they would pick up out in the country. These were not family songs handed down, but things they had heard in the mountains that they had learned and could sing, ballads and all kinds of things.

NOR: Where in West Virginia was that?

WELTY: It was in Clay County, which is near Charleston, up the Elk River, quite wild and lonely up there in the high mountains.

NOR: That experience is like Laurel's in *The Optimist's Daughter.*

WELTY: That's true. I used my own memories of about the age of three. I was there many other times, but I used those sharp memories you have when you first begin to notice things and gave them to Laurel. And also, memories of my grandmother and of my mother at that age. I used some of that personal memory in that book, about the first time I ever did do that, without translating them entirely into fictional characters.

NOR: My grandmother used to tell stories more in the fashion of Miss Katie Rainey when she's talking to this obvious stranger in the opening of *The Golden Apples.* My grandmother used to do that for the children—sit on the front porch and snap beans or something like that and entertain us; really to keep us out of trouble, I think, she would tell us stories.

WELTY: Well now, those were the kind of thing that I would hear in my neighborhood at home under the same circumstances. My mother would tell us that she remembered, but they would be too important to throw out like that, to her, you know. She would tell them to us, but maybe after we were in bed at night wanting a story. She'd tell us something, but that's very serious to her—it's about her family. I don't mean pompous; it meant a lot to her.

NOR: Did she make up stories for you?

WELTY: No.

NOR: She just told you real experiences. My grandmother tended to make up stories for us (I think they were made up), and she would put riddles in them to keep us quiet for a while. How did you first become interested in telling stories? Did you take courses in high school where you wrote short stories or poetry?

WELTY: No. As I remember in high school we had composition, which would be grammar and themes. They were severely corrected and criticized for grammatical mistakes, for which I'm thankful. I remember the Latin grammar, which teaches you English. I liked to write simple narratives—"How I spent my vacation" or book reports. It's all beginning to come back to me. We had to do many book reports, and I used to write the book reports of a good many others besides me, because they didn't want to read the book. That was fun. I used to enjoy that, this early book reviewing. And we had oral themes and written themes. So, I think we were given a sense of being able to express ourselves on a piece of paper, and we had a pretty good literature course, too.

NOR: Did you write in reaction to this literature?

WELTY: I guess we did give reports on things, but whether we were asked such personal things as our opinion, I rather doubt. I think it was all too formal. Of course, I contributed to the St. Nicholas League in *St. Nicholas Magazine* and to the children's page of the *Commercial Appeal.* I liked to write at home.

NOR: You've said before that you wanted to write, as far back as you can remember. All this time in school, even elementary school, were you, on your own, writing stories?

WELTY: I think so; my mother kept some. They are so-called comicals and poems, you know, funny poems that take off on something. We used to write plays and give them in the garage for the neighbors. Oh sure, I was always doing that. I won a prize at an early age. It was a patent something called "Jackie Mackie Pine Oil," and they gave me a prize for the best poem about it, and I won twenty-five dollars. Wasn't that great?

NOR: That was; that's a lot of money for a child to win.

WELTY: I'll say. That's the reason I remember it; luckily I don't remember the poem.

NOR: As a student in the Jackson, Mississippi, public schools, did you feel that any course or teacher was especially important to you as a writer?

WELTY: The level of excellence in the schools was really outstanding. I'm not speaking only from my memory, but from that of all the kids I know that have grown up and are my contemporaries. We remember with much admiration how well we were taught. We had somebody sort of like Miss Julia Mortimer (*Losing Battles*) who was principal of my particular elementary school—Miss Lorena Duling, who was marvelous. And there were a number like her—wonderful teachers. I think they were missionaries in a sense; I think they felt they were. It was marvelous; we had good schools. The year I entered Jackson High School, or somewhere along there, there were only eleven grades. They added on to make a twelfth grade and they picked a class to make a graduating class. There were about sixty altogether, and we were the entire twelfth grade class. I think I know what happened to just about everybody in that class. We had a reunion (I hate to tell you the number) last year, and just about everybody came that was still in the land of the living. The summer I worked on the *New York Times Book Review*, one of my jobs was to recruit new reviewers for the summer. Robert Van Gelder, who was the editor, wanted to bring fresh reviewers from time to time, in contrast to the *New York Herald Tribune*, which used the same stable of reviewers week after week after week. He wanted all new. One week, as it happened, there were seven or nine members of my high school class all reviewing books from different parts of the country. One would be a professor at Duke, one would be a clergyman on the Gulf Coast, and one would be a teacher at Sewanee, but we were all members of that same high school class. I think it was rather extraordinary; it shows the way we were taught. I mean, it proves what I said, that we were well grounded in getting an education later in college.

NOR: How did Robert Van Gelder know of all these people?

WELTY: He didn't. He interviewed me about a book I'd written, and then offered me a job. I was amazed, naturally, but I was quite young and I thought, "Why not try it?" He knew exactly my limitations; it was just a summer job. So, I stayed in New York and did it, and I was the one who suggested these other people that was part of my job.

NOR: That was after the first collection of your stories. A friend has a letter from you just before that first collection came out, in which you ask him and others you knew in Raleigh, North Carolina, to help you find a title. How did you decide on *A Curtain of Green*, also the title of one of the stories, though not a central one?

WELTY: The way it was decided was funny; no one could agree. And so the editors decided. That was the only story that there wasn't a strong feeling about from everybody. Nobody really cared about that title, but they wanted a title of one of the stories. The editor said no one objects to "A Curtain of Green" and then he laughs (this is John Woodburn, who's so wonderful) and says that settles it for the future; you can call your next book "A Curtain of Red," and "A Curtain of Blue," and a curtain of so on. And then he laughed and said the last book can just be "Curtains."

NOR: "June Recital" from *The Golden Apples* was once entitled "The Golden Apples." Did the editors change this?

WELTY: Yes, and they thought, and quite rightly, that this book, being connected stories, should have a title that none of the single stories had. I think that was proper. All my life I've been plagued by the inability to find a title for anything.

NOR: Can you remember any other special teachers?

WELTY: I think, without question, the teacher who influenced me because he showed me something about the profundity or the scope of great literature was at the University of Wisconsin—Mr. Riccardo Quintana, who taught me Swift and Milton.

NOR: He's got a wonderful name.

WELTY: And he was a wonderful person, and he's still there. I asked the other day when I met somebody. I think he's retired, but he's around. This was not a class where we did much reciting. It was a lecture course and, really, he began with the seventeenth century which he said Swift was the child of. So, we had almost a course in John Donne and all of those other people, and then on through Swift. It gave us a whole (concept). I never heard a teacher use—like "passion"; he really made us realize the strength and truth of poetic feeling and depth of feeling and emotional drive. I saw what a vast force literature was and the seriousness of the whole thing. It was exhilarating. It really opened the door to me.

NOR: The vast force, the connection in all of life. That's what a good teacher does, I think.

WELTY: Yes, exactly, exactly. It really does come as a revelation. I always loved the things he was talking about, but I had never realized that it was all right to be so wholly enraptured by things. That it was part of it, you know, those were the feelings it reached. And there was also another teacher, I can't think of his name right now, I'm sorry. I had a course in logic under him that was a great help to me to show me how to organize my thoughts, which I'd never learned, to make an outline of things and to set things in order. How to take notes, that was very valuable. A course in art history was wonderful, too. I sort of minored, I suppose you'd call it, in art history.

NOR: In college?

WELTY: Yes, that was just out of love for painting.

NOR: What about art courses? You did paint and sketch.

WELTY: I was no good, and I found it out when I went to Wisconsin and entered a class. I knew nothing whatever about anatomy or anything, I had no training whatever. I didn't even know enough to know that I couldn't draw the human figure without more knowledge. The teacher told me to go on over to the library and practice drawing on the statues that were over there. To learn how people were made instead of drawing these people in their clothes without knowing how a foot was made or where a shoulder went into its socket or anything. Well, I realized I was in over my head. I took that course and liked it, but I learned that I couldn't do it.

NOR: Did you go practice on the statues?

WELTY: Oh, sure. I did all right. I made good enough grades, but he had to tell me I didn't know about the human body; I didn't know it.

NOR: But it seems to me that there is so much of the artist in your stories—the perception of scene and the colors and the depth of the whole scene before you begin to delineate other things.

WELTY: I'm sure it helped me to take these courses regardless of whether I was good or bad in them. It helped me to see more clearly. But I, of course, have a visual mind.

NOR: Did any of these special teachers encourage your writing or your art work?

WELTY: No, to the art work part, I'm sure. All my teachers thought I did well in composition; I always made good grades. They encouraged me, for instance, or probably put me on the staff of the college magazines or things like that.

NOR: How did you finally come to write a story that was published?

WELTY: You mean "Death of a Traveling Salesman?" It was the first one I sent to a magazine. I had written a lot of others and, in fact, I doubt if I would have sent this one anywhere except for Hubert Creekmore. He was my neighbor up the street who was a poet. He was ahead of me in years and accomplishment, and he was getting things published. He had never read anything I had written; I was too shy to show anything. But he said, why don't you send things to magazines? I said, where? Either he suggested *Manuscript* or he told me to go look in the back of *Best Short Stories* and see the list of magazines consulted. I used that all the time to send stories out to. That was the first one I sent off and it was accepted. But I remember writing a story at the University of Wisconsin that was pretty silly. It was a murder story laid in Paris. You know that was about how crazy I was; it couldn't have been taken seriously. Although I wrote things all my life, I was, in fact, a late starter.

NOR: So it was the neighbor who really was encouraging you?

WELTY: No, I really wanted to do it.

NOR: But you didn't know what to do?

WELTY: I was shy of doing it. I had never shown anybody anything I had written outside of college. You know, nobody. I was trying to teach myself and to learn. In fact, Hubert and some other boys had gotten out a little magazine called *Southern Review* ahead of the real *Southern Review,* which we had published. I helped them work on that, but was I ever asked to write anything? No. I mean, see it was secret, and I worked on the business end and got ads for it and did typing for it and everything. But I did nothing toward contributing, nor was it ever thought of. And all this time I was writing stories. The stories weren't worth printing, and I hope I destroyed all of them.

NOR: But this friend, Hubert Creekmore, knew you were writing?

WELTY: Well, yes. See I read his things; he was getting them published.

NOR: So then you showed him your stories.

WELTY: He was always published. Our families were close. We lived right along the street from one another. Later, he published seven or eight novels and books of poems and translations from various things, and edited *A Little Treasury of World Poetry* or something like that. He worked at New Directions for a while. You know, he really had a literary life, and I knew he was somebody I could ask. I didn't show him anything, but I asked him.

NOR: He didn't see the stories?

WELTY: No, nobody saw them.

NOR: He just told you how to go about doing something about it.

WELTY: Just the way children have asked me in class, "How do you go about it?"

NOR: Well, you sent it off to *Manuscript*. Did you send just that one story?

WELTY: Yes. No, I didn't. I think I sent the one that came out second, come to think of it. They took two at once, I believe. One I never have reprinted; I've forgotten the name of it. "Magic" or something like that. l believe I did send them both at once.

NOR: Yes, that's it, "Magic."

WELTY: I hadn't thought of that in years. If not, they asked me for another one, and I sent that. And they took it; they were the first two.

NOR: That was in 1936, and five years later a collection of stories came out. That's fast moving.

WELTY: I was writing just every minute, and I never revised things. I didn't know enough to. Some of those stories in *A Curtain of Green* were about six years old when the book came out because I was writing one after another and sending them out all the time. See, I would try places like *The Atlantic Monthly* or *Harper's* or something first, trying to get published in a national magazine. Of course, *The Southern Review* had started taking them early, and they were a great help because they published so many. But then I got my agent, Diarmuid Russell, after about four years of writing. He had seen some in the little magazines and wrote to me.

NOR: And volunteered to be your agent?

WELTY: Volunteered to be my agent; I'd never heard of an agent. He said, "You get all these stories back in from the folds (you know they were all out) and send them to me." And then he sent them out for about two years before *The Atlantic* finally took one. And when that happened, then other magazines of national circulation wrote and asked for things. And some, as you can imagine, took the very ones that they had been rejecting. You know, that always happens. That was my break, when Diarmuid wrote to me. If it hadn't been for him, I don't know if I'd have ever been published. I really mean it, because he worked like everything just because he believed in the stories. And that's the only reason he ever took any writers.

NOR: Everybody says that about him, and I'm sure he was marvelous; but he simply had an eye for what was good material, too. I mean, he knew who should be published.

WELTY: I believe he did, and that was true consistently in all of his work. And when he did think you were good, he was tireless and very astute in what he was doing. He never sent a story anywhere when he didn't think the editor would think it was for them or think it was good. He wouldn't take anybody whose work he didn't like, even very well-known people who tried to get him.

NOR: Of course, that's what makes a good agent.

WELTY: Absolutely. Everybody trusted him implicitly, not just his writers but editors. Gee, was I ever lucky. If there were more like him today.

NOR: When you were writing the story "Death of a Traveling Salesman," did you see the whole story as an actual event, or did you see it as an hallucination or even as part of each?

WELTY: I saw it as an event; I saw it as real.

NOR: This man Bowman actually had been sick, and he is back on the road from this illness.

WELTY: Yes. I think in all my work I try to write things that can be seen and taken as an event. I want them to stand on that solid ground all the way through with anything suggested that might work out of the material as I go. But in that case, that was a first really full-fledged solid story, and I was writing it absolutely like that. I was fascinated with various almost fairytale connotations in it, like go out and "borry some fire." But the reason I used that was that I heard the expression from a neighbor who bought land for the highway department. He had heard somebody way out in the country say "we have to borry some fire." I think that's really why I wrote the story, so I could use that. That's why I used that for what it was worth, you know, that's a little more than an event, but it is an event. I mean, it's got one foot on the ground.

NOR: A friend refers to that act as the Prometheus image of bringing the fire to man, but, you know, that just goes to prove the realism of the legend, rather than the legend in the realism.

WELTY: I agree. I've always thought that. I wouldn't use it without its realistic hold on us, I don't think. In my way of looking at things as a writer, I rely on it, that you have one hand on it.

NOR: In "Keela, The Outcast Indian Maiden" there are such dark tones, especially in the ending when Little Lee Roy wants to relate this new episode in his story, and his children will not listen to him. This seems to show a lack of communication; Little Lee Roy is related. When the younger man who is guilt-ridden comes to find him, he fails to see that the past which was so horrible to him is Little Lee Roy's greatest memory. And then the ending is so dark when Little Lee Roy cannot even talk about the day's event with his children. Am I misinterpreting it?

WELTY: I'll tell you what I was actually trying to do. I hadn't thought about it like that, and I can see how that would apply. What I was trying to do in the story was simply to present three insights into what had happened. One was from the guilt-ridden Steve, and from the rather callous older man Max, and one from Little Lee Roy. Steve and Max are the ones that are so concerned; they haven't even thought of what he might feel. Everybody is thinking about how *he* feels, Steve and Max and Little Lee Roy, to whom it happened. I just wanted to show how he felt by starting to tell the children. I think it was the children who are the ones that really knew the reality of it, that it was almost too terrible. They knew what it really was, what had happened to him, and they just don't want to hear any more of it—it's just too terrible. It was kind of a sign-off for the story, too. The whole thing was just too awful to contemplate, what had been done to this little man. That was all I meant to do. I didn't think about the lack of communication; that is, I think the children knew. It wouldn't be lack of communication, just not wanting to hear it.

NOR: I see. I think that's my own misreading.

WELTY: Well, I wouldn't call it a misreading. What you said is perfectly legitimate, but I didn't mean to suggest too much isolation except they were all isolated from each other. But nobody felt it, really, except Steve; he felt that no one understood his feelings about it. Each for his own reasons couldn't really express it, what it was. I have worked on that story. I sometimes read it (I was asked to) and I made it better than it is in the book, to make it clearer what I meant to do. Maybe the way I fixed it, it is clearer—mostly with transpositions of things, revealing things in the right order. That's my greatest failing; I tell something too quick, I mean too early, and it needs to be spaced out.

NOR: The ending of "Flowers for Marjorie" seems dark to me, too.

WELTY: That's a poor story; I had no business writing that story. That's a kind of an artificial story that is written about a city. I think I wrote it in New York during the Depression. It's too literary.

NOR: But that oppressiveness that must have permeated the time and place is there. The characters are victims of their time and place. I think it is a successful story.

WELTY: I haven't read it in a long time, but the only thing that sticks in my mind about it is a small detail. The thing I think of on hearing its name just now is how he walked up the subway between those heavy, fat, warm ladies. That was oppressive all right.

NOR: In *The Golden Apples,* why did King MacLain run from his twins the first time he saw them on Halloween day?

WELTY: Oh, I haven't read these things in so long, I don't remember specifics. Oh, when he comes home and sees them?

NOR: They're all dressed up with their masks.

WELTY: He's somebody who comes and goes at will, and I think almost anything could have driven him off. But the sight of those little boys on roller skates with masks on must have been rather scary.

NOR: Because it seemed like an entrapment?

WELTY: I think so, but I'd have to read it again to be sure of all the ramifications. He was pretty easy to run off; he's just passing through. I think he came out of curiosity to see what had come of this. I don't think he was even prepared for twins.

NOR: In the ending of *The Golden Apples,* Virgie Rainey is sitting on the steps just outside of Morgana, and the old black woman with the hen under her arm comes by and sits down, too. It's raining and Virgie thinks of Miss Eckhart and the Perseus as he chops the head of the Medusa three times. Then, she hears the running of the bear and the other images. Now, I see those as other legends you refer to, but I see those images also as constellations belonging in a Mississippi sky in October.

WELTY: Good, I think so, too.

NOR: I'm glad to hear you say that. Of course, they are the legends that have been made into constellations.

WELTY: They belong in Mississippi. I really let myself go on that last page, as you can tell.

NOR: You said in a television interview that you didn't know what this page means.

WELTY: I didn't know what it means in the sense that people ask. You know, this is supposed to be this and this is supposed to be that, and the old black woman with the chicken means, as if everything has an equivalent. I just say that the whole thing was supposed to be a mesh of suggestions and insinuations that just sort of showed the whole mysteriousness of experience. I didn't want anything explicit. I couldn't go into this on the program; in fact, I never have been able to. What you say is such a key kind of thing that I wanted it to end up, not in the abstract world of ancient mythology, but in reality. To Virgie all of this was real, and there was a genuine photograph of the Perseus and the Medusa. Everything was real along with many connotations. So I'm glad you said that; I'll remember that.

NOR: Somehow I feel with Virgie at the end of the book, and I feel that she is at last free because she knows who Virgie Rainey is.

WELTY: Yes.

NOR: And she is just stopping outside Morgana to assimilate all this. In the process she is finding her own kinship with humanity, with everything. And so I see that as the sky.

WELTY: That's exactly what I tried to do. I do, too. And she has a companion in the old black woman who's sitting down for reasons of her own. This old woman has got something out of it with the chicken. To me, it all seemed a very natural thing to do. As I remember, she goes out after her mother dies, after the funeral; she goes out and swims. She was very beautiful, she was kin to the earth and the sky and all that. Oh, I think that's fine; I'm delighted to hear you say what you did.

NOR: I'm glad you agree with it—that it is not farfetched.

WELTY: It's so hard to say what you're trying to do with something. I know, but I don't know how to put it into any other words than the fiction.

NOR: You've said you intended for your stories be actual events. In "Old Mr. Marblehall," some critics see Mr. Marblehall as being either an actual life or fantasy life, with Mr. Byrd as the other. One life actual, one is fantasy. Do you intend it to be that way, or do you intend that the man is actually leading a double life? Someone has pointed to the title as a reference to the song "I dreamt I dwelt in Marblehall." Is that not the reference?

WELTY: I can't claim that; it never occurred to me. I meant to express the fantastic life of Natchez, Mississippi, which is where I laid it, where all kind of crazy stories about families are always going around. I was trying to write a kind of Natchez fantasy. It too, was a very early story; I didn't feel too responsible for making everything hang together. But that kind of story could so easily happen in Natchez. I'm sure there are so many double lives going on there.

NOR: I see it as an actual story. Did you use the song as reference?

WELTY: I think it is an actual story. I didn't know the song.

NOR: It reminds me of the movie *The Captain's Paradise*, which we spoke of earlier; Alec Guinness leads a double life.

WELTY: Right.

NOR: None of these stories ever seems like an hallucination to me, though I see fantasy in them. More and more critics seem to interpret them hallucinations or dreams.

WELTY: I'm sorry about that.

NOR: It seems to me that what is so real in the story is the fear he has that he will be caught. And that fear can't be real unless there are two lives.

WELTY: Well, he delights in that fear.

NOR: That's his adventure.

WELTY: That's his adventure. "What a thing I'm doing," he thinks.

NOR: He sees himself "netted like the butterfly."

WELTY: The story really is crazy, but I loved writing it.

NOR: In several stories, "Old Mr. Marblehall" and "Petrified Man," for instance, you use references to science fiction or detective stories. Both Mrs. Pike and Mr. Byrd read pulp magazines such as *Startling G-Man Tales* and science fiction. Do you mean to imply that one's reading influences his life—actions, imagination or fantasy?

WELTY: No, I thought that *Startling G-Man Tales* would be exactly what would be on the table at home in the stories. I just thought that's what they read. I think probably it was the magazine in that beauty parlor I went to, that they'd be reading.

NOR: It's more the extension of the personalities of the characters than a shaping force.

WELTY: It's just what they would be reading.

NOR: A friend recently remarked about your writing in *The Eye of The Story* that if you had never written fiction, you would still have made your mark through criticism. How does that thought strike you?

WELTY: Well, I think I'm a natural fiction writer. I only wrote critical things because they were assigned me as a job. I never would have normally done it I think, except I was asked to do book reviews or asked to give lectures, and in order to do these, I would write them. The only piece in that book that I wrote because I just plain wanted to, out of love for something or someone, was the piece on Henry Green, which I never supposed would be printed. For the other lectures, of course, I chose my subject, mostly, and worked hard on what I did. The "Place in Fiction" in the book, I did because I was invited to go to Cambridge University in England on one of those American Studies in English Schools programs, and it was the only subject I could think of that I could possibly speak on with any authority. I'm not a teacher and not a scholar. And the other things were requests like: "Will your write the Jane Austen biography for Louis Kronenberger's *Brief Lives?*" I wouldn't tackle something that didn't strike a congenial note. I liked doing it, but I don't believe I *ever* would have originated any of those pieces.

NOR: It is rare for someone who tries fiction or poetry to also write criticism. I know a lot of people attempt it, but you write good criticism, not only about other writers, but you have an idea of what it is you do that makes a story successful. I'm not sure that most writers have that ability.

WELTY: Well, I would have had no idea that I either could or wanted to if I hadn't tried and worked it out. I enjoyed the teaching of myself that writing such pieces made possible for me. I never would have thought I could write anything on writing. Those things I did at Smith College when I had to give three public lectures about writing, I did by trying to seize some handle where I already thought I knew something and to work into it. Well, a lot of it is journalism, then an effort to support myself with book reviews and lectures, too. It was what I did on the side to help pay my way. But I've enjoyed what it's brought to me, and I love, I really love, writing about other writers. But I'm not an analyst in the real sense. I analyze, maybe, my response to something.

NOR: In responding to it, you get right to the heart of the thing you're talking about.

WELTY: I'm glad you say that because that would be its only justification.

NOR: On a recent PBS interview, you remarked about your story "Why I Live at the P.O." that you saw the writing of it sort of as a schoolroom type theme. Can you think of other schoolroom type assignments that have instigated others of your writing?

WELTY: I don't think so; I believe that's *the* only one. I just wanted to write a funny story about how I'd heard people talking. I just wrote that title at the top of the page to amuse myself. I believe that's the only one that started like that; it is a high-school theme thing in the way it starts.

NOR: How did you think of "Why I Live at the P.O."?

WELTY: I don't know. I did see an ironing board behind the window in some little post office once, and I thought somebody must live back there. And probably they did.

NOR: I have a theory that Laurel in *The Optimist's Daughter* is a grown-up version of Laura from *Delta Wedding.*

WELTY: There may be something in that. I've never thought of it because I don't think of people in one novel as existing outside of the book but probably that sensibility is the same. I can well see that there is a thread between them, but it never occurred to me.

NOR: It's the same sort of sensibility, but more matured as the result of having lived through the situation. I thought that sometime I might pair these two and see what I could do with them. I didn't know whether it had come to your mind or not. Some critics have seen "Petrified Man" as a demonstration of how women emasculate men, and the theory is largely based on that final line from the child as he runs out of the beauty parlor: "If you're so smart, why ain't you rich?" Then, of course, there is the image of the petrified man. Did you intend such an interpretation?

WELTY: No, I was just trying to express how people talk in the beauty parlors, and I kind of made that story up as I went, although the freak show next door was certainly talked about in my beauty parlor. And a lot of those horrible quotes, some of which I've cut out when I read it aloud, were really said. But I wasn't trying to say anything about men and women except how women talk about men. How *they* talk about them. I wasn't trying to make a statement, and I love "If you're so smart, why ain't you rich?" That's something I've heard all my life.

NOR: I've heard it all my life, too.

WELTY: Sure, it's just an old saying that this little three-year-old has just heard. And it fit so well because it was his parents that had gotten rich off the petrified man, and it was Leota who said that they had made all this money from her magazine. And he was pretty precocious anyway, you know, learning about the beauty parlor business. He was the most precocious one in it, and always present; he was the go-between. But I didn't mean anything except the terrible way people talk, and I thought it was funny. I wasn't trying to be horrifying. Someone had said it was the most horrible story they'd ever read. I thought it was funny.

NOR: Well, I always tell my students that such a theory exists, but I try to show them the absurdity of it by saying that someone could equally as well say the story shows how adults tyrannize the children of the world. They see the humor in that. I say that women in beauty parlors do talk about men just as men in pool halls talk about women; that is exactly the same sort of talk.

WELTY: I agree with you; I wish I had thought of saying that. At a recent conference I said, as a panel member, that I had not intended such a ponderous statement about the sexes. I just want to quietly assert that. I was just using dialogue to show the extravagant way people talk. It had no more ambition than that.

NOR: So often, especially since the mid-1960s critics have tended to look for some kind of social statement in works of fiction. I think they picked up your essay "Why Must the Novelist Crusade?" for sort of license to do this with your work. I tell students that the comments you make are not just about you, but about all writers, and that they concern human nature, the universality of the human character and personality, and not on a given situation in a given time and place. The message is larger than a single event; it's about the human situation.

WELTY: I think they do it, too, and I have answered a couple of things. This whole year, while talking with students, I often say that they haven't read anything of my work except the early stories. They say, why don't you write about things that are happening today? I explain that I have, but today is not in those early stories. Then I say that I was always writing about justice and injustice and man's inhumanity to man and so on—that those things don't need to be explained by trends or whatever is stylish to write about. No writer can write without moral commitments and moral feelings at the very root. They think that if you don't write about the Civil Rights movement, that means you don't care about people, that you don't have any sense of right and wrong or anything. Of course, that's just nuts.

NOR: Maybe it's because we're living in a time when so many people see morality as an abstract concept which isn't viable in today's world. They don't know how to handle an abstract concept; things are relative to them.

WELTY: I know it, I know it. They think it's all right to do so and so. Anyway, I think we are all agreed.

James Tate

Interviewed by Joe David Bellamy
(1980)

James Tate was born in Kansas City, Missouri, in 1943. His first book of poems, *The Lost Pilot*, won the Yale Series of Younger Poets Award in 1966. Subsequent volumes include *The Oblivion Ha-Ha, Hints to Pilgrims, Absences, Hottentot Ossuary, Viper Jazz*, and most recently, *Riven Doggaries*, published by Ecco Press in 1979. His poems have appeared in such magazines as *The New Yorker, The Atlantic, The Paris Review, Poetry*, and *The American Poetry Review* and in many anthologies, including *The Norton Anthology of Modern Poetry, The Best Modern Poetry*, and *The Contemporary American Poets: American Poetry Since 1940*. He has received a National Institute of Arts and Letters Award for Poetry and a Guggenheim Fellowship, and has taught at the University of California at Berkeley, Columbia University, and since 1971 at the University of Massachusetts.

This interview was conducted over a period of two-and-a-half-years, from the fall of 1975 to spring 1978, by Helena Minton, Lou Papineau, and Cliff Saunders, working together, and by Karen Florsheim. The three sessions were edited and combined from over a hundred pages of manuscript by Joe Bellamy.

NEW ORLEANS REVIEW: In 1966, you received the Yale Series of Younger Poets award for *The Lost Pilot*—the youngest poet ever to receive the award. How did that affect your writing? What pressures, if any, were put upon you?

JAMES TATE: I wanted to take it very seriously at first and thought it was supposed to mean something profound. It shook me out of something; even if you're totally dedicated to your writing, you don't necessarily imagine it actually affecting anyone. So I had to consider the possibility of an audience, which was probably a phony consideration—it was a waste of time. But I thought I had to.

It had a muddied effect on my life that lasted over several years, and I never knew when I solved it or what exactly it was I had ever solved. It involved such things as giving poetry readings and receiving little strange clippings in the mail that insulted you all the way from London. But then it just once again felt natural writing poems without having to think that somebody expected something from me.

NOR: Are there any poems in *The Lost Pilot* where you feel you come closest to your true voice?

TATE: There are things that are true for a time. The voice I had then I don't think would be true now. It was only perfect and true for the time. I say perfect in the way Williams uses it when he says, "When will they realize I am the perfect William Carlos Williams." So that's what I mean by perfect, perfect for the time. I think "The Lost Pilot" is, in a way.

NOR: How did you come to write "The Lost Pilot"?

TATE: First, there was a false start. I used to go into trances when I wrote. I was at Iowa at the time, living in a very tiny doll's house with someone and had an office in a quonset hut about a mile away. When I made that walk I would float, hoping to zero in on something. Must not have been in a very good trance that day because I remember sitting there working on this poem for about five hours or something, and it wasn't any good. It was construed. There was something false about it. It wasn't the poem I meant to write at all. So I did what I normally don't do. When I went back to writing the next night, I left the poem at home. And I started all over again.

NOR: How did you write the final draft?

TATE: The real source of the poem came during an afternoon nap, not one of my normal vices. We all know what those subterranean afternoon-nap dreams can do to us. A mystical experience swept through me, really shook me, and left the image of my father circling the earth in his B-17 continuously, refusing to come down.

I understand that it is some kind of shame that keeps him there the past twenty-two years. And in the dream I somehow sensed that I was passing him in flight, I was changing roles with him, I was becoming his father, he was becoming my son. The sensation was vivid and quaking. The point of this is that, as far as I can ascertain, the dream took place literally at the time I passed the age of my father when his plane was shot down (and never found) over Stettin, April—whenever it was—9th of 1944. At 22 I was passing him on the clock. We talked about my father so much when I was a child, my mother and all her family that we lived with my first seven years, that I didn't really think he was dead. And then when I did realize it, I really didn't want to think about him for awhile. Or else his name got sacred, and I refused to speak of it for the pain it caused.

Anyway, to this day, I continue to relate to a man I never met, who never saw me; some kind of steely determination to make him my best friend, or at least make him like me; maybe fear me, I don't know what. But then I may go on for years without thinking about him. Some people aren't close to their families at all. I can never understand those people.

NOR: To get back to the poems themselves in *The Lost Pilot*—you said you felt you had found your voice for that particular time. Would you like to elaborate on this?

TATE: For a while at Iowa I felt comfortable with a certain voice I had found or developed, sort of electrified existential. I felt I was refining this thing, this triadic stanza and syllabic line, floribund images, if only there were such a word. There for a while everything was dripping orchids and I loved it. But there was some psychic damage done when I won the Yale prize.

NOR: Had you anticipated winning it?

TATE: No, not at all. And I remember being shaken by the sameness of the shape of the poems when I corrected the galleys. I was immediately frightened by the thought of getting stuck in a rut and spending the rest of my life as that triadic-syllabic fellow in the grey pin-striped suit. I wanted to change; I knew that I had to open up a bit. There followed some pretty awkward poems.

NOR: What do you think would've happened if you'd stayed with that form?

TATE: I would have grown up to be Wallace Stevens.

NOR: Are you still recovering from winning the prize?

TATE: No. I forgot all about that, but I've never been as fixed into one form as I was then, which can keep you on pins as a writer. Probably I've been more fixed than I know. Maybe to other people the poems look more alike than they do to me. I've been writing for eighteen years; I allow myself "an old trick" only if there's no other way out of a tight corner.

I had been going on such a nice wave there for a while; I had a really creative period of seven or eight months. I was writing a poem a week, and the whole week centered around this new poem; there was a joyous sense of something being born. The sudden little exposure I got as a result of *The Lost Pilot* forced me to reconsider everything. When given the tangible possibility of an audience—not necessarily a poetry-reading-event audience, but any contact with strangers—I felt that my poetry was too acquiescent, quiet and lovably defeated. Those poems are okay, but that attitude in a grown person today I don't find lovable. There is room for anger, love, violence, humor, all in one poem, but if it can't keep up with life's most interesting moments, it's out of the game.

NOR: *The Lost Pilot* is filled with formal structures: syllabics, "loose syllabics," and symmetrical stanzaic forms. Do you still try working with some of these forms, or have you abandoned them completely?

TATE: Now it seems as though I'm resorting to something not quite natural when I do. It's usually when I'm in trouble with a poem that the free verse seems arbitrary and unnerving in some way not natural to the poem. If I can't find a form, I'll go back and work with syllabics and stanzas, but it'll never feel as necessary as it did then. Then it was a very integral part of the writing, and even in the abstract conceptions of the poem, I quite often felt those formal things as strongly as I felt about the images of the poems.

NOR: Did using those forms in the beginning help focus your writing?

TATE: The forms helped me define a voice that I, at that time, considered my voice, that I was looking for. The form was literally a part of it; it was a kind of faltering, tense voice. It wasn't somebody I was particularly obsessed with at that time, but it's not so distant from Wallace Stevens. There's a similarity in my poetry and Stevens'—in only one way because in tone and everything else it's completely different—but my poetry is also dense with images. I think the density of the images in that tight structure—and in my case fairly wild images and different languages—provides a real tension between the strict-form and the sometimes outrageous voice of the poems.

NOR: How do you structure stanzas? Do you just think of, say, tercets and work that way? I'm thinking particularly of *The Lost Pilot*.

TATE: It's hard for me to answer that question because you're sitting there looking at a book that I wrote thirteen years ago. It changes all the time, I'm sure. Now I tend to think of them more as entities. They may run on syntactically but still I think of them as thought entities and still write in even numbered stanzas quite a lot, but it's for different reasons. But in those poems, again, there was something artificial about it, something slightly arbitrary that I liked.

NOR: How important is the physical appearance of the poem on the page, in a visual sense?

TATE: I'm most involved in the poem on the page. Maybe other poets are thinking about how it's going to sound out loud, and I'm sure unconsciously you care about that anyway since that's one of the things you can do as a poet. But the appearance on the page is a big part of my consideration in the poem and that in itself will keep the poem from being finished for months, not finding the appropriate form for it.

NOR: How do you view your progressions from *The Lost Pilot* to *Hottentot Ossuary*? There's an obvious shift from book to book, and I was wondering if your approach to each group of poems reflected a conscious change or just something you found yourself doing differently.

TATE: First of all, I guess it isn't true of other poets I can think of, but for me I almost never thought I was writing a book. I never knew what the outcome was going to be. You start getting a sense of something whole much later. It's turned out almost in all of my writing time except for *The Lost Pilot* that in my mind if I thought of books at all I thought there were two different books going at the same time. So the times that I've finally gotten around to bringing out a book, it doesn't really mean much in terms of exact progression.

For example, *Hints to Pilgrims* and *Absences* were more or less written simultaneously over a three-and-a-half-year period. It's the same way with *Hottentot Ossuary* and *Viper Jazz*; both were written simultaneously, and I didn't even know they were separate books for a long time, and then suddenly it started occurring to me. So I can't give a very precise answer. As for the way poetry evolves, it must have something to do with bio-rhythms, metabolism, things beyond our control.

I seem to explore—more or less exhaust, write myself into a corner—a kind of poem or particular obsession. It's not an arbitrary or artificial thing; it's what is truly obsessing every part of my self. But then after maybe three years of being troubled and obsessed with certain things, poetic and personal and philosophical, it comes sort of naturally. I need to be reborn a little bit and start moving into something else. I've almost never been able to put my finger down and say, "Ah, this marks a change."

NOR: Do you go about structuring your collections in any specific way?

TATE: Though you don't expect to meet many readers who are going to tell you that they perceived the movement and statement of the book the same way as you did, I have in my mind almost a story line moving in and out of whatever that obsession is— getting different takes on it and hopefully moving some kind of investigation, some inquest, through as far as I'm able to carry it. I spend a lot of time thinking about the structure of it, but for me it's never been chronological.

NOR: You said that often the reader doesn't perceive the movement. Does that bother you?

TATE: I always feel lucky and flattered if I think even a few people do—literally—because I don't know what most people's responses are anyway. It's an anonymous relationship. So if a few people seem to, I'm pleased—that's all it takes. Reviews aren't the thing I care about.

NOR: Many of your poems, such as "The Wheelchair Butterfly" and "It's Not the Heat So Much as the Humidity," are built upon a succession of images that often seem disparate and irrational, if you will. Do you consider yourself a poet of symbolic imagery rather than a narrative poet or a personal poet?

TATE: I wouldn't consider myself much of a narrative poet. There are certain poems that are completely structured around a succession of images, and you hit on one of them: "The Wheelchair Butterfly," which a few people have liked, but I never liked that poem much myself. I have some prejudice about it. I must not like those poems that I think are solely structured from, as you said, a succession of images, and that one sort of is, at least it was to me, because I know how it was written, and I was just seeking images. But that's not true of "It's Not the Heat So Much as the Humidity." That's one where I get a better balance of the images being more integral to something that's being said in the poem. Whereas in "The Wheelchair Butterfly," to me at least, they're not ornamental, but they're plenty whimsical.

NOR: Irony and wit play an important part in your poetry. There's a line in "Shadowboxing" which reads, "how come you never take your life / seriously?" Are you afraid of getting too serious?

TATE: I do believe in some kind of humility, which I think keeps you from being morbidly serious about your own fate, and for better or worse—whether taking the good parts seriously or the bad parts too seriously—and I don't think I have a right to do that. Irony . . . well, I like to be able to look at things from more than one direction at once, but it's not as flat as serious and humorous. It's just trying to see the richness of the situation.

NOR: What do you see as your common themes?

TATE: I don't want to write poems about incidents particularly unless they lend themselves to a larger expression of a viewpoint. Love poems are always just accidents for me. I want to catch the way our brains really do think and perceive, and the connections that they make.

My primary intention is to try to express how I see the world at the time. I'm trying to exhibit a way of seeing. Rimbaud says the poet's mission is to measure the amount of unknown present at any time, and that's part of it.

NOR: Many writers have seen themselves as social historians—would you accept that tag?

TATE: I wouldn't mind it particularly, but I think it happens to you unwittingly. If one succeeds in being spoken through by one's times, then you're bound to reflect it. I don't know where the individual talent or genius comes in there, but it does, obviously; you don't escape yourself entirely.

NOR: Some poems in *Hints to Pilgrims*, like "Boomerang" and "Pocamoonshine," seem at first glance to have the appearance of automatic writing. Did they start that way?

TATE: I stayed with George Hitchcock for a month in the summer of 1970. We did a lot of it together, in a very fun way by making it a very intense measure. With George, it was a combination of seriousness and offhandedness. He was very good at it, and it taught me something about the great quality of spontaneous, accidental combinations. It's no new discovery at all, but for me I think that despite the density of my imagery in earlier books I still had more rational connections. So I was trying to loosen up.

None of the poems in *Hints to Pilgrims* are legitimate automatic writing, but I'm sure a lot of them started that way. They may be collages of a number of different experiments put together at once; just some of the poems, like "Pocamoonshine"—not necessarily "Boomerang." But even with those poems there's a lot of revision and a lot of intention behind what I was doing, contrary to the impression of the wild recklessness of them. I believed in those words as they were put together. I'd like to see more of that excitement in American poetry.

NOR: What else do you think about "poetry now?"

TATE: There's always some direct connection between what's going on in the world and what's going on in poetry; and I feel this great uncertainness about, at least, American poetry, the same way I feel about the future of the world. And that is that nobody knows exactly. I feel a lot of poets are treading water, holding back, getting drift of what's to come. You can change your mind on these things about every three months. If one really good book comes out, it gives you a lot of excitement and you think that's a promise for the future of poetry. So maybe there hasn't been anything that startling for a while—a few disappointments here and there. There's no focus to it right now, I think that's part of the uncertainty I'm talking about—nobody knows what the real poetry is or what's speaking most closely to our times. Most poets take some kind of center-of-the-road voice that is popular for that decade and it gets used by everybody except those few leaders who lead you into the next decade.

For the first time in a long while, there is some concern for a criticism that can speak intelligently of the new poetry, the poetry of the last fifteen years. This is an area that has been lacking. The new poetry needs a criticism to go with it, and the previous criticism was completely outdated. It was written by critics who were unaware of the discoveries and techniques of the new poets.

As for the poetry itself, I think of it as being a reactionary or conservative moment, and I really mean moment. It's just been true of the last couple years, and it's impossible to foresee how long this return to modified formalism may go on and in what direction it may develop. There seems to be a retrenching, a reexamination of the poetics that were to come out of the Vietnam war years, and the more socially engaged times.

NOR: What do you see coming out of this period?

TATE: It's still new. People were saying that the 1970s were amorphous. They have been, but now they're coming to a close. There does seem to be a kind of coherence and something emerging. Nobody's quite put a finger on it yet. I see it as a cautious time. It seems that there is a resort to a very genteel and civilized view of the function of art, just because there isn't a direct social conflict to play the aesthetic off of. There seems to be a new clarity settling now. There is some kind of establishment screening process. I'm not sure what kind of aesthetic they are promulgating, but there is something very civilized.

NOR: *The Antioch Review* said *Hints to Pilgrims* contained "poems of great personal risk." Do you like taking poetic risks?

TATE: Yeah, I do. I hope I always make the challenge, and when I'm reading other people's poetry, I judge them in that way, too. With a lot of poets I love most, I admire their courage to try something that hasn't been tried before—when you know you're stripping yourself of all trained responses. And with the *Hints* book, it's true, I accept that: they were poems of great personal risk. I was literally frightened by a lot of them and was really terrified to show them to anybody and would hide them. And this publication was a perfect format because though he [Halty Ferguson] did an excellent, exquisite, beautiful job of printing—a very tasteful presentation of the poems—I had the feeling that nobody was going to see the book, and that was just fine with me. I've enjoyed the way that's turned out. The book was published in 1971, and some people will still find it and buy it, and it'll be a new thing for them.

NOR: What was it about the poems that frightened you?

TATE: Well, their apparent disconnectedness and their willingness to use words completely detached from their original meanings and to have a combination of startling effects of incredible seriousness and absolute slapstick, embarrassing jokes, and to combine them all into one view of the world which, for me at the time, was pretty terrifying and violent. So I don't think of the book as being incomprehensible, obscure, arcane work at all. I felt that it was speaking directly to . . . the war [*Tate laughs here*] because that was the strongest awareness—it sort of defined all of your relationships at that time.

NOR: Did you ever write blatantly anti-war poems?

TATE: I find that all too obvious; you can usually get all that matters on the news, and I'm not a bit interested in some poet's righteous opinion. In fact, I find it offensive to be slapping yourself on the back because you don't believe in killing babies, as so many poets were doing at that time. I mean, did you ever meet anybody who said, "Yeah, I *like* to kill babies"? [*Tate laughs.*] But the way the poets wrote about it in their poems, you'd think they were the only ones who had this deep feeling. They were congratulating themselves on their great sensitivity.

There's a lot of disintegration in *Hints to Pilgrims*, and I don't mean to say that it's all directed at the war. I'm sure a lot of it has completely personal roots and is also tied up in poetics. So I don't mean you select a subject matter and aim your weapons at it, because it was evolving poetics and personal turmoil at the same time. It's probably full of a lot of distrust for some kinds of poems which one needn't get so excited about, as it turns out. There's room for all kinds.

NOR: Have you ever written what you would call political poems?

TATE: What is obvious is seldom worthy of poetry. I do think poets must be committed to being certain kinds of "outlaws." They can't "fit in," as it were. Supposedly, if you are aware of a social structure you can never again be a natural, interacting part of it. Maybe we will cross that threshold now, when we will reach such a high level of consciousness we can be natural again, forget about all the differences and be natural. I definitely mean for most of my poems to ridicule our performance in life: it is shoddy and not what it should be. But this will not make me righteous now: now I see failure as what unites us. I am political in that I speak for failure, for anger and frustration.

Jorge Luis Borges

Interviewed by John Biguenet
and Tom Whalen
(1982)

Jorge Luis Borges, the distinguished Argentine author of short fiction, poetry, and essays and the winner of the International Publishers Prize, was interviewed by *NOR* on a recent trip to New Orleans to receive various academic honors. His most recent collections in English include *Borges: A Reader*, *The Book of Sand*, and *The Gold of the Tigers*. The interview was conducted in English on January 27, 1982.

NEW ORLEANS REVIEW: In your work, your devotion to Buenos Aires is obvious.

JORGE LUIS BORGES: Yes, I don't know why for such a drab city, and yet ten million people, it sprawls all over. Of course, since I was born there, the city has really changed. Now there are tall buildings. When I was a boy, tall buildings had two stories, not more than that. The houses had flat roofs, patios, cisterns; that was not just the downtown, the whole city was like that. And we had apartments; that was all the way back in 1899. And the first apartment house for rent—I think it was erected in 1910 or so. The whole city was different. Of course, it was a small city, but a growing city, often very elated. Today we're rather, in a quiet way, hopeless—in a quiet way.

NOR: That sounds like New Orleans.

BORGES: No. I think of New Orleans as brimming over with music and jazz. They speak of the tango. But you may spend several years in Buenos Aires and not hear a single tango. Usually you can spend a long time in, well, Brazil and not hear any music, as far as I am aware. But here, the city is brimming over with jazz. You're hearing it all time and enjoying it and taking it in. But the tango in Buenos Aires, as most people have written about it, was evolved in the brothel houses about 1880. And the people didn't accept it because they knew whom it came from. When people heard that they were dancing it in Paris, then they took it seriously. They were a nation of snobs. Paris, of course, they took for reality. So then people said, "Ah, the tango." They all knew it came from the brothel houses and shouldn't be talked about. It wasn't accepted by the people, but when people knew that the right people were dancing it and it was being sung in Paris, then it was taken up by them. When I was a boy, yes, I can remember only two tangos. I was hearing all the time French music, Italian music, now and then perhaps Spanish music—no, that was rare.

NOR: When you describe the city, it often sounds like the sort of labyrinth that some of your fiction employs. Is the city a kind of labyrinth for you?

BORGES: Well, it is today because it's very large. When I was a boy, it wasn't. It was quite small, but, somehow, very hopeful, very proud in 1910. But since then—well, of course, we had that awful scoundrel Peron. But even before Peron things were falling down, falling down. And I was declining and falling. I don't suppose anyone would disagree, the whole thing has gone beyond it. But on the other hand, I don't think anything can be done about it. Elections would be a mistake, of course, in which we would have lots of scoundrels like Peron; and the military do their best, but inefficient best I should say, maybe their well-meaning best, as far as I know. I was a conservative, then left the conservative party, and now I'm just a writer and not too conspicuous in my country. They know I'm there and that's that.

NOR: As a writer, although you seem very rooted in Argentina and Argentinean history . . .

BORGES: You shouldn't say Argentina. There's no such word. It's *Argentine*. Because you see, Argentine means *silvery*. The Rio de la Plata means the *Silver River*. You don't have to add Argentina, because that's non-sensical. Someone invented it to rhyme with

Bolivian and *Peruvian*, but *Argentinean*—there's no such word. If you said, "Argentiniano," the Spanish people would laugh at you. No, it's *Argentine*. The Argentine Republic, yes, but the Argentine, not Argentina, wherever that may be.

NOR: Despite the fact that you are a citizen deeply rooted to your home, Pablo Neruda, even though he criticized your work, said you are one of the very few universal Latin American writers.

BORGES: Yes, of course. I'm a kind of world-wide superstition. I don't take myself seriously as all that. I dislike what I write and I like what I read in my other writers, not my own stuff, my own output. I don't like it, but I put up with it. I'm 82, too old to attempt new tricks. I just go on writing. Yes, what else can I do? I'm 82. I'm blind. I've been pensioned off with two pensions. From the library, of course, then as a professor of English literature. Then when the time came, I had two pensions and royalties, but royalties— you can't make a living in my country from books. Perhaps the booksellers can, but not the writers. And the publishers can't either, because they only get 20 percent for a book sold. They have to pay for the printing, for the propaganda, for sending the book all over. While the writer, whoever writes the book, has no expenses but he may be paid royalties every six months (that's theoretically), but really quite possibly he might not get a cent. And then there are the lectures. I lecture in Buenos Aires. If I lecture, let's say, at a library or a school, then of course I don't charge them anything. But if it's an institution, people pay for hearing me or chatting with me then, of course. They give me something. But who would make a living out of my literature? Nobody can. Even if you condescend to pornography. But even then, you are obscene and still poor, no?

NOR: Even someone as widely translated as you doesn't make—

BORGES: No, because it goes through so many hands before it reaches the writer. Yes, I've been widely translated. I don't know why, because there are far better writers than I in my country. Somehow they don't get translated, and I do. I don't know why it is. I never thought in terms of fame or selling or even of finding readers. The only reason was that I felt an inner urge to do so. And my father advised me, "Don't, above all, don't rush into print. Publish as little as you can." I published my first book when I was

24, a book of poems and already I had destroyed three or four books before I published that one. Not a very good book, either.

NOR: You have said that translations are different perspectives of an object in motion.

BORGES: Yes, I suppose they are. But every translation is a new version. And every book is really a rough draft. As [Alfonso] Reyes said to me, we publish our books in order not to spend our lifetimes going over rough drafts. We publish a book and then we're rid of it. We can go on to other or perhaps better things. When I publish a book, I let it find its way in the world. I don't worry about it. I haven't read a single line written about me. I haven't read the translations, either. I never reread my own work because I'd get very discouraged if I did so. So I go on writing. Because what else can I do? I'm blind. I would like to go on reading, that would be far better than to go on writing. But unhappily that is forbidden me. But I keep on buying books. I don't know why. I like being in a bookish atmosphere. Of course the books, well, they might as well be in Timbuktu since I don't read them. Friends come and visit me and then we read, we reread; then generally, we take some history or philosophy or Schopenhauer or if not, well many favorites of mine. We go in for poetry; generally we read Browning or Emerson. I love Emerson. He was somewhat influenced by Whitman.

NOR: And Emerson was the only one to see Walt Whitman as a great poet.

BORGES: Yes. You know what he called Poe? He said, "Oh, Edgar Allan Poe, the jingle man." He was thinking of "The Bells," I suppose; it was really a jest. It was all the same. These things don't have to be right or not. The jingle man.

NOR: I would like to ask you about a writer that most American readers are still unaware of and that's the Austrian Gustav Meyrink.

BORGES: Well, they should not be. I taught myself German in order to read Schopenhauer (just for reading purposes, I don't speak German). I taught myself German with this method. I recommend it to everybody. I got hold of Heinrich Heine's *Buch der Lieder* [*Book of Songs*]. And then, a German-English dictionary, since English was the only language they had. And then I began reading. I was looking all the time in the dictionary. The only German I had was "*Der, die, das, die. Den, die, das, die.*" Then I began reading. Then after three or four months, at another moment (it was in Geneva; I must have been seventeen at the time), I cried because I was reading a poem in an unknown tongue, in German, "*In der Fremde*" ["Abroad"] It went thus:

> *Ich hatte einst ein schönes Vaterland.*
> *Der Eichenbaum*
> *Wuchs dort so hoch, die Veilchen nickten sanft.*
> *Es war ein Traum.*
>
> *Das küsste mich auf deutsch und sprach auf deutsch*
> *(Man glaubt es kaum*
> *Wie gut es Klang) das Wort: "Ich liebe dich!"*
> *Es war ein Traum.*

> [Once I had a lovely fatherland
> The oak trees
> Grew high there, the violets nodded gently.
> It was a dream.
>
> It kissed me in German and said in German
> (It's hard to believe
> How good it sounded) the words: "I love you!"
> It was a dream.]

And then I cried. Not only was it the beauty of the verses, but I was reading in German, actually. I had conquered the German language. It's the best method. When you are Spanish speaking, then I think the best writer would be Oscar Wilde because Oscar Wilde writes with many Latin words, where for example Browning or Kipling, no, they use plain Saxon words.

NOR: I was wondering if you agreed with a character of yours, Dr. Zimmerman, who says in the story "Guayaquil" that *The Golem* is the only book by Meyrink worth reading. Didn't you edit a collection of short stories by Meyrink, translated into French?

BORGES: Yes, I did. A book called *Fledermäuse* [*Bats*]. Then he wrote the story about a wandering Jew. In German it's the everlasting Jew. That book is called *Das grüne Gesicht* [*The Green Face*]. Then a book about English wizards, with a beautiful title *Der Engel vom* *westlichen Fenster*, *The Angel of the Western Window*. But his book is *The Golem*. It was the first book I read in full in German. After Heine, I went on to prose, and then I found a fascinating book, *Der Golem*. So, it was two Jews who led me to German, Heine and Meyrink. Meyrink was actually called Meyer, but that was too commonplace. He changed his name. Meyrink sounds better, no? Meyer in German is like Smith or Lopez. Borges is a very common Portuguese name. Every other man is called Borges in Lisbon.

NOR: There are many American, European and British writers that you have recommended to us for whom we're grateful. I was wondering if there are some South American writers that you think we should be reading?

BORGES: Yes, perhaps. But I know very little about them. Still I think we have a pretty fine poet; her name is Silvina Ocampo. She's been done into English now. And, well, I won't go in for any more names because all people notice is the omissions, the exclusions. Someone is left out, he stands out, in a sense. Well, I know very little about those writers. Garcia Marquez is a fine writer. Of course, Alphonso Reyes, I think, wrote the finest Spanish prose ever written on this side of the Atlantic. He was a great writer. A great prose writer. He was my master—well, I had many masters. Lugones, in my country. But Lugones here is an unknown quantity, I should say. You see, you have been in the world so much, and we in the world so little. I mean, what we have done is important to us and to Spain but not to the outside world. Such writers as Edgar Allan Poe, Emerson, Melville, Walt Whitman, Emily Dickinson, Thoreau, Frost, Faulkner—well, you can't think them away. There they are; they influence us all the time. What have we given the world? A few words simply, no? For example, Bolivar, *pampas*, *gaucho*, Rio de Janeiro, Montezuma, Cortez, Pizarro, perhaps tango—well, that's that.

NOR: Many people would argue that Borges, too, belongs on that list of writers.

BORGES: Oh, no. Not him. Not him.

NOR: What do you think of the young poet Borges who wrote *Fervor de Buenos Aires*?

BORGES: Well, he was trying to imitate Walt Whitman and failing, of course. He did his best to be Walt Whitman; he failed miserably.

But somehow, people remember him still. No, maybe there are one or two pages that may still be readable. But I don't know since I don't read my own output.

NOR: How do you weigh your poetry against your fiction? Do you prefer your poems to your stories?

BORGES: I suppose they are essentially the same. I like my poems. My friends tell me, no, my verses are a mistake. Well, I say maybe my poor friends are also mistaken. I like my poems. Well, of course, if I'm writing in verse about something, I'll write about it. A story, after all, is a kind of verbal object you invent. It's outside you. But poetry should surely be flowing. But maybe there's no great difference. After all, you have to fall back on inspiration. I don't think books can be explained. If they're explained, they're explained away. See, you can't say that in Spanish. It can't be said because the language wouldn't allow it. Remember some very fine verses by Rudyard Kipling, the famous "The Ballad of East and West." There you have a British officer who is pursuing an Afghan horse thief. They're riding. Then Kipling writes, "They have ridden the low moon out of the sky, their hoofs drum up the dawn." Now, you can't ride the moon out of the sky and you can't drum up the dawn in Spanish because the language doesn't allow it. It can't be done.

NOR: So the translations in Spanish are infinite, then?

BORGES: Well, you have to find some way or you fall flat, I suppose. For example, you can say in English, you are dreaming away your life. Well, that can't be said in Spanish or any romance language as far as I know. It might be said perhaps in German or one of the Scandinavian tongues, but not in a romance language. There are many words that have no Spanish or French translations. Somebody in English will say, "Uncanny." That's Scots, I suppose. In German, *unheimlich*. But you can't say it in Spanish, because the Spanish never had that feeling. They had no need of the word.

NOR: So does that mean that a Spaniard can't dream his life away because he can't say it?

BORGES: Yes, he can do it, but he can't say it. He can do it, of course. Just as we can die even if we don't think of death. But English has another virtue. The virtue of Anglo-Saxon words: they're short. If you say *selini* in Greek, that's far too long—three syllables. In Spanish, *luna*, or in Latin, two syllables. In French, just one syllable really, *lune*. But in English that beautiful, lingering word *moon*. It's the right word, no? But in Old English the word is quite ugly, *mona*. Moon and sun, those two were the right words. Or the difference between sky and heaven. In Spanish, you say *cielo*, or for example, well, in English you have a difference between weather and time. In Spanish, no, it's *tiempo* and that's that. In French also. Such a beautiful English word as *dim*. You don't have any Spanish equivalent for *dim*. In German, of course, you have *Dämmerung*, the twilight, and *Götterdämmerung*, the twilight of the gods.

NOR: When you were speaking about your fiction and your poetry, you spoke of fiction as if it were a perfect little object and poetry as a kind of song?

BORGES: Yes. I suppose that they both come from the imagination. I mean inspiration comes to you; it may be a story or it may be a poem. I suppose the starting point is the same.

NOR: And the experience finds its own way to the right genre?

BORGES: Yes. And the less you meddle with it, the better. The writer shouldn't allow it, should not try to meddle with his writing. His opinions should not be allowed to find their way into his writing. Since opinions, after all, come and go. Emotions, well, emotions go away.

NOR: I was teaching this morning H. G. Wells's "The Country of the Blind"—

BORGES: What a fine story, eh? I read that in the *Strand Magazine* when I was a boy. It came with its own pictures, the *Strand Magazine*. In it I read "The Hound of the Baskervilles," also. What a fine story, eh, "The Country of the Blind"?

NOR: A beautiful story—it echoes for me your short story "The South." The possibility that Nunez's fall down the mountain is his fall to his death, that Dahlmann's journey south is only a dream on the operating table. Many times when one reads your work, there are echoes from literature, "The Book of Sand" echoing "The Blast of the Book" by Chesterton.

BORGES: Of course there are. I try to be a good reader even if I am a bad writer. And Wells was a man of genius, of course.

NOR: Literature that begets literature—some critics see this as a sign of literature being exhausted.

BORGES: No, I think that Emerson wrote that poetry comes out of poetry. Whitman thought that poetry came from experience, no? I don't think so. I think Emerson was right. I think Victor Hugo said, "Homer, of course, had his Homer." "*Homer avait son Homer.*" I suppose he had; he lived in a literary tradition. It's like time, really, beginningless.

NOR: Maybe that's why you say that you are quite incapable of invention. Why should we invent when we have Wells and Stevenson and Chesterton to draw from?

BORGES: Yes, because we keep on inventing the same stories, eh?

NOR: Many critics come back again and again to the subject of time as your most profound concern.

BORGES: Yes, it is. I think time would be the central riddle, no? If we knew what time was, of course we would know ourselves.

NOR: The other evening, you spoke of the metaphor, "Time is a river."

BORGES: Yes, I think that's the real metaphor, no? When you think of time, you think in terms of a river, no? Well, the Mississippi, why not? You think of it as being a river. Yes, I was quoting that verse, that line that Tennyson wrote when he was fourteen. "Time flowing through the middle of the night." A fine line. He wrote it when he was fourteen or fifteen. Then he forgot all about it, and it was somehow dug up by his critics.

NOR: Living on the banks of the Mississippi, we see things washed past us by the river, but it seems that you're able to swim upstream to get back to Homer and Chesterton.

BORGES: Well, I do my best, after all. Homer and Chesterton are really desirable goals. I wish I could. Really, I am unworthy. My writing is unworthy of my reading, eh? I'm beginning to see language. You see, at home we spoke English and Spanish. My maternal grandmother was English, spoke both languages. Then I went to Geneva when I was fourteen. There I was taught French, and there I was taught Latin, a very fine language. After all, I spoke

Spanish and French; I just said, "Now Latin." I'd just think of it in that way. And then, I taught myself German. And when I went blind, I said to myself, "I won't abound in loud self-pity," quoting Kipling. And then I began studying Old English, Anglo-Saxon. And now I go in for Icelandic, for Old Norse. (I love all things Scandinavian.) Old English is a very beautiful language; it's a large language like modern English. If I give you a piece in Old English, it will be—what do you prefer, elegy or epic? I can tackle both. What do you prefer? Elegy or epic?

NOR: Elegy.

BORGES:

> Mæg ic be me sylfum   soðgied wrecan,
> siþas secgan,   hu ic geswincdagum
> earfoðhwile   oft þrowade,
> bitre breostceare   gebiden hæbbe,
> gecunnad in ceole   cearselda fela,
> atol yþa gewealc,   þær mec oft bigeat
> nearo nihtwaco   æt nacan stefnan,
> þonne he be clifum cnossað.

That's Old English ["The Seafarer"] with a line of French, I think. And the other verses are the same. That was done into English by Ezra Pound. He wrote, although he was off his head, he wrote, "May I for my ownself song's truth reckon." Because he was translating the sounds, when the literal translation is "I can offer a true song about myself." And "to tell my travels" he translated as "journey's jargon."

NOR: When you speak of Chesterton and Stevenson and other English writers, you seem most delighted by their styles.

BORGES: In the case of Chesterton, there are many other things, eh? Of course, Stevenson was a great poet. I mean the plots, the style, the metaphors are overwhelming really. Do you remember, for example, "Marble like solid moonlight, gold like a frozen fire." Those are wonderful metaphors. "I shall not be too old to see enormous night arise. A cloud that is larger than the world. And the monster made of eyes." "A monster made of eyes," that's weird, isn't it?

NOR: Can you speak about your own style?

BORGES: Well, when I was a young man, I did my best to be Chesterton, to be Lugones, to be Quevedo, to be Stevenson. Then after that, I said, no, I'll just be Borges, and that's that. A very modest ambition. But after all, people like it.

NOR: And you think Borges is more plain-spoken than these authors?

BORGES: Oh, of course he is. I began by being baroque, because all young men are. I tried to astonish, I went in for far-fetched metaphors; now I try to avoid that kind of thing. I like to use, well, easy words that aren't dictionary words.

NOR: "Blindness is a confinement," you have written, "but it is also a liberation, a solitude propitious to invention, and an algebra."

BORGES: Yes, but I was cheating myself. No, really it's not. Well, of course, you're lonely. I mean you have to read. I used to read all the books in my house. I used to read all the books.

NOR: So you think blindness is a kind of loneliness?

BORGES: It is. One feels lonely. And most of the time. After all, my friends cannot afford to give me all their time. I spend most of my time at home. Most of my contemporaries have died; they're in the cemetery.

NOR: You still have your good friend Bioy Casares?

BORGES: Yes, he's far younger than I am, but he forgives me for being an old man. We meet, perhaps, once a month. Buenos Aires is far too big a city. Ten million inhabitants. Somehow, we drift apart. The telephones don't work, because they're no good.

NOR: Do you think your work has lost something by your being blind?

BORGES: Well, I try to think that it has gained. But really I'm cheating myself. But I want to go on.

NOR: How has your work changed since your blindness?

BORGES: For example, when I had my eyesight, I attempted free verse. But now that I have to make a rough mental draft, of course I go in for sonnets or rhymed verse—those things make the memory easier. You can remember a sonnet. I can remember many sonnets. Both in English and French and Spanish and Italian. But I can't remember free verse to memorize. Even in the case of Walt Whitman, who I've read and reread. I wonder if I can quote a page of Walt Whitman for you, if I may. I might decline and fall at any moment.

> These are the thoughts of all men in all ages and lands—they
>   are not original with me;
> If they are not yours as much as mine, they are nothing, or next
>   to nothing;
> If they are not the riddle, and the untying of the riddle, they are
>   nothing;
> If they are not just as close as they are distant, they are nothing.
> This is the grass that grows wherever the land is, and the water
>   is;
> This is the common air that bathes the globe.

He says at the end: "I love you. I depart from my materials." (That's rather ugly.) "I love you. I depart from my materials, I am as one disembodied, triumphant, dead." The words get shorter and shorter. "I am as one disembodied, triumphant, dead." It rings out, as it should. Whitman was a great poet, of course.

NOR: In reading your work, I often feel as if there are many Borgeses, perhaps an infinite number of them.

BORGES: There should be. Let's be endless.

NOR: Which Borges are we talking to?

BORGES: Well, you pays your money and you takes your chances.

NOR: Can you tell about the books you still have to write, your future projects?

BORGES: I have many future projects. What else can I have but projects at my age? I am translating with Maria Kodama from the German Angelus Silesius's *Der cherubinishe Wandersmann*. He was a seventeenth-century German mystic. That's about to be printed in Chile. Then I am going to write a book about the great historian and writer Snorri Sturluson. That will be the first book on him in Spanish. Then I'm also preparing a book of short stories and another book of poems. Then, at this moment, a book of mine has just come out in Madrid, *The Cipher,* a book of poems. Then, I have two anthologies. One of the Argentine poet Lugones, selected and with a foreword by me, and the other of the famous Spanish writer Quevedo, also selected and with a foreword by me. That's that at the moment, but I keep on writing.

NOR: That's a busy schedule.

BORGES: Yes.

NOR: If you were the headmaster of a school for young poets, what would be your curriculum?

BORGES: Well, when I taught English literature, I said to my students (I had classes for twenty years, and they were always in Buenos Aires), I said, I can't teach you English literature because I don't know it. But I can teach you the love of English literature. Don't go in for dates or place names; don't go in for bibliography. Try to find a way into the book itself. Some of them fell in love with Old English, others fell in love with Chaucer, others with Dr. Johnson, or else with Shakespeare or Marlowe or Milton or Bernard Shaw or Chesterton or Edgar Allan Poe or Emerson, whatever the case might be. They all fell in love with some book or another, and that's the gist, that's the important thing, yes?

NOR: I was wondering if you ever thought of the universe as being designed by a divinity in a state of delirium.

BORGES: No. I think what Bernard Shaw said is true. God is in the making, and we are the making, of course. The whole cosmic process is the making. The universe is history and so on. I don't think of God as a person or a being at all, except he may be. He may be myself for all I know. I may be one of his many disguises. I believe this is more or less the Buddhist idea. I wrote a small handbook on Buddhism, and that was done into Japanese. When I went to Japan, I saw the book on Buddhism. Of course they know far more about it than I do. Buddhism is one of the two or three religions of Japan. Shinto and Buddhism. There is a very strange word in Japanese: *hotoke.* According to the context, it may stand for the Buddha. It may stand for Jesus Christ, or it may stand for anybody who has died. The thought is really the same, no?

NOR: You mentioned this week that you looked very hopefully toward death, as a great adventure.

BORGES: No, not as a great adventure, I should say as a liberation. My father said, I want to die all together. I want to die body and soul. I'm looking forward to death as a kind of sleep. My father, in a sense, committed suicide. He got himself killed on purpose. One of those small battles in the civil wars. That was in 1874. Yes, Colonel Borges. And his death was more or less famous, because he rode a white horse, wore a white poncho, he rode very slowly toward enemy lines, and he got two shots fired into him. The first time the Winchester rifle was used in my country. Of course, it was used in the War between the States, the Civil War. The first time the Winchester rifle was used. The Remington came afterwards I think.

NOR: Do you have something you consider your greatest weakness as a writer?

BORGES: I don't know. Maybe I'm impatient. I'm very clumsy. I take many pains with my writing. Usually it seems to be, well, spontaneous and it isn't. I worry carefully over it. Every page of mine stands for at least a half a dozen rough drafts. They are mental, of course. I have to dictate, I can't write. If I tried to write, it would overlap, the writing would overlap, it couldn't be read by anybody. I've read but few novels, but I've read many short stories. In the beginning, of course, I read Grimm's fairy stories, I read the *The Arabian Nights*. And then to Stevenson, to Chesterton, to Edgar Allan Poe, to Jack London also. The first novel I ever read through in my life was Mark Twain's *Huckleberry Finn*. Then I went on to *Life on the Mississippi* and to *Roughing It*, and *Flush Days in California*, those books few folks seem now to have read. Enjoyable books. He was a man of genius, of course, Mark Twain. He was unaware of the fact that he was a man of genius.

NOR: Why do you consider Borges a "minor" writer?

BORGES: Well, because I have read him, but not only read him, I have written him, I know all about him. Still there may be something in all that stuff for all I know, since so many people have taken it seriously, taken it in earnest. There should be something there.

NOR: There are many people who are very grateful for your having devoted yourself to your stories.

BORGES: They're very generous. Very mistaken, I should say. Generous mistakes.

NOR: What does literature have to offer us?

BORGES: I should say everything, eh? The universe at least. Literature, of course. I am tone deaf, I am blind. I have never greatly enjoyed architecture. Painting, yes, perhaps—Turner, Velasquez. And that's that. Words have meant much to me, and languages. I am very fond of words, etymologies.

NOR: So, literature is like an aleph, a little window onto the universe?

BORGES: Well, thank you for remembering that story. It's quite a good story, I should say, even though I wrote it.

NOR: I can tell you a story that may please you. I worked with a program where poets went into school classrooms and taught poetry to children. And one of the games we played with them was to give them invisible alephs. And they could hold them up to the light we told them, and they would see the universe pass in front of them. And they would write down what they saw.

BORGES: Oh good for you. Far better than the story I wrote.

NOR: I think it's the same story. And the children wrote wonderful poetry by looking through the invisible alephs.

BORGES: It was a prism, no? Of course, it had to be a prism.

NOR: For the children, we said it was an invisible prism and gave each one his own.

BORGES: That's far better than what I wrote.

NOR: We learned from you.

BORGES: What's good for me, was good for you. Good for me especially.

NOR: And good for the children.

BORGES: A man in Spain asked me whether the aleph actually existed. Of course it doesn't. He thought the whole thing was true. I gave him the name of the street and the number of the house. He was taken in very easily.

NOR: But perhaps, as you say, if literature gives us everything, then the aleph is the short story and the poem. Because through it we see everything as through that small prism.

BORGES: Yes. That piece gave me great trouble, yes. I mean I had to give a sensation of endless things in a single paragraph. Somehow, I got away with it.

NOR: Yes, it's a beautiful catalogue.

BORGES: Yes. But a lot of trouble.

NOR: Is that an invention, the aleph, or did you find it in some reference?

BORGES: No. I'll tell you. I was reading about time and eternity. Now eternity is supposed to be timeless. I mean, God or a mystic perceives in one moment all of our yesterdays, Shakespeare says, all the past, all the present, all the future. And I said, why not apply that, well, that invention to another category, not to time, but to space? Why not imagine a point in space wherein the observer may find all the rest. I mean, who invented space? And that was the central idea. Then I had to invent all the other things, to make it into a funny story, to make it into a pathetic story, that came afterwards. My first aim was this: in the same way that many mystics have talked of eternity . . . that's a big word, an eternity, an everness. And also neverness; that's an awful word. Since we have an idea of eternity, of foreverness in time, why not apply the same idea to space, and think of a single point in space wherein the whole of space may be found? I began with that abstract idea, and then, somehow, I came to that quite enjoyable story.

NOR: Physicists came up with the same idea when they thought of the big bang theory, that the universe might be moving toward a single point, which would condense and then explode into a universe again. Perhaps they, too, learned from you.

BORGES: Well, I don't think so. I don't think they would trouble about a minor South American writer, no?

Catharine Stimpson

Interviewed by Mark Lussier
and Peggy McCormack
(1984)

With the founding of *Signs: Journal of Women in Culture and Society*, Catharine Stimpson's place within the brief history of feminist literary theory was secured. Her essays have appeared in prominent anthologies and journals, such as *Writing and Sexual Difference*, *Feminist Literary Criticism*, and *Literature and Society*, as well as *Women's Studies*, *Boundary*, *Critical Inquiry*, and *Signs*. Dr. Stimpson is professor of English and director of the Institute for Research on Women at Rutgers University. The interview was conducted at the 1984 Modern Language Association Annual Convention.

NEW ORLEANS REVIEW: The first question I wanted to ask you is whether it is possible to define feminist poetics, and if it is, is it needed or would such a definition be useful?

CATHARINE STIMPSON: The real difference is among looking for a feminist poetics, looking for a female poetics, or looking for a poetics of the woman writer. Let me try to separate them out. A poetics of the woman writer would be a theoretical description of writing by women that could incorporate a number of reasons as to why women write as women. Do they write as women because of their historical situation, because of complicated biological reasons, a combination of them? A poetics of women's writing would also see the common stylistic features of an entire sex without necessarily tying us to a specific reason for why women write as women. However, a female poetics, through the very use of the word "female," implies that women write as women out of biological causes, out of the body, out of the fact that they are born female, born into a biological class. The corollary of that would be a male poetics, a way in which men write as men because they are born into that biological class. The search for a "female" poetics now emphasizes bodily rhythms, bodily metaphors, which often seem multidimensional for women, linear for men. An old article in *Critical Inquiry,* studying a male poetics, especially in Hemingway, suggests that a male style is like a male orgasm which ends in death and silence. Finally, a feminist poetics would be a poetics of politics, a style that self-consciously incorporated a feminist ideology that begins in protest and revolt and seeks to affect equality and gender transformation. More a thematic than a stylistic venture, feminist poetics would have to involve a political and ideological reading of the world that was then taken into the literary text.

NOR: If a male poetics is defined by a linear progression towards orgasm, then is it also connected to what [Jane] Gallop calls in her book "the chain of metonymy"? She discusses metonymy as a male-erected trope. Are the two terminologies compatible at this point?

STIMPSON: It could certainly work that way, but if you are looking for a male and a female poetics, you must ask if your underlying reading of the world is a psychoanalytic one in which you see all tropes as substitutes for a sexual dilemma, all tropes as a displacement for a terrible dilemma between the infant self and its parents before you are six years old. I'm not sure that a female or a male poetics has to work that way. A female and a male poetics can simply mean a sense of language and the text springing out of the body. Obviously, the text is a series of displacements of the bodily experience, but you need not use psychoanalysis to define it. What distinguishes women as women and distinguishes men as men? A bodily state. What distinguishes you from me right now? Lots of cultural things distinguish us, but what is the one difference that we could not will? The body. A female and a male poetics would have to look for a writing that springs from bodily, erotic, reproductive differences.

NOR: In summary, it depends on the lens through which one wishes to examine the text; if one selects the psychoanalytic model, it inevitably leads to a reading of the text as displacement.

STIMPSON: If you are going to talk about maleness and femaleness and how they might be inscribing themselves in the text, you are going to have to talk about a series of tropes for the body and for eroticized experience.

NOR: One cannot help noting a strong element of eroticism in your own writing; certainly the presentation last night on [Gertrude] Stein was tied to the body, and also what I have read both in *Signs* and in *Women and Sexuality*. Perhaps I should define what is meant by "eroticism" in your writing. You seem to understand and take as given that we must address the body, and that alone would probably make men uncomfortable.

STIMPSON: What class was to the nineteenth century, the body is to twentieth-century literature. This is an eroticized century that is taking, at least in the West, a founding text from Freud and founding ideas from D. H. Lawrence. This is the century that has used sex and sexual differentiation as a form of social organization and as a way of reading the world. I am a creature of the twentieth century; I mean we are taught to read the world erotically. In fact, I think we are consumed by sexuality. In a couple of places, like my essay on the lesbian novel, I ask how historians will judge us and our obsession with seeing the world erotically. What does it mean about us that we look at childhood and see these poor libidinal creatures, seething, these cauldrons of desire and frustration. If you are a feminist, you have to look at the body for several other reasons. One is because women have been taught to live in the body and to serve as metaphors for body. In social structures, women are treated as body, either the beautiful or the erotic or the maternal object. Feminist criticism has to analyze these practices. Feminism, too, teaches us to look at the importance of sexual differentiation in the building of social structures and says that sexual differentiation is not the right foundation for these structures.

NOR: So one goes through the body to exhaust it as the primary critical lens through which to see the world.

STIMPSON: Yes, it is a deconstruction of the importance of the body, which at the same time recognizes that it has a place in the world. We are creatures of the flesh as well as creatures of the mind. This is ironic for me because I'm basically a "blue-stocking," a proud and wonderful title.

NOR: In your essay on the lesbian novel, you mention a novel in that article entitled *Labyrinth*, in which the main characters are two sisters, one who marries an ambitious egocentric man and the other who lives with an ambitious generous woman. I found it most interesting in light of what another feminist stated last night, in [Annette] Kolodny's session on re-reading the canon, about Brockden Brown's *Ormond* and what happens at the conclusion of that novel, which she read as a very strong statement by Brown about the nature of the forms that govern our lives and as Brown calling for a radical reshaping of those forms because without such there is no re-formation. In regard to re-shaping the structures by which we live our lives, at the past several MLAs, the best criticism and without doubt the most powerful voices are those from the feminist "camp," and by camp, I mean that as we sit within the structure of MLA, the good old boy system that still exists, they must perceive you still as a hostile camp, a source of hostility and conflict.

STIMPSON: We are to some of them.

NOR: This goes back to the women's caucus held in Houston at its MLA in 1980. I wonder if you still perceive a sense of that hostility?

STIMPSON: Oh, yes, but we women in the MLA really are very mild, polite, decorous. If this is a revolutionary movement, it is a revolutionary movement with teacups.

NOR: Well, you know what the attitude would be if a male said that.

STIMPSON: But the consequences of feminist criticism are far-reaching. What actually is being called for is a way of re-reading the world that asks us to look at the fact that gender matters in the construction of the world and of culture. It asks for a reading of new texts; it asks for equality in the administration of knowledge. It doesn't ask for triviality or for silence. It asks for equality and heterogeneity in the distribution of knowledge.

NOR: So where's the fear if that is what I hear you saying?

STIMPSON: What's scary? The call for change. But are women going to be vengeful? I don't think so. If they achieve power, are they going to be exclusionary? Are men never going to be allowed to read papers? I don't think so, except power does tend to be exclusionary. Fortunately, a feminist critique carries with it a self-consciousness about the abuses of power. Whether when feminists achieve more power they will remain true to their principles is another question.

NOR: What is apparent from everything heard by feminists at this convention is that there is an invitation to the men that was not there a few years back.

STIMPSON: It depended on whom you talked to. However, I do think men are more receptive now; there have always been sympathetic men, but you are right to pick up a sense of feminist criticism feeling less besieged. It is not what it was fifteen years ago. Feminist critics are still being denied tenure, but there are also feminist critics who have tenure. There are some feminist books that are not published, but for the most part, feminist criticism is well published, particularly in the United States.

NOR: This brings the discussion back to why feminists are bringing out the best theory at the moment.

STIMPSON: In terms of a form for approaching various texts, there are three things to look at: the representation of women, which also means looking at "male prosy"; at the women's tradition, the gynocritical tradition; and, three, the cause and consequences of sexual difference. Given those questions, there is no area of culture that feminist criticism can't help; there is no area of culture that feminist criticism shouldn't move in. Moreover, not just academics are drawn to feminist criticism. Some of the most important work comes from outside, from non-academic writers. Who is our saint? What is our *locus classicus:* "A Room of One's Own." It is still the text where one can find the promise and perils of feminist criticism. Alice Walker's *In Search of Our Mothers' Gardens* was first in *Ms.* magazine (May 1974). Having this group both inside and outside the academy helped to give feminist criticism some of its volatility and energy. It still has some of that founding wildness, which I hope it never loses. It's poised between its founding days and becoming a boring, standard subject.

NOR: This is precisely why we included our question on institutionalization and the women's movement. This is, in fact, what the argument has been for.

STIMPSON: The institutionalization of feminism? I want it to have happened. No one wants to stay crazy forever. Anybody who says that they love existence on the margins, and that they want to spend their lives on the margins, is kidding him or herself and you. Who, unless you're a saint, wants to eat cat food when you can have a decent meal? Nobody wants to live on the periphery. The real question becomes how do we avoid becoming self-enclosed. How do you make connections? One is with students, through students. A second way is through a connection with other analytical systems, between feminism and Marxism or post-structuralism or black studies. A third way is to keep links with the women's movement. Am I saying that all academic movements should be primarily political movements? No, because I think one of the tasks of academic life is constantly to deconstruct ideology. Ideology, by definition, is a set of blinders, and if we made the academy a place that had to be political and ideological, it would destroy some of its virtues.

NOR: This returns to a previous statement. Who are our saints? Certainly those that would figure prominently would have to be politicians like Shirley Chisholm, Barbara Jordan, Bella Abzug and others. Yet these memories are, in fact, new and just were not there twenty years ago. Feminist theory was just not there.

STIMPSON: Nor could it be. It just did not exist twenty years ago.

NOR: So to maintain the connection with the movement is to maintain the connection with your primary energy source?

STIMPSON: Yes, and with a passion for social justice. A fourth way is to keep in touch with actual living writers. We sound so dull, don't we. It is very useful to talk to writers other than oneself. The writers are looking at theory. Do you know a poet named Kathleen Fraser? She's working with a wonderful little poetry magazine called *However.* They're trying to bring together modernist and feminist principles.

NOR: To return to something discussed previously, it would seem to hold that we can deal with each other not through the body but beyond the body. You said earlier that one reason for focusing attention on the body was to get beyond it as a way of dealing with each other. What steps might be taken to assure this?

STIMPSON: What you have touched on is one of the principles of feminist (or all) criticism: a need for critical self-consciousness. The feminist critic, in theory, asks herself, "How did I come to think what I think; how can I show my reader how I came to think what I think?" Feminist critics have an initial assumption that we think badly, so that feminist criticism begins in suspicion. The process of the feminist critic, male or female, is one of de-mystifying one's own presumptions about literature and culture, and then to try and make public the process of unraveling so that the next stage of reconstruction can begin. But the second and third generation of feminist critics will be different. Why? Because if you go to a college classroom now, you can read de Beauvoir to begin with. You don't discover her on your own. You see some of the insights of feminist criticism as a part of the world as it is.

NOR: As a given in that environment?

STIMPSON: Right. The younger feminist critics have to become suspicious of us, and that's good. I see this happening. I was having lunch with a couple of people while I was evaluating women's studies programs at universities, and there were a couple of next-generation young assistant professors, saying, "Look, we don't have to say these things anymore."

NOR: Part of what I heard at our first meeting at the Houston MLA was a young assistant professor asking, "Why is there this tone of hostility, because I don't think it's needed any longer? I can understand it in the mid-1960s, but we are at the dawn of the 1980s, and it is counter-productive." The question did evoke a sense of generational conflict within the feminist movement. What is your sense of this development?

STIMPSON: Are things different? Yes. So, are certain oppositional stances still totally necessary? No, they are not totally necessary. But can we deceive ourselves about how much change has happened? Can that young assistant professor be kidding herself? Has she come up for tenure yet? Has she really hit it yet? The important point is that change is not symmetrical; change is asymmetrical, sloppy, certainly in those gender relations that concern both our public and private lives. We have to reconstruct the structures of intimacy as well as the structures of governments. Because change is so sloppy, you are going to see some places that are utopian visions right next to places that are perfectly awful. The techniques that are obsolete in one place may still be necessary in another. One must think of the situation as a patchwork. This is one reason why I resist the metaphor of margin and center. This spatial metaphor of margin and center means that there is one place of centralized power, with the rest of us dispersed around the edges.

NOR: And fighting to get in.

STIMPSON: But is that really the way things work in the United States today? What's a more appropriate way of looking at it? I think another appropriate way of looking at it is that we are circuit boards. Our life, in terms of cultural and political power, is like a circuit board; power is flowing every place. At one point in the circuit board, we have power, but at another point we may not. There are some people at the edges of the circuit board who have nothing whatsoever, but most of us above the poverty line have power in some places, where we are little centers, but we lack power in other places. As we charge around this vast circuit board that is America, at some places we are blinking with power, but in other places we're dim and dark. There is a scene in Thomas Pynchon's *The Crying of Lot 49* where Oedipa is looking down a hill at a California town; she's gazing at the lights of the town and the patterns lights make when they interlock with each other, and she believes it looks like the back of a transistor radio, all these lines and squiggles going in all directions. That's the way power and force work in our lives—in analyzing the complexities of the lines of psychological, political, and cultural forces. There is some good work coming out of women studying popular culture or the media, but I think too many of us are only looking at the literary text, insufficiently at the electronic text.

NOR: We agree here; while it is popular to assert that we live in a visually saturated environment, what most people don't realize is that our culture remains a basically visually-illiterate society since to read any medium requires training in a process of reading that ultimately gets transferred to reading the world around us. Didn't you, in your presentation on colonization, mention something about being in a group of feminist filmmakers?

STIMPSON: What I said was that I was reading an essay by English feminist filmmakers, and I thought they were misusing the metaphor of colonization. They talked about how invasive capitalism was and how it was always looking for new areas to take over. The example they used was the way that Virginia Slims cigarettes had taken over the women's movement with the slogan "You've come a long way, baby!" Now what does that slogan mean? It's saying to women, "Your life is better than it was." The ads have pictures of the old oppressed woman and the true, new, wonderfully liberated woman. What the ads have taken over from the women's movement is the principle of the value of women's autonomy and the principle that men have dominated women in the past; that has not been good for men or for women. But to what end? Why have they taken this over? Virginia Slims has taken this over to make money for Virginia Slims and also to teach women to smoke. I hate smoking. It is a killer habit. If all this is true, then why did I object to the feminist filmmakers using the term "colonization"? Because colonization, as we understand it in the modern world, is an economic, cultural, and political process that began in the fifteenth or sixteenth century, that later saw England running India and now sees America helping to dictate the policies of Central America. That process is a specific, historical one that hurts people, and if we use the word *colonization* as a metaphor to describe any dominating process, we lose sight of what colonization itself actually is. It blurs our vision. As much as I hate the Virginia Slims ad, I can't compare my experience of reading a Virginia Slims ad to what my experience would have been if I were not a tenured college professor in the United States but rather an illiterate woman working on a coffee plantation in Central America or a textile worker in Guatemala or an electronics worker in Taiwan.

NOR: You mentioned earlier that you did not want to get into a discussion of feminism outside of the Western democracies, but it would seem that issue would be the most burning issue for feminists and feminism.

STIMPSON: Absolutely, and let me tell you why I'm reticent. I don't want to get into it because I don't want to look like I know everything about everybody. Do we have to understand colonization? Do we have to know about it? Yes, but am I the person to teach about it? No. I don't want to be in the position of a First World woman saying, "This is the reality *there*." I've seen too many errors and mistakes coming out of intellectual imperialism. What we have to do is read, and listen, to the voices that are coming out of their own experience. I have been reading an article by Gayatri Spivak in an issue of *Yale French Studies*. She begins with a wonderful anecdote of being a well-born, Indian woman, educated in the West—an intellectual. She hears two old, illiterate women as they wash clothes in a river that is flowing through her family's land. Then she goes into this powerful analysis of what French feminist theory is saying about women, how it cannot work for the Third World. Then she returns to the washer women to say, "What can we say to each other?" Another text I've been reading is a collection of writings by Native American women edited by Rayna Green. One hears the voices from a place itself. They have always been there, but now they are rising in power and beauty. My task as a First World feminist critic is to try to frame the voices in a way that is respectful, tactful. Our job is to open up the walls of ignorance, and not to rebuild the walls of ignorance, even while claiming that this is a transparent mirror to the new reality. In the future, I think more and more of women's studies work will be done outside of the United States. It may take different forms, which I cannot predict. What I see happening within the United States is the increasing institutionalization of feminist criticism and women's studies on all levels without becoming just another subject that students feel they have to learn.

NOR: What one might call another industry?

STIMPSON: Yes, another industry.

NOR: So that is, as you see it, the future direction?

STIMPSON: It's a big job.

NOR: It is also fraught with problems. With those walls of ignorance you're talking about, institutionalization may be merely a device of separation under the guise of protection. We have covered a lot of ground. Speaking more personally, I was surprised that the Tolkien book was your first book.

STIMPSON: It was a monograph, not really a book, and I did make a couple of mistakes. I asked, "Why are people reading this; why is it so popular—this empty pastiche?" Well, despite my strictures, Tolkien keeps on selling.

NOR: Speaking of power, that is one manifestation of power. Why do you think it continues to sell?

STIMPSON: Because it is a wonderful story.

NOR: We're very plot-oriented, aren't we?

STIMPSON: As well we should be. I am now working on my second novel, and the hardest thing to do is plotting. To tell a story is a real gift. I respect Eudora Welty so much because she tells a story, because she gives us a sense of a beginning, a middle, and an end. To get from the beginning to the middle and then to the end is the hardest of work. It's much easier to be a critic.

NOR: The same might be said for poetry as well since it is not as time-consuming and does not require the organization.

STIMPSON: Human beings need plot; we need stories, and Tolkien's is an intricate story. It appeals to the same part of us as "Dungeons & Dragons." Tolkien is also moral. There's good and bad; it's easy to tell who's who. Good and bad are always in arduous combat, and bad may win. So it's the intricate story that scares us.

NOR: Indeed, bad seemed to be winning constantly until the end, and then he pulled it out.

STIMPSON: He pulled it out; we're going to be safe after all. Tolkien is pretty banal and narrow on women, though. I say that even as I insist that we cannot think of the world only in terms of men and women. Now feminism does because that's its project: to look at relations between men and women, and see where they work and don't work. But it also may lead us to think of the world only in terms of men and women. What's going on in this convention? There is talk about literary theory, about Asian-American literature, about Spenser and the Renaissance. There are a great many things that these men and women share. We cannot reduce the world to men and women, even as we try to reconstruct their relations. I hate binary thinking.

Carolyn Heilbrun

Interviewed by Mark Lussier
and Peggy McCormack
(1985)

Carolyn Heilbrun has written works that continue to affect the ongoing development of feminist literary theory, most notably *Reinventing Womanhood* and *Toward a Recognition of Androgyny*. She served as President of the Modern Language Association in 1984 and teaches in the English department at Columbia University, where this interview was conducted.

NEW ORLEANS REVIEW: This is in certain ways not an original question, but do you feel it is necessary to assert a cohesive feminist theory? This question arises out of a reading of Elaine Showalter's new book and the theorists that have been included.

CAROLYN HEILBRUN: Maybe we need to, but we're not about to. The theoretical aspect of feminism, I think, is very important. As one of the people who writes in a plain English that dogs and cats can read, I'm really sort of unhappy about a certain intellectual group of feminists who are anti-theoretical, because I think we need them both very much. The dialogue between them is very important, but the idea that there will ever be one theory, I don't think is true of anything, and where it exists, I think it holds things up. I mean they're very caught up in both Freudian and Marxist theory, and to some extent I think this is regrettable because they are both such stunning theories; it's like shooting a tank with a peashooter to try and get at them. So all I, for one, try to do is to be clear. Hopefully, some genius will come along with a theory that will relate to Freud and Marx, but as to having one coherent theory, I don't think you will, and I don't think I'd want it.

NOR: Is it sufficient to have earned respectability for the consequences of gender in writing?

HEILBRUN: If you mean as a subject, it's more than sufficient, and I just wish we could do it more. We're still waiting for the generation of "old boys" to die out who don't think it's respectable, who don't think there's such a thing as gender. There's the universal writing, you know, neutral.

NOR: And in relation to them, you really have to keep putting a name "feminist" to what we're doing, but when I looked at the series of essays in Showalter, the question occurred to me: should there be any single feminist theory any more than there is single masculinist theory?

HEILBRUN: No, but naturally they have to debate the point of view, and Showalter herself has been very much a leading figure in this questioning, but even she changes her mind, as every intelligent person does. Many of us, those of us on what is called the "cutting edge," are very concerned about the relation of men to feminism. And now that has become a very important topic.

NOR: Whether men can even practice feminist theory at all is another of our questions along with the question of reading texts and the effects of gender difference on both sides of this reading activity.

HEILBRUN: Speaking to some students in graduate school, we've come across an interesting version of this. I now have a number of male students in my feminist classes, and they pick up a lot of feminism. Then they give a report in another class using it entirely, but they never call it feminist, and they never mention the feminist critic they got it from. That is one of the big points in male critics. Even if they become feminists—and there are rare exceptions to this: Jonathan Culler is one—for the most part they are now learning the techniques, which are very exciting and very good, but they don't credit anybody.

It's like they just saw the light and were converted, and there was no one between them and Jesus. There is someone between them and this view. I'm probably the oldest feminist around, and I tend to be a little tempered by the winds, being very much a shorn lamb, and so I'm glad if this happens at all. If a young man can get up and say, "The interesting thing about Isabel in *Wuthering Heights* is that she has no story; there is no script. She's living by a romantic script. How is she going to live?"—as if he just picked this out of the air—I'm not quite as upset as some of the younger feminists are, but maybe I should be.

NOR: After all, they are just appropriating an insight as their own and crediting no one.

HEILBRUN: I guess in the end you have to ask yourself what is more important: the credit or the insight. And the male ego in our society is such that it can't credit women for something. But that's one of the problems; it's not how men read women's texts, which intelligent men—in particular younger ones—are getting very good at. It's the whole position of really taking seriously women, feminism, and the like. The biggest problem I've had all my life and have yet is to get the very brilliant, serious younger critics to recognize that Woolf is as important as Joyce. Now bit by bit they begin to see that the fact that they don't know how to talk about her, and yet they can talk so easily about Joyce, perhaps indicates that she is a little more revolutionary than Joyce, who appears, I think, considerably more revolutionary than he is.

NOR: We're continually struck by men informed by but who never cite women and women who laboriously and concentratedly respond to those men. The women are having arguments with the men in their texts, and the men continue to ignore those women, most particularly at a theoretical level.

HEILBRUN: That's very true. I know of male scholars who have a whole book about plots or a whole book about melodrama and never mention women writers, novels or even characters. But this just takes time.

NOR: You're optimistic. Catharine Stimpson was also optimistic and encouraged us to be also.

HEILBRUN: It is because some of these same scholars are very supportive of women scholars and scholarship behind the scenes. The men whom I have the most trouble with are the older men who don't admit there is such a thing as women's studies, who don't understand why you might want to be out on that fringe when you could be studying the center. We can only wait for them to die off.

NOR: Are they more frustrating to you than your allusion to Edward Said, in your essay from the Showalter book, where his *Orientalism* made you see your own situation in a different light but then you said of him that perhaps he wouldn't want to study feminism as a discourse or want it in the profession?

HEILBRUN: Here again I'm talking about a colleague. He and I in the last few years have been serving together on committees, so I've seen how he works. And it's true he doesn't mention women very much in what he writes although what he's doing is very allied to what feminism is doing. And yet here again I've found he will support good women. Believe me, what I have seen at the university over my life—there is such a change, at least in the English department at Columbia and other places, that I can't despair. Also, Edward Said does so much we can use; we can learn so much from him, and it would be nice if he could learn something from us. As it happens in this case, what's happened is really parallel.

NOR: How long have you been at Columbia? There's that part of the sentence in your essay in Showalter that's so wonderfully expressed. You say, "I, thirty years a girl and woman, in the feminist discourse. . . ."

HEILBRUN: And now it's been even longer. I took my degree here.

NOR: And they never let you go. That's a wonderful compliment.

HEILBRUN: The days when I came here, it was very easy to get tenure. Well, not for a woman, but it was much easier. I first taught here in 1960, so that's twenty-five years I've been teaching here.

NOR: They have certainly been twenty-five crucial years for this whole subject.

HEILBRUN: Lionel Trilling, I hear, used to object to me in the early 1960s in faculty meetings because I was a feminist, so I'm interested in how I was perceived as being too interested in women's writing.

NOR: Returning for the moment to your work, what do you feel will last from your work—your best work, the one work you found most useful?

HEILBRUN: Oh, I don't think any of it will last. One of the fascinating things about feminism is that it moves so fast that already everything I have written has been written by somebody else. I would never write it the same way. Now what I have found is that *Toward a Recognition of Androgyny* and *Reinventing Womanhood* are still important to women who are, in relation to feminism, where I was when I wrote them. I mention, and am always asked about *Androgyny*, and in Montana I mentioned before an audience that I would not do the book the same way.

Incidentally, androgyny is coming back, and a lot of the ideas in the book are coming back. The fact is that in the world where I am, they're already out-of-date. Yet even there it is appalling to me to discover how I've changed. A young man who wrote a long essay on me said, "She has grown so much more liberal and broad-minded over the years. For example, she no longer makes fun of homosexuals." Well, I called him up and asked, "Where and when did I do this?" And he was right; I was not making fun of them, but I was using the kind of language which we used in those days. I referred to a group—I said to someone—as a bunch of queers. Now you know I changed the entire thing when it was re-issued, and I took this out at considerable expense, but I have to admit to you I have never been homophobic, but nonetheless that was how we talked. And there are other things; in the very first book, I know that I mention the fact that Freud found out that all the women who said that they had been sexually assaulted by their fathers later admitted that it was all fantasy. Of course, we know now that it probably wasn't; we now know, in fact, how many women were sexually abused by fathers. And this is also what I mean; even there one changes.

NOR: And we also know now that Freud, at the end of his life work, was changing his entire view of the economics of the female libido and feminine sexuality. So even Freud was changing.

HEILBRUN: If you are dealing with very current issues, you are going to date yourself, and I have no illusions about this. I'm just trying to do what I can to keep this movement going. There are people who are encouraged, to whom you give courage, who find themselves in difficult situations, and that's what it comes down to.

NOR: Are there some you remember, dare I say, that were more fun to have written or enjoyable to have written?

HEILBRUN: Well, yes. In *Reinventing Womanhood*, for the first time I spoke personally, and I felt we had to get away from the high-up-on-Olympus mode; that was an enormous thing for me to do, an enormous hurdle to get over, an enormous risk to take. I no longer find it difficult, but then, of course, you're called confessional. Women are "we" and I find I no longer can stomach a book, for instance, like Diana Trilling's book on Jean Harris, that absents the author;

she takes these moral stands about Jean Harris without ever saying anything about herself. This is a male stance that I find—I don't know exactly why I call it male other than that they set the standard—troubling. Susan Sontag has such a style. Showalter refers to it as the Olympian stance of Susan Sontag and Elizabeth Hardwick. So there are certainly women that do it, and most of the women who write for *The New York Review of Books* or *The New Yorker* have it.

NOR: This would seem a shift of voice to form.

HEILBRUN: You have to say, "I am a woman; I have suffered; I was there."

NOR: What about other people's work? Are there books that you feel were particularly helpful or useful to you?

HEILBRUN: I can't tell you what the excitement was like. I have lived in an all-male world; all my friends were men. One did not have women friends. It's hard to think of now, but one didn't if one were a professional woman in the 1960s and 1950s. And women were all playing this back-to-the-suburbs role—no men all day except for diapering one, and you don't even have him now. Women were dull at dinner parties; they didn't talk about anything but their children. Anyway, these same women are now fascinating, so it's not the women. Everything that came out was so exciting that I almost couldn't bear it.

I was talking recently with the woman who owns Woman's Books on 82nd Street here in New York, one of the biggest women's bookstores that sells only women's books. She said that when they started all their customers had the same books they did, and I was one of them. Now it's quite out of hand; they can't carry it all, and I certainly can't buy it all, but everyone who wrote in those earlier years I found extremely exciting. And you know Betty Friedan's *Feminine Mystique*—you can never repeat what that work meant. That book is one, and I read *The Second Sex* in 1953, and I remember that my whole generation of men became analysts, and all the women went to analysts, and all the men used to say, "She's suffering from penis envy." One had to be a closet feminist. There are certain texts that defined and fueled the movement like Kate Millett's *Sexual Politics*. It now looks naive to us. I just read two reviews of feminist criticism: one by a Norwegian woman who studied in France, and one by an Australian man. It's very easy for them to say that she [Kate Millett] only looked at men, and she was so obvious in what she said, but that book had a lot of power, and it still does. I like the way she confronted things and the way she spoke politically. She understood that she was talking about something political. People like Elaine Showalter have done wonderful things, and Mary Jacobus' collection, *Women Writing and Writing about Women*, is excellent. Gilbert and Gubar's *The Madwoman in the Attic* is an incredible book.

NOR: In fact, last year it was hard to keep up with what just Cornell was publishing. This raises a question from another interview where the interviewee was worn out with this whole conceptual model of marginality, being on the margin. She felt it does not work because feminism itself is pushing out on all fronts, so it's not like being on the margin any longer but being at a center. Do you get a sense of that shift as well, a sense of the replacement of one metaphorical description by another?

HEILBRUN: It depends where you are. If you are at Columbia or Yale or Princeton or University of Wisconsin (Madison), sure you can think of yourself as a center. But women, mainly, are still marginalized. If you study marginalization, as one of my young colleagues is doing, then you constantly re-discover that women are marginalized. We in the East tend to think that we're the world, but I've done two NEH summer seminars which taught me a great deal. College teachers from small colleges out there come here; the NEH pays them: it's one of the best programs they've ever had. I would say something, and they would say, "Well, maybe in New York!" If you go out to the Midwest—Indiana, Ohio, the big smokestack towns—it's different.

In one of those towns I said something about how I would like it to come to a point where no teacher would make a joke about a woman any more than anyone would now make a joke about a black student in the classroom. Well, several people came up to me afterward and said, "I have news for you." Women are still marginalized here, not to mention the whole rest of the world. No matter what the society is, there's always one more oppressed within the oppressed group, so I don't agree, but I understand what she meant. So much is going on, and it's becoming discussed in such a central way that we cannot go on telling ourselves that we're marginalized because what we're trying to be is not marginal. We're all trying to mainstream, and obviously the way to mainstream is to discontinue saying we're marginalized. So I think politically that was probably a good statement.

NOR: What is your sense of how your own voice fits in with this avalanche of interest in feminist critical theory, women's studies and feminism?

HEILBRUN: Because of the privileged life I lead—and it is privileged in the East at a prestigious university and so forth—I get to talk to a lot of the very smartest people; I'm also at the same time immensely aware that the real problem of feminism is taking place somewhere in a classroom with a group of students who either couldn't care less about this or who are going to say, "Men have a hard time, too," or whatever. And you have to keep these two groups in touch with each other. It's more important than that because the young women, or the older women who are teaching feminism for the first time, on the one hand, want to talk about the intricacies of the text while at the same time the students are back where feminism was before Betty Friedan wrote her book.

They need to be encouraged and supported all along the line, and I tend to talk to groups of people and to somehow convey to them the excitement of feminism. I try to write in a way that's understandable while at the same time I try not to sound or be foolish in the knowledge of all that I hear. It's not an easy position because you're not quite theoretical enough for the theoreticians and a little too heavy for the others, but it's what I aim at. Well, I don't so much aim at it; it's what I discovered to be my destiny.

NOR: That is a very difficult position to maintain. Does that mean that you look back and reflect upon the places in which you have chosen to publish or now you see that there are certain places in which you want to publish if, indeed, you are turning from one group to another?

HEILBRUN: It's not that conscious; like I said, this is more a discovery than an intention. First of all, when speaking there are always a large number of women who have never really heard of feminism before, who are afraid of feminism, but they come from an academic world. I mean that I don't go out and talk to the gardening club; I'm usually talking at a university. And I have learned that I get up on the podium with my pearls and my grey hair and my wedding ring and being a full professor and so forth, and I say very radical things, and I don't frighten them that much. They think, "My God, if she can say these things, then there's no danger."

Now I do notice that sometimes it frightens the men and some women, particularly fundamentalists, Mormons and so on, but for the most part you get radical ideas over, and it's reassuring, and because I am where I am, there's nothing they can do to me. So I don't worry anymore. I used to worry frightfully. I was the world's most sensitive creature; if anyone said "boo," I went away and cried, but not about reviews. I feel that once you've written something, you've laid it on the line. I have had to learn if men—and it mostly is men—and certain kinds of women don't like what I do, okay. I can't be everything to everybody. That was very, very hard to learn. I should also say that I'm asked again and again, "Where did you get this self-confidence to talk?" It wasn't easy, and it took many years. I had to keep myself literally from crying if a man said something negative to me.

NOR: How long ago was this sensitivity present?

HEILBRUN: Certainly fifteen years ago, and it didn't come overnight. I remember the first time I really had the nerve to say something; it was when I heard a group of faculty men—and I was the only woman present and we were discussing something—say, "Okay, we'll give it to the girls to type." I had been working myself up to this for the last four years, and I said, "You know, they're women, and they have names."

Believe me, I didn't feel that a braver act had ever been done. And I've since noticed that men would come into the English office—we have a rather large English office as you can imagine and we also now have a rather large number of male secretaries—and look around at the secretaries and say, "Nobody's here."

NOR: Yours is a difficult world, but it strikes me as a happy one.

HEILBRUN: It isn't, because I spend half my time feeling that I ought to be more involved with theory and the other half thinking I'm really making this too complicated.

NOR: I know that the NEH summer institutes for college professors that you mentioned before are clearly geared to walk that middle path that you're attempting to describe. Not only for that reason but for others, as well, it's a wonderful program. It's comforting to know that no matter how theoretical you get, you still give thought to what might be called the trenches.

HEILBRUN: Except that what you say sounds a little like still talking from on high. It's a matter of discourse. That's what I'm really talking about, and I really have discovered that I obtain a sort of median discourse. You have to understand that I'm in the position of whenever I'm with a group of feminists, I'm always by at least ten years the oldest person in the room. And this means that you are, through no choice of your own, in a certain role. Now a lot of my younger colleagues who think that I think too much about this keep telling me that nobody notices; it doesn't make that much difference, but, of course, it does, and they do.

That role, in a sense, has affected the way I talk, but it has also given me a way out of one of the more difficult problems women have within the women's movement, that women as figures of authority are relatively new; they used to be the odd one. Concerning the female role, growing out of Freud's family romance, the mother is not "naturally" invested with authority on the one hand, and on the other hand, she is supposed to be a nurturing figure. So you get a great deal of displacement from students and younger colleagues on both grounds; they're not being nurtured enough or whatever. You have to be aware of this and deal with it, and it is a lot easier to deal with it at my age. My age invests me with a kind of authority that ends the question. What sort of mother am I? I don't know. Now in dealing with younger colleagues, I'm very careful not to take any sort of authority position because what I want are friends, and since I am in a position where I've got to be older than my friends, that does not matter. With students, it helps. Younger women teachers often have a problem, and in fact a book was just published on the subject entitled *Gendered Subjects*, and the entire book is about the problems women have when teaching feminism.

NOR: If Showalter's book represents many or most of the important speakers within the feminist discourse in the last twenty years, what do you see on the horizon? What will happen within feminism in the next ten years, and in relation to that role you spoke of, is one of the things you see happening in the future that more American women scholars will respond to the strong generation of French feminists?

HEILBRUN: Yes, American feminists have been responding to them and to their masters for about six years, so that dialogue is, at this point, fairly well established, and there's been a great deal of discussion about the book *New French Feminisms*. That dialogue is there and will continue.

The first question, about where feminism is going, is much harder to answer, and everyone at the moment is being rather retrospective. Feminism sees itself as being at something of a crossroads, I would say, for two reasons. First, at its cutting edge, it has developed so many techniques, and there is so much it can do, that the question becomes much more how to mainstream it: how to get men into it, how to convince the men and how to get it into universities.

After all, back on the ranch, you still have to be at the first stages, which is one of the mistakes I find some feminists making. Where they are or where we are, it looks like we're somewhere, but they're forgetting the people in small towns across the country. And that, I think, is a mistake. I think we are doing a great many things; I think we are retrospective, and I think we are in great danger. Every wave of feminism has been destroyed, has stopped. Not that there were that many waves because all of this began in the nineteenth century.

NOR: Could you expound on your sense of the destruction of various waves of feminism?

HEILBRUN: For example, there was a wave to get women the vote. Before that, there was the wave to get women into the professions, to start into colleges. There was the Married Woman's Property Act in England. Elaine Showalter's book, when it comes out, on madness as a female thing shows that women who didn't work or fit into these things were just considered mad. They were put in madhouses; they were operated on.

NOR: Both our mothers and almost every other woman we know of from the age of the ascendancy of psychoanalysis in this century, especially in the 1950s, have undergone shock therapy for such an inability to cope with such a radical male model.

HEILBRUN: This is my generation of women.

NOR: So these are the historical moments where the movement was stopped, but do you see a present way to stop this movement?

HEILBRUN: Each time you get an undergraduate generation who calls it strident and shrill and who are embarrassed by the whole thing, they don't see what the problem is. Kate Stimpson is the one who is best on this subject, and Gloria Steinham said, "They'll never be more equal again than they are now in Princeton." And she goes on to say that they have not done the four things that make them feminists: marriage, parenthood, jobs, and aging. That's one danger: the younger generation's inability to see this. Being scared of the feminist is another danger. This one group has gotten a great deal of backlash from the fundamentalists and the right wing of this country. It is very interesting to me that women are at the heart of it; people fail to notice this.

It is no accident that abortion is the major issue, and these people couldn't care less about the life of a fetus or of a cornfield. They want to control women's bodies because that's how you control the next generation of women. Obviously, if someone is against abortion, then they shouldn't have them. We are now facing a tremendously rich enemy and a lot of very scared women. Remember that there are over forty-five million women in this country who have totally internalized the male "plot," who are Mormons, born-again Christians, fundamentalists of all sorts, and we haven't touched them.

NOR: They run for the cover of the "Word."

HEILBRUN: That's right; that race can be a question, or whether or not evolution is taught, is a result of the women's movement. On the other hand, we are never going back to the nuclear family; that is fact. Women are going to be out of the homes; they're going to be working. In short, whatever aspect of feminism you talk about, I think it is always in very great danger, and one gets tired of the fight; one gets tired of being abused because of it. I could see where a lot of women would say, "To hell with it. If they don't care, why should I care?"

NOR: Especially if one characterizes feminism as having two major and very different fronts at the moment, one of which is in small towns across America—the one we've just been speaking of—and the other in major universities. Concerning this second one, are you concerned that they might turn their back on the movement?

HEILBRUN: Reagan has done everything possible to make that so. Affirmative action is now virtually toothless and so on, but fortunately the major Eastern universities—Harvard always excepted—have continued this commitment.

NOR: Yet it's localized. Do you know the MLA book *Stepping Off the Pedestal: Women and Academics in the South*?

HEILBRUN: I know the book; it's a good book, and the South, I think, is where the most trouble still is. I mean the South and the Midwest—the Bible Belt—is still a problem for women. I'm told that it's tough to get any male faculty member in the South to take sexual harassment seriously.

NOR: You mean, other than as a privilege. To its credit, that issue is taken very seriously at Loyola [New Orleans], whereas at state universities we have been affiliated with, it was a problem for women.

HEILBRUN: Particularly young, attractive undergraduates where these men are in positions of power—it's an unbelievable position to be in. My feeling is that this is the other argument about the women's movement being an upper middle-class, white elitist, classist, racist movement. Sure it is, but those are the people who have the time to do this. All movements start there; they don't start with women with eight children, a husband who drinks and no income. How is she supposed to do it? And I feel very much that if we can demonstrate that it works at Yale, then that is going to help everywhere. Other places should take very seriously what's being done at Yale.

NOR: There's Columbia and Yale, then there's our university [Loyola New Orleans], but what's left unconsidered is the black woman in a Third World situation, and neither of our situations speak to that.

HEILBRUN: Yes, that's exactly right, and another problem to be addressed in the near future. Still Alice Walker says that when she was studying at Howard, she studied black men because it was a black university, but she didn't study black women or any women.

I think on this question of the ideal sisterhood and so forth that I follow Teresa de Lauretis, a feminist film critic who wrote *Alice Doesn't*. At the very end of it, she says that she thinks we should get back to a certain quality we had in the 1970s of seeing groups and women working together and helping each other to talk through things, and I tend to agree with this, so I'm not sure I know what sisterhood means, but I think we need much more to talk to each other. I think that's the essence of feminism—to be able to talk things out in a group—but there are problems.

Women don't know how to deal with competition; they've never competed. We, including me, are all out there as though someone handed us a violin and said, "There's the audience." It's not easy. There is nothing easy about it, and these women who buy the romance structure, the marriage structure, "I'll support you and so on . . . ," know what they're doing; they get lots of rewards. What do we offer in exchange: risk, anxiety, excitement? I was recently in Idaho with Sonja Johnson, who had a bodyguard. She was a Mormon woman who had begun to speak out in favor of feminism, and the Mormons were very upset. They drummed her out of the church and so forth; it's a very powerful organization. Do you know that in Mormon families little girls iron the little boys' shirts? I have had a number of students in seminars who were Mormons, but this is frightening; you were supposed to take pride in being the servants of men. I don't think it's good for men, either.

NOR: That harkens back to your notion of the fierce protectivism by women who have so much invested in their position as downtrodden slave. It strikes me that there's some troubled moments for feminism, for the future of feminist theory and writings. I was struck by the last sentence of Showalter's dedication of her new book to the daughters for whom all of this is history.

HEILBRUN: My children grew up in the 1950s—a boy and two girls—and, a while ago, they watched *The Women's Room* on television. I know that Marilyn French was writing about my generation, although it wasn't my life, and they couldn't believe it. They asked, "How did you escape this?" It was as if they were watching something that was taking place in Salem in the 1750s. This is one of our real problems; there is no sense of history. And now women have everything; what more could they want? Now they're caught up in being in law firms. I think women should do exactly what they want, but they now see themselves very much torn between the job, the children, or this and that.

It's just as though new problems come up all the time; it's the hardest question in the world. What we need is each other to talk to for support, and I think where we get through our troubles is when we can just talk it out. Every woman I know thought she was personally a monster because she didn't enjoy staying home all day with her children, and when they began to understand that they all felt the same way, you can imagine how that felt. That was what Betty Friedan did.

NOR: It certainly wouldn't be the first movement to have undone itself, or seriously damaged itself, to let the second generation become divided.

HEILBRUN: Every movement does. It's a danger for every movement, but feminism has, in addition to all the dangers other movements have, an additional one—no, two additional ones. One is the obvious one; as Robin Morgan put it, we sleep with the oppressor, which means that you have to make the private public. The other more dangerous one, because I think it is so difficult and anxiety producing for women, is that they tend to slip off, even if they remain radical, into other causes: race, nuclear arms, South Africa, South America. And these are all wonderful causes, and they all need help. The fact is that women have been indoctrinated with the idea that it's better to do things for others and never for themselves, and the women's movement suffered and will continue to suffer.

NOR: What are you working on? You said you couldn't take any more speaking engagements because you have a book on autobiography.

HEILBRUN: Biography. It began as a book on the theory of biography, which I decided was indistinguishable from fiction, and here is Roland Barthes' notion that biography is another way to a novel. He said it a little more elegantly than that, but of course having discovered that a lot of other people are doing the same thing, this is really where the discourse is now. And I became interested in a second question to do with women, which is precisely that they have no script to their lives. The only obvious script is the one where you get married and have children, and so we're all making it up. What are other scripts that might exist for various parts of their lives? I mean Rachel DuPlessis has just published a book called *Writing Beyond the Ending*, and it discusses the ending of what might be called romantic throw-over. I'm very interested in age and women, and friendship in men's and women's lives. Many successful women, over the years—achieving women—have had very nurturing husbands. Now their numbers are not legion, but it's an interesting phenomenon that's totally not talked about. If you look back you can see it: George Eliot, Virginia Woolf and so forth. This interests me.

Armando Valladares

Interviewed by William Marling
(1985)

Poet Armando Valladares spent twenty-two years in Cuban prisons. His crime: criticizing Fidel Castro in a student newspaper in 1960. Although he fought to overthrow the Batista regime and became an official in Castro's Ministry of Communication, Valladares disliked Cuba's status as a Russian satellite.

Valladares was convicted of "undermining state security" after a two-hour trial before a military tribunal. "I can still recall," says Valladares, "how the President of the tribunal spent the whole trial with his military boots on the table, reading comics." The sentence was thirty years in jail.

Confined first at the Isle of Pines and later at the notorious Boniato prison, Valladares and other political prisoners were beaten, showered with human excrement, and denied medical treatment. In 1974, they were kept in isolation without food for forty-six days in an attempt to make them join a political re-education program. Valladares could not walk when he emerged, and prison officials refused to let him use a wheelchair sent by Amnesty International.

His first book was written on cigarette papers with Mercurochrome and smuggled out of Boniato in a toothpaste tube by his future wife, whose father was a prisoner there. She published *Desde mi silla de ruedas* in Paris in 1976. Mounting international pressure forced the Cubans to release 3,000 political prisoners in 1977 and to send Valladares to a military hospital. There he was asked to recant the charges in his book: he refused, medical treatment stopped, and he was held in solitary confinement in a Havana jail until 1981.

Deliverance came as a result of a campaign by Spanish writer Fernando Arrabal. He persuaded French president François Mitterand to intervene with Castro on Valladares's behalf. After his release in October of 1982, Valladares was flown to Paris and rushed directly to the hospital.

Today, Valladares and his wife live in a small *piso,* or apartment, in a nondescript building typical of the sprawling new suburbs of Madrid. He is a small man, and seated among the stacks of books, magazines, and papers that he collects to document human rights abuses in Cuba, he looks even smaller, a tiny, inoffensive ex-bureaucrat. When he speaks, however, a secret switch seems to have been thrown. He gestures rapidly, nervously, continuously. A range of emotions—from compassion to disdain—passes across his face.

NEW ORLEANS REVIEW: What do you think of when you recall your twenty-two years in prison?

ARMANDO VALLADARES: I consider it a stage in my life that I must not forget so that I can tell what it was like. Fortunately, I have no bitterness, not even against those who tortured me—remembering it does not upset me.

NOR: How long were you held incommunicado?

VALLADARES: I was held that way many times, but the longest time was nine years, during which I neither saw anyone from outside, nor received letters nor telephone calls. When I left solitary I almost couldn't walk.

NOR: Is it true that you finally wrote poems with your own blood?

VALLADARES: Yes. Being in a punishment cell, I didn't have anything to write with, so I cut my finger and with a splinter I wrote that poem.

NOR: How did you keep your spirits up?

VALLADARES: By my religious convictions and my love for my wife. I was absolutely convinced that I had acted correctly, that I was right. The important thing in any circumstance is to live according to your own conscience. When you make yourself whole this way, you give yourself a force that is indestructible.

NOR: During that period, what did you do; what did you think about?

VALLADARES: I took refuge in a fantasy world, I wrote . . . other times I analyzed the situation, I thought. Luckily, I had years and years to think about everything: man, life, my situation, Cuba . . .

NOR: And to dream about freedom, I suppose. What is freedom for you?

VALLADARES: The possibility of thinking, expressing yourself and acting according to a set of convictions. Above all it is an internal attitude: there are a lot of people walking the streets, going from one place to another and, nevertheless, they're not free. I never felt myself a slave: inside I was free and that is the only real way to feel free. I was also afraid; there were times when I was terrified, but they never succeeded in breaking me.

NOR: In addition to your activity as a writer, you're a human rights activist. How would one describe your activity?

VALLADARES: As helping the foundation of committees throughout Europe. In October I founded one in Spain that people as ideologically opposed as Alvarez de Miranda, Javier Tusell, Sanchez Drago and Xavier Domingo belong to. I offer all the material on the violation of human rights that I receive from Cuba to organizations like Amnesty International. It's a job that has to be done in a coordinated way among all those who advocate it, and not just denounced when it's a dictatorship.

NOR: Nevertheless, it seems that violations and torture are denounced with more frequency in Chile or Uruguay than in Cuba. Why is that?

VALLADARES: Because there has always existed the idea that Castro is the just *guerrillero* who saved the Cubans from dictatorship and gave them back their freedom. But one has to have the honor to recognize that the revolution that so many helped and admired was betrayed. It is immoral to criticize Pinochet and justify Castro, or vice versa.

NOR: What is the situation of political prisoners in Cuba?

VALLADARES: There are in Cuba really about 150,000 prisoners, of whom some 15,000 are political, out of a population of nine million inhabitants. Havana, with two million people, has a penal population that varies between 45 and 50,000 prisoners, distributed in forty jails and concentration camps.

NOR: How many remain from the era of the revolution?

VALLADARES: Some 200, who have always rejected plans for rehabilitating them and have been there now between ten and twenty-four years. The majority of these "historic prisoners" were collaborators close to Castro, commanders who made the war and fought with him in the mountains, like the Spaniard Gutierrez Menoyo.

NOR: Can you tell us anything new of his whereabouts?

VALLADARES: For two years I haven't heard anything of him. We can only trust what [Spanish cabinet member Fernando] Moran said when he came back from Cuba—that they told him he was alive. When I left jail, he was isolated in a tiny cell without sunlight, without clothes, without adequate medical assistance, and without either visits or mail: absolutely incommunicado and under a regimen of torture. I was with him many years and I was witness to the brutal beating that they gave him and without doubt it caused his detached retina. It seems inconceivable that the Spanish government has not secured his release. How is it possible that France gained mine, when I'm Cuban, and the Spanish government is not capable of freeing one of its citizens? At the least someone ought to demand that some Spanish authority visit him and that he be treated like a political prisoner.

NOR: It is said that Castro has this personal charisma. Is it true?

VALLADARES: It is true. He has a personality that attracts people, especially European politicians. It's something similar to what happened to Roosevelt with Stalin, when he called him "Papa Stalin." Castro is also this manly, virile type, very much the protector. . . . Surely if he were short and slender he would not be so attractive.

NOR: Attractiveness gains him the masses?

VALLADARES: No, you can't "gain" the masses. What happens is that it is mandatory to attend the rallies of Fidel; the chief of personnel of every business has his employees sign up to assure their attendance, and the same occurs with the so-called voluntary labor of "Red Sunday," and those who don't go can lose their jobs.

NOR: Did you participate actively in the revolution?

VALLADARES: Yes. I even finally held a high post in the Ministry of Communication. I will say that 90 percent of Cubans supported the revolution. During the dictatorship of Batista there was tremendous corruption in the administration and this was one of the reasons, among others, why Castro received so much sympathy. I believed that it really would be the solution of Cuba, that he was a type of Messiah.

NOR: Do you believe that Castro was sincere in his initial plans, that he was pursuing a policy of freedom?

VALLADARES: Castro was always a charlatan. He called himself a democrat because he knew that with the title of communist there was nothing he could do: back then communism was like "the bogeyman." Nevertheless, a few months ago he declared for TVE [Spanish National Television] that he was always a communist.

NOR: Tourists are coming back from Cuba with the impression that now, at least, the people eat.

VALLADARES: Sure, people eat starch and eggs until they're stuffed, but many important foods are rationed, like meat, to which each person has the right to one kilo per month. Other foods, like seafood, are only offered in stores for tourists or for directors of the Party. A few months ago, the *Washington Post* reported that 70 percent of the wages of Cubans go to the black market. The scarcity of goods, not only foodstuffs but clothing, is impressive.

NOR: Is there any self-criticism, or any organized political response?

VALLADARES: There is some self-criticism; for some months now the government has opened up the possibility of "constructive criticism." On the other hand, they are talking about organizing independent unions, but listen to the attitude of the government, in this respect, in the declarations of the vice-president of the republic to *Diario 16* this past October: "Perhaps there exist in Cuba people with fanciful ideas of union liberties, but I foresee for them ridicule." A few months before this, eleven farmworkers who had organized a free union were executed. Exile is the major reply in Cuba, and, at this moment, there are a million Cubans with their passages paid to leave the island as soon as they can get the "papers."

NOR: Is there a chance things will change?

VALLADARES: Of course. I hope to return to my country free of communism, to a free Cuba, a place like Spain is today.

James Baldwin

Interviewed by David C. Estes
(1986)

As essayist, James Baldwin has written about life in Harlem, Paris, Atlanta; about Martin Luther King, Malcom X, Jimmie Carter; and about Richard Wright, Lorraine Hansberry, Norman Mailer. In examining contemporary culture, he has turned his attention to politics, literature, the movies—and most importantly to his own self. To each subject he has brought the conviction, stated in the 1953 essay "Stranger in the Village," that "the interracial drama acted out on the American continent has not only created a new black man, it has created a new white man, too." Thus he has consistently chosen as his audience Americans, both black and white, and has offered them instruction about the failings and possibilities of their unique national society. Several of the essays in *Notes of a Native Son* (1955), published two years after his first novel, *Go Tell It on the Mountain*, are regarded as contemporary classics because of their polished style and timeless insights. *The Price of the Ticket: Collected Nonfiction 1948–1985* marks his long, productive career as an essayist. It includes over forty shorter pieces as well as three book-length essays—*The Fire Next Time* (1963), *No Name in the Street* (1972), and *The Devil Finds Work* (1976). Baldwin's most recent book is *The Evidence of Things Not Seen* (1985), a meditation on the Atlanta child-murder case. It is his troubled and troubling personal reencounter with "the terror of being destroyed" that dominates the inescapable memories of his own early life in America.

NEW ORLEANS REVIEW: Why did you take on the project to write about Wayne Williams and the Atlanta child murders? What did you expect to find when you began the research for *The Evidence of Things Not Seen*?

JAMES BALDWIN: It was thrown into my lap. I had not thought about doing it at all. My friend Walter Lowe of *Playboy* wrote me in the south of France to think about doing an essay concerning this case, about which I knew very little. There had not been very much in the French press. So I didn't quite know what was there, although it bugged me. I was a little afraid to do it, to go to Atlanta. Not because of Atlanta—I'd been there before—but because I was afraid to get involved in it and I wasn't sure I wanted to look any further.

It was an ongoing case. The boy was in jail, and there were other developments in the city and among the parents and details which I've blotted out completely which drove me back to Atlanta several times to make sure I got the details right. The book is not a novel nor really an essay. It involves living, actual human beings. And there you get very frightened. You don't want to make inaccuracies. It was the first time I had ever used a tape recorder. I got hours of tape. At one moment I thought I was going crazy. I went to six or seven or eight places where the bodies had been found. After the seventh or the eighth, I realized I couldn't do that anymore.

NOR: There is a sense in the book that you were trying to keep your distance, especially from the parents of both the victims and the murderer. In fact, you state at one point in it that you "never felt more of an interloper, a stranger" in all of your journeys than you did in Atlanta while researching this case.

BALDWIN: It wasn't so much that I was trying to keep my distance, although that is certainly true. It was an eerie moment when you realize that you always ask, "How are the kids?" I stopped asking. When I realized that, I realized I'm nuts. What are you going to say to the parents of a murdered child? You feel like an interloper when you walk in because no matter how gently you do it you are invading something. Grief, privacy, I don't know how to put that. I don't mean that they treated me that way. They were beautiful. But I felt that there was something sacred about it. One had to bury that feeling in order to do the project. It was deeper than an emotional reaction; I don't have any word for it.

It wasn't that I was keeping my distance from the parents. I was keeping a distance from my own pain. The murder of children is the most indefensible form of murder that there is. It was certainly for me the most unimaginable. I can imagine myself murdering you in a rage, or my lover, or my wife. I can understand that, but I don't understand how anyone can murder a child.

NOR: The carefully controlled structure of your earlier essays is absent from *Evidence*.

BALDWIN: I had to risk that. What form or shape could I give it? It was not something that I was carrying in my imagination. It was something quite beyond my imagination. All I really hoped to do was write a fairly coherent report in which I raised important questions. But the reader was not going to believe a word I said, so I had to suggest far more than I could state. I had to raise some questions without seeming to raise them. Some questions are unavoidably forbidden.

NOR: Because you are an accomplished novelist, why didn't you use the approach of the New Journalism and tell the story of Wayne Williams by relying on the techniques of fiction?

BALDWIN: It doesn't interest me, and I've read very little of it. Truman Capote's *In Cold Blood* is a very pretty performance, but in my mind it illustrates the ultimate pitfall of that particular approach. To put it in another way, when I write a play or a novel, I write the ending and am responsible for it. Tolstoy has every right to throw Anna Karenina under the train. She begins in his imagination, and he has to take responsibility for her until the reader does. But the life of a living human being, no one writes it. You cannot deal with another human being as though he were a fictional creation.

I couldn't fictionalize the story of the Atlanta murders. It's beyond my province and would be very close to blasphemy. I might be able to fictionalize it years from now when something has happened to me and I can boil down the residue of the eyes of some of the parents and some of the children. I'm sure that will turn up finally in fiction because it left such a profound mark on me. But in dealing with it directly as an event that was occurring from day to day, it did not even occur to me to turn it into fiction, which would have been beyond my power. It was an event which had been written by a much greater author than I.

Reflecting on the writing of the New Journalists, I think the great difficulty or danger is not to make the event an occasion for the exhibition of your virtuosity. You must look to the event.

NOR: In other words, style can take away from the event itself.

BALDWIN: In a way. I'm speaking only for myself, but I wouldn't want to use the occasion of the children as an occasion to show off. I don't think a writer ever should show off, anyway. Saul Bellow would say to me years and years ago, "Get that fancy footwork out of there." The hardest part of developing a style is that you have to learn to trust your voice. If I thought of my style, I'd be crippled. Somebody else said to me a long time ago in France, "Find out what you can do, and then don't do it."

NOR: What has been the reaction to *Evidence* in France, where you are living?

BALDWIN: Because of some difficulty in arranging for the American publication, it appeared first there in a French version. They take it as an examination of a social crisis with racial implications, but a social crisis. The most honest of the critics are not afraid to compare it to the situation of the Algerian and African in Paris. In a way, it's not too much to say that some of them take it as a kind of warning. There is a great upsurge on the right in France, and a great many people are disturbed by that. So the book does not translate to them as a provincial, parochial American problem.

NOR: Were you conscious of the international implications of the case while you were writing?

BALDWIN: I was thinking about it on one level, but for me to write the book was simply like putting blinders on a horse. On either side was the trap of rage or the trap of sorrow. I had never run into this problem in writing a book before.

I was doing a long interview in Lausanne, and it suddenly happened that I could see one of those wide intervals. I was asked a question, and with no warning at all, the face, body, and voice of one of the parents suddenly came back to me. I was suddenly back in that room, hearing that voice and seeing that face, and I had to stop the interview for a few minutes. Then I understood something.

NOR: What seem to be the European perceptions of contemporary American black writers in general?

BALDWIN: A kind of uneasy bewilderment. Until very lately, Europe never felt menaced by black people because they didn't see them. Now they are beginning to see them and are very uneasy. You have to realize that just after the war when the American black GI arrived, he was a great, great wonder for Europe because he had nothing whatever to do with the Hollywood image of the Negro, which was the only image they had. They were confronted with something else, something unforeseeable, something they had not imagined. They didn't quite know where he came from. He came from America, of course, but America had come from Europe. Now that is beginning to be clear, and the reaction is a profound uneasiness. So the voice being heard from black writers also attacks the European notion of their identity. If I'm not what you thought I was, who are you?

NOR: Now that your collected nonfiction has appeared in *The Price of the Ticket*, what reflections about your career as an essayist do you have as you look back over these pieces?

BALDWIN: It actually was not my idea to do that book, but there was no point in refusing it either. But there was also something frightening about it. It's almost forty years, after all. On one level, it marks a definitive end to my youth and the beginning of something else. No writer can judge his work. I don't think I've ever tried to judge mine. You just have to trust it. I've not been able to read the book, but I remember some of the moments when I wrote this or that. So in some ways, it's a kind of melancholy inventory, not so much about myself as a writer (I'm not melancholy about that), but I think that what I found hard to decipher is to what extent or in what way my ostensible subject has changed. Nothing in the book could be written that way today.

My career began when I was twenty-one or twenty-two in *The New Leader*. That was a very important time in my life. I had never intended to become an essayist. But it came about because of Saul Levitas, who assigned me all these books to review. I will never know quite why he did that. I had to write a book review a week, and it was very good for me. You can always find turning points looking back, but there was one very long review of *Raintree Country*, a novel about an America I had never seen. Between the time that I turned in the review and its publication, the author, Ross Lockridge, committed suicide. It was very shocking because it was such a sunlit, optimistic book that had won every prize in sight. But he had blown his brains out. That marked me in a way. I didn't feel guilty about it since he hadn't read my review, but it struck me with great force. It was from that point, in hindsight, that I began to be considered an essayist by other people.

Later, at *Commentary* I had a marvelous relationship with one of the editors—Robert Warshow, my first real editor. He asked me to do an essay about the Harlem ghetto. When I turned it in, Robert said, "Do it over." He didn't say anything more. So I did. And then he said, "You know more than that." I began to be aware of what he was doing. When he saw me come close to what I was afraid of, he circled it and said, "Tell me more about that." What I was afraid of was the relationship between Negroes and Jews in Harlem—afraid on many levels. I'd never consciously thought about it before, but then it began to hit me on a profound and private level because many of my friends were Jews, although they had nothing to do with the Jewish landlords and pawnbrokers in the ghetto. So I had been blotting it out. It was with Robert that I began to be able to talk about it, and that was a kind of liberation for me. I'm in his debt forever because after that I was clear in my own mind. I suddenly realized that perhaps I had been afraid to talk about it because I was a closet anti-Semite myself. One always has that terror. And then I realized that I wasn't. So something else was opened.

NOR: What major artistic problems have you had to confront in your nonfiction?

BALDWIN: I was a black kid and was expected to write from that perspective. Yet I had to realize the black perspective was dictated by the white imagination. Since I wouldn't write from the perspective, essentially, of the victim, I had to find what my own perspective was and then use it. I couldn't talk about "them" and "us." So I had to use "we" and let the reader figure out who "we" is. That was the only possible choice of pronoun. It had to be "we." And we had to figure out who "we" was, or who "we" is. That was very liberating for me.

I was going through a whole lot of shit in New York because I was black, because I was always in the wrong neighborhood, because I was small. It was dangerous, and I was in a difficult position because I couldn't find a place to live. I was always being thrown out, fighting landlords. My best friend committed suicide when I was twenty-two, and I could see that I was with him on that road. I knew exactly what happened to him—everything that happened to me. The great battle was not to interiorize the world's condemnation, not to see yourself as the world saw you, and also not to depend on your skill. I was very skillful—much more skillful than my friend, much more ruthless, too. In my own mind, I had my family to save. I could not go under; I could not afford to. Yet I knew that I was going under. And at the very same moment, I was writing myself up to a wall. I knew I couldn't continue. It was too confining. I wrote my first two short stories, and then I split.

NOR: You said earlier that you never intended to become an essayist. Did you ever consider one or the other of the genres in which you worked as being more important than another?

BALDWIN: No, as a matter of fact I didn't. I thought of myself as a writer. I didn't want to get trapped in any particular form. I wanted to try them all. That's why I say I remember having written myself into a wall. Significantly enough, the first thing I wrote when I got to Paris and got myself more or less together was the essay "Everybody's Protest Novel"—a summation of all these years I was reviewing those "be kind to niggers" and "be kind to Jews" books. There was a mountain of them, and every one came across my desk. I had to get out of that, and "Everybody's Protest Novel" was my declaration of independence. Then I began to finish my first novel and did *Giovanni's Room*, which was another declaration of independence. And then I was in some sense, if not free, clear.

NOR: A striking feature of your work is the great amount of autobiographical material that finds its way into essays which are not primarily autobiographical.

BALDWIN: Well, I had to use myself as an example.

NOR: When did you realize that you should use yourself in this way?

BALDWIN: It was not so much that I realized I should. It was that I realized I couldn't avoid it. I was the only witness I had. I had the idea that most people found me a hostile black boy; I was not that. I had to find a way to make them know it, and the only way was to use myself.

NOR: Does it take some measure of audacity to write autobiography, to expect readers to find your personal life of interest to them?

BALDWIN: It didn't occur to me to be audacious. It occurred to me, first of all, to be very frightening. Rather than audacity, it involved a great deal of humility to use myself as a witness, which is different from an example, to the condition of others who are in your condition but cannot speak—or cannot be heard. Jimmie Baldwin himself as a subject is not very interesting. There's nothing special about my life in that way at all. Everybody suffers. Everybody has to make choices. It was only in my social situation that I had to use my personal dilemma to illuminate something. I repeat, I am not speaking from the point of view of the victim. I am speaking as a person who has a right to be here. That's where the humility comes in, for you're setting yourself up to be corrected.

NOR: Which works have given you more insight into yourself, your fiction or your autobiographical accounts?

BALDWIN: The essay called "Notes of a Native Son" was risky— I was trying to deal with the relationship between me and my father and to extrapolate that into a social question. On the other hand, *Giovanni's Room* was risky, too, in a very different way. I wouldn't say in a more personal way, but I knew very well what I was setting myself up for when I wrote that book. I knew that, too, when I wrote "Notes," but it was much more direct. It involved not only me and my father, but also my family. There was always that delicacy because you are revealing not only your own secrets but those of other people. You simply have to realize that is what you are doing and you don't quite know what the consequences will be.

NOR: As you have grown older, have you ever wanted to retell an incident in your life about which you have already written?

BALDWIN: No. I couldn't anyway. Every writer has only one tale to tell, and he has to find a way of telling it until the meaning becomes clearer and clearer, until the story becomes at once more narrow and larger, more and more precise and more and more reverberating.

NOR: On numerous occasions, you have written about your teenage years. Yet the focus always changes. For example, the most recent account in "Here Be Dragons" touches on homosexual experiences, a subject not mentioned in "Notes of a Native Son."

BALDWIN: You begin to see more than you did before in the same event. It reveals itself—more. There's more to it. It's not a conscious decision to refashion the anecdote. In time, one of those things that happens is that you become less frightened because there's less to be frightened of—quite unconsciously. This is not something which is cerebral. I don't know whether you can hunt more and more of your own life or if more and more of your own life will hunt you, but it comes back to you during points in your life in another light. One's relationship to the past changes. Yet that boy, the boy I was, still controls the man I am. If I didn't know as much as I think I do know about that boy, I would still be his prisoner. This happens to many people who are effectively stopped between the ages of seventeen and twenty and when they are fifty or sixty are still imprisoned by the boy or the girl they have been. Perhaps what I'm saying is that all the action is to understand enough to be liberated from first of all one's terror and then one's self-image, to keep moving into a larger space.

NOR: In the preface to *Evidence*, you state that "no one wishes to be plunged, head down, into the torrent of what he does not remember and does not wish to remember." Am I correct that this suggests your reluctance to write autobiographical accounts?

BALDWIN: Certainly not so very long ago I was reluctant—terrified. Well, I'm still terrified. But I think that in time terror begins to be a kind of luxury; you can't do anything with it, but it can do a lot with you. You have to learn how to ride it. When I was writing *Just Above My Head*, I'd never been more frightened in my life, either as a man or as a writer. Yet I knew it had to be done. That book is not directly autobiographical at all, but it is autobiographical on a much deeper level. There are elements which you can place in my life. My brother was once a member of a quartet in the Deep South, for example. Yet there are no direct, one-on-one relationships between my life and the lives of the people in that book. It truly is a composite. A novel or anything I write begins with an incoherent disturbance, and you can't run away from it. You have to sit and wait and see what it is. It may be things I've forgotten or think I've forgotten that suddenly begin to stir.

NOR: What do you think readers hope to find in autobiographies?

BALDWIN: Somebody said to me once that it's not so much what happens as who it happens to. The sound of the voice is the key; without that, it's false.

NOR: In *No Name in the Street*, you say that "no one knows how identities are forged, but it is safe to say identities are not invented." What do you feel is the relationship between writing an autobiography and the forging of an identity?

BALDWIN: You have to be aware of the temptation to invent, which is the same thing as the temptation to evade. You have to be aware that you would not like to violate your self-image, and on the other hand, at the very same moment, you have to be aware that your self-image is entirely false. You have to discard your self-image. You don't have to be corrected by your public; you can be corrected by your friends or your lovers. They see you quite beyond your self-image in a way you don't see yourself. And without that, you couldn't live at all. I'm writing for the people who would know if I were lying. They can call me on it. Otherwise, I'd be locked into my own fantasy.

NOR: The stormy reception of William Styron's *Confessions of Nat Turner*, although fictional, seems to illustrate what you are saying about how the image an autobiography presents can be challenged. What are your reactions now to that controversy and your defense of Styron at the time?

BALDWIN: Looking back, I feel I would do the same thing. I happen to like the novel. I was working at Bill's house when he was doing *Nat Turner,* and we used to talk about it—or around it—from time to time. Bill comes from Virginia, where the insurrection occurred. So it seemed to me that it was part of my inheritance and was also part of his. I didn't read the book so much as a confession of Nat Turner but as a confession of Bill Styron, and I don't mean that as a "put-down." He had taken an historical event which belongs to everybody and especially to the man it torments the most, and he tried to make some kind of peace with it, to tell the truth—very much like Faulkner, although I didn't always agree with Faulkner, especially as he got older. It's one of those books which proves what I'm always saying, that history is not the past, but the present. In any case, I thought Bill's book was a very honest, very honorable job, and when he was attacked, I didn't think it was fair at all. My position was if you don't like his Nat Turner, write yours.

NOR: What is your vision of the America to which you must respond as a writer?

BALDWIN: This is a curiously and dangerously fragmented society while, perhaps unlike any society in the past, it has all the stirrings of well-being. It has at its back the resonance of the American Dream and the history of conquest. But it is also based on a lie, the lie of Manifest Destiny. So it's a country immobilized, with a past it cannot explain away. That's why everyone's so cheerful, and the Americans who are crying have to be cheerful. Everyone is friendly, and nobody is friends. Everybody has something to hide, and when you have to hide, you have to cry for despair. Despair is the American crime. So one is trapped in a kind of Sunday purgatory, and the only way out of that is to confront what you are afraid of. The American image of the black face contains everything America most wants and everything that terrifies it. It also contains the castrations, the lynchings, the burnings, the continual daily and hourly debasements of life, and you cannot do those things without doing something to yourself.

NOR: Do you feel that artists in such a nation as ours can find an audience willing to listen to them?

BALDWIN: The artist cannot attempt to answer that question because if he does he'll go mad. The public is going to assume you are a success or a failure, the book was a hit or not. The publisher looks at the market. But if you depend on the market, you might as well become a traveling salesman. The artist has to assume that he creates his audience and that the audience won't be there until he starts to work. The artist is responsible for his audience, which may exist in his lifetime or may never exist until long after he is dead. The artist has to realize that commerce is only a detail. If you try to beat your last success, you stop writing. It's a high-risk endeavor.

John Ashbery

Interviewed by Paul Munn
(1990)

Born in 1927, John Ashbery is the author of twelve books of poetry and the recipient of numerous prizes and awards, including the Pulitzer Prize, the National Book Award, the National Book Critics Circle Award, and the Bollingen Prize in Poetry. Readers who value poetry committed to a clear and progressive vision of society or language distinctly referential and determinate sometimes attack Ashbery as too cerebral, even as nonsensical. But several of America's most influential literary critics consider Ashbery to be among America's strongest living poets, citing his complex responses to his poetic precursors (such as the English Romantics and Wallace Stevens), the openness or profound indeterminacy of his work, or his postmodern linguistic playfulness.

The title of a poem in his 1984 volume, *A Wave*, suggests the difficulties or pleasures or pleasurable difficulties of his work: "But What Is the Reader to Make of This?" The reader is obliquely asked—in a strikingly colloquial manner—to take on the task traditionally reserved for the poet, to become a maker of the poem or to make meanings out of linguistic possibilities. T. S. Eliot's notion of poetry as "superior amusement" may have found its greatest example in the work of Ashbery.

This interview, sponsored by Third-Century Poetry and Prose, University of Minnesota, Minneapolis, took place on April 9, 1987, before an audience of about forty people.

NEW ORLEANS REVIEW: Besides writing poetry, what are your current projects?

JOHN ASHBERY: I was fortunate enough to get a MacArthur fellowship, which has relieved me of the necessity of earning a living for five years at least. But during this time it seems that I have agreed to write a number of articles, essays, art reviews, and so on, all of which I procrastinate about, and I can't seem to do anything with the time I am procrastinating about these other things. Basically, I have written more or less the same amount of poetry I normally would have if I had been working at a job. I'm trying to get out from under these other commitments, and when I do that I would like to try to write some different kinds of things. I wrote some plays years ago in the 1950s which I never really did anything with, although I still like them. And I would like to go back and do something in that form. And also, I would like to write some fiction, which I haven't really done, except for a novel I collaborated on with the poet James Schuyler, called *A Nest of Ninnies*, which was published—which I don't really consider to be a novel. It was really a kind of game we played to amuse ourselves, never expecting when we began it at a very young age, both of us, that anyone would ever publish it. I'd like to try to write some fiction with the idea of publishing it rather than from the standpoint of its never seeing the light of day—which was the understanding I wrote the other one out of.

I've never enjoyed writing art criticism. For a long time it was the only way I seemed to be able to make a living, especially when I was living in France for ten years. There I wrote for the *International Herald Tribune* for five years. And although this wasn't enough to live on—they only gave $15 an article when I began working for them; it was up to $30 by the time I left five years later, so I actually got a 100 percent raise somewhere along the line—nevertheless, this enabled me to write other things about art and I was able to subsist that way. But I have always been a somewhat reluctant art critic. And now I would like to think that I'm not going to write any more art criticism. To celebrate this, I have completed a book of my art writing. As long as I was in the business of writing it, I didn't want to publish it, because I was afraid some reviewer would come along and attack it and I would lose my job. But I no longer have this to worry about.

NOR: I'm interested in your selection process for the *Selected Poems*? How did you decide what to include and what to exclude? Did others take part in determining what finally went into your *Selected Poems*?

ASHBERY: No, I selected them myself. I've had friends and other people—who knew my work—not be happy with the selection because of things I've left out. No one has yet complained about anything I have included, but I suppose there are complaints on that side too. But there were some poems that I realized were fairly well known, so far as any are, which I never really liked and therefore didn't include. There were others which I did like but which seemed somewhat repetitive of other poems which I like slightly better. I didn't intend this to be a sort of codex or ultimate choice, since my other books are in print, and I had no intention of disavowing any of the ones that are not included in the book.

NOR: If you were to put together a collected works, are there any poems that you would exclude? I'm thinking of the later W.H. Auden, who re-thought his career. Would you re-think yours or throw out some poems or re-edit?

ASHBERY: I think this is about as much of a collected poems as I'll ever do, and so, in a sense, I've already done or not done whatever that is. And I don't think I've been too harsh on my early work, one reason being that I felt that Auden did a kind of disastrous number on himself, leaving out many of his most cherished poems. This seems to be a congenital affliction of writers who reach a certain age. Henry James also kind of massacred or re-did some of his early works which were better in the original versions. So I'm leery of doing this. I don't think, I hope, at any rate, that I wasn't too harsh on early works, which I can see flaws in but which nevertheless seem to have a kind of redeeming freshness, which maybe later works, which are in some ways better, wouldn't have. It's kind of a narrow line you have to follow in doing something like that, I guess.

NOR: You don't feel a strong self-censoring or self-editing impulse, then, as you look back at the earlier work?

ASHBERY: Much of it had already happened before the books were published. It takes a long time for a book of poetry to come out. Sometimes the poems in it are five years old or more when a book finally appears, so you've had ample time for self-criticism or winnowing out. I certainly have written a lot more than I have actually published.

NOR: Critics have seen sources or analogues for your poetry in a considerable range of poets, and even composers and painters:

Rimbaud, Whitman, Wallace Stevens, the current Language poets, John Cage, and Jackson Pollock are just a few. You have expressed an early admiration for Auden and Elizabeth Bishop. How important do you feel it is for readers such as us to be familiar with these earlier poets in order to get at your work?

ASHBERY: I would hope not at all. Because even though I've been influenced by many different poets and artists and things not even related to the arts, I would not like to feel that a knowledge of any source material is necessary or even desirable before reading my work; I think that's true of any writer that one admires. It's interesting afterwards if you wish to go back and see where these things originated, but I hope at any rate that it's not a condition of reading my work.

NOR: Do you have any tips if there were someone in the audience who was just beginning to read your work? Is there any advice you might give them to facilitate their way into your work?

ASHBERY: Well, much has always been made about how difficult my poetry is. I never thought of this until it was first pointed out to me. It has been many times since. This has become a kind of self-fulfilling prophecy, I think. This reputation of being difficult I think really discourages people from looking at my work. I found in a number of cases that people who somehow have never heard of me and who don't even read poetry and happened on it have read it with enjoyment and not found it puzzling or enigmatic. I'm thinking particularly of a handyman who occasionally worked for me who heard indirectly that I was a writer and went to the library and found some of my books. Then he began collecting them, even insisting on first editions, even though I don't think he ever had read anything before, not *any* book. I could see that he was really very fervently involved in these poems. That doesn't happen every day, of course, but I think it can happen, and perhaps one suggestion would be to pretend that you haven't heard that it's very difficult, to read it and see what happens. And also, not to worry if you don't understand it; it doesn't make that much difference. There are other things in life. And not to look for a structure or a framework underneath it. But as they say, go with the flow, which I hope is there.

NOR: From your example, you almost suggest that those of us who have sought a structure and applied the traditional ways of looking at poetry might actually be handicapped a little bit, and this other person you were talking about had an advantage by coming to it without preconceptions about how he should read.

ASHBERY: That could be. He was perhaps an extreme example, but other people more literate than he have occasionally come up to me and said, "People are always saying your work is so difficult, but I think it means something to me." I've never quite understood about understanding anyway or about the meaning of poetry. Eliot, I believe, said that you don't have to understand poetry to enjoy it, and I think that's true. And I think the converse might be true as well. In fact, it's necessary not to understand it in order to enjoy it. I don't get much pleasure out of poems that offer no resilience or crunch, where you can tell almost from scanning the poem exactly what the message is, something like "The Star-Spangled Banner," even though that has a few obscurities in it. In fact, I find that much so-called clear poetry is full of murkiness that I seem to be the only one to pick up on.

NOR: Maybe this next question will lead into the murkiness in what's often thought to be more clear poems. Some of your poems might be characterized and have been characterized as anti-voice poems. By that I mean that your poems resist being thought of as speech originating from a presumed personality, attitude, or clear situation. I can think of a few poems of yours where you seem to have a poetic speaker who is a relatively consistent "I" and is also grounded in a time and place. "The Instruction Manual" is one. "Self Portrait in a Convex Mirror" may be another. "Evening in the Country" and "Ode to Bill" also seem to have that sense of the present speaking voice, relatively coherent. In any of these poems, were you aware—and this is a psychological question which may not help us with these poems—of the Wordsworthian, Yeatsian, and maybe Frank O'Hara background—the personality poet? Were you consciously playing off that in these sorts of poems?

ASHBERY: I don't think I was, even in those examples that you just cited. I've never really had much of an idea of who I am, and I feel that Rimbaud put it very well when he said, "Je est un autre": "I is an other," meaning using "I" in the third person as someone who's not speaking that statement. I am constantly using different voices without being aware of it, of different people who seem to be talking in these poems without bothering to indicate to the reader where one stops and another one starts up again, because I'm interested in a kind of polyphonic quality that attracts me in music. I seem to be somewhat notorious for what I have come to think of as the floating pronoun. I coined this from my own practice. I didn't mean it to be that way. But it often seems to be enough to know that "you" is someone that the speaker is addressing, that "he" or "she" is someone who is neither of these two people, that "we" could be a number of people, including the speaker of the poem, the person he may be talking to, and all possible readers as well. For me this is actually enough. And it seems to be an attempt, possibly a misguided one, at a kind of more realistic approach toward what one learns, what one sees, hears, and what happens, what one's mind does during the course of a day, something like that. I'm interested in the movement of the mind, how it goes from one place to the other. The places themselves don't matter that much; it's the movement that does.

NOR: I have one more question before we turn to reading and talking about "At North Farm." You have written in a considerable variety of forms, some of which seem to be your own nonce forms or free verse, others of which are traditional or derived from traditional forms—quatrains, couplets, prose poems, and sestinas, for example. You have spoken yourself of "the tyranny of the line" ["The Experience of Experience: A Conversation with John Ashbery," with A. Poulin, Jr., *Michigan Quarterly Review* 20 (1981): 254]. One way of looking at your work might be to see it as a continual struggle with or response to form. Please excuse the baldness of this question: Why write a sestina?

ASHBERY: Well, that's a very complicated form which I first discovered in Auden and in Elizabeth Bishop, although many poets, particularly twentieth-century ones, have used the form. And that's a kind of special case, really. I often use this as an assignment for students because the complexity of the form involves making so many conscious decisions that one's unconscious is kind of left free to go ahead and proceed with the poem, which is as it should be. Eliot said something like meaning in poetry is like the piece of meat that the burglar throws the watchdog so that he can get at the treasure or whatever he's looking for. Frequently, it has a kind of therapeutic effect on students. When they get all done and realize that they have fitted all the pieces into place and stand back, they suddenly realize that they have written a poem while they thought that they were just solving a puzzle. There are not too many forms that I find useful for that kind of exercise. The canzone, which is actually a more constrained version of the sestina, has sometimes produced interesting work in class and the villanelle, which I have assigned. I have never actually been able to write a successful one myself, but I've had students who have done so. But when you get into the sonnet and things like that, there are forms that are really too loose to have this liberating effect that I'm looking for, especially in teaching. I don't use these forms such as the sestina very much for myself anymore. I probably did when I was younger, when I was finding it more difficult to write and used them as a kind of exercise to get going.

[At this point, by agreement, he read the first poem in his collection *A Wave*, "At North Farm."]

At North Farm

Somewhere someone is traveling furiously toward you,
At incredible speed, traveling day and night,
Through blizzards and desert heat, across torrents, through
    narrow passes
But will he know where to find you,
Recognize you when he sees you,
Give you the thing he has for you?

Hardly anything grows here,
Yet the granaries are bursting with meal,
The sacks of meal piled to the rafters.
The streams run with sweetness, fattening fish;
Birds darken the sky. Is it enough
That the dish of milk is set out at night,
That we think of him sometimes,
Sometimes and always, with mixed feelings?

I'll tell you a little bit about how I happened to write the poem, although I would caution you against thinking that this is the key to the poem, because it doesn't have any key, like all poetry. Frequently, I find that questions in a situation such as this are actually someone asking for the recipe, and the recipe is always in my head. I can't give it to anybody, just like one's grandmother. The title, "At North Farm," although it could have come from anywhere, actually was suggested by the Finnish epic folk poem the *Kalevala*, which you may know from some of Sibelius's tone poems. They were based on a fascinating body of folklore, copied down in the nineteenth century but actually much older. North Farm in the epic is a place near hell but not in it, and it's always referred to with the epithet "gloomy and prosperous North Farm." And as I recall there are always a lot of beautiful serving girls there, whom the hero, Lemminkainen, is very attracted to; he is always dropping in at North Farm to see what's cooking. So the "gloomy and prosperous," I think, gives you a little note to the stasis in the second part of the poem. Although nothing grows there—it's not fertile—nevertheless it's full of the evidence of fertility, such as these sacks of meal, fish in the streams, and so on.

The first part of the poem, I think, seems to me to come from some cinematic memory, maybe *Lawrence of Arabia*, somebody galloping across a desert stream. And "will he know where": this person is heading in your direction, but there's some doubt as to whether you will receive the thing that he has for you. It might also have been a kind of memory of that legend that's mentioned in the beginning of "Appointment in Samarra," by John O'Hara, where the man says he has to go to Samarra to avoid death, and death comes and says, "I have an appointment with him there." At any rate it's something ominous, I think, and it reflects a relationship that I had at the time that I wrote it with a person whom I felt to be sort of fascinating but somewhat alarming at the same time. There are a lot of people like that one encounters in the course of one's life—not too many perhaps. I think the idea is that somebody, maybe one of these maids-in-waiting, is waiting back there at the farm where nothing ever happens, where it's fertile but somehow sterile, waiting for this kind of electrifying arrival of a messenger of something, we don't know quite of what. The dish of milk is traditional in fairy tales, something you set out at night to pacify the elves so they won't spoil your crops. It's an image I also use in another poem called "Hop O' My Thumb." A lot of my imagery comes from fairy tales and things I read when I was young, which impressed me more than much of what I've read since. The line in the other poem is "Nocturnal friendliness of the plate of milk left for the fairies / Who otherwise might be less well disposed."

I wrote this poem with great ease. And I enjoyed writing it a lot. I enjoyed the feeling, I was somehow able to use clichés, like "at incredible speed," "birds darken the sky," "travelling day and night," that sort of thing, that kind of very colloquial, not quite clichéd speech which I found at that moment very appealing. I frequently find colloquial, overheard speech to have a kind of beauty that I'd like to steal and put in my poetry. This was one case where I felt that I had been able to do that. At the end, this ambiguous person seems to be the thing that everything hinges on—"That we think of him sometimes"—which is immediately contradicted by "Sometimes and always, with mixed feelings," again a further feeling of contradiction. So it's left up in the air whether the person is going to arrive and what will happen when he does; and that's very often the case.

NOR: It sounds as though I'm a victim of too much reading when I'm hearing Yeats and Keats all through the second movement. I'm thinking particularly of Keats's "high-piled books, in charactery, / [which] Hold like rich garners the full ripened grain," and the closing stanza of "To Autumn," which has that sublime stasis, that end of the season fruition. And maybe even Yeats's "The young / In one another's arms, birds in the trees /—Those dying generations—at their song, / The salmon-falls, the mackerel-crowded seas"—that sense of richness and the sensuous life, which is there, and that's certainly in my head.

ASHBERY: That might well be. We all have read these poems. They are all part of our subconscious, if not our conscious; I'm frequently finding that I'm rewriting something that I read thirty years ago and had completely forgotten. Perhaps indeed the Yeats line was in the back of my mind. I was also thinking of the Welsh epic poem the *Mabinogion*, where there's a scene in which I think a lot of soldiers are disguised as sacks of meal as in *Ali Baba and the Forty Thieves*, and the unfortunate warrior comes and accosts this man surrounded by sacks of meal. He is about to put him to the sword and the man says, "There is in this sack another type of meal," and then at that point, as I recall it, the armed men all jump out of the flour sacks. But even though this is material that I used, I don't know that it proves anything. It doesn't make the poem any better or worse. That's why I don't have footnotes or explanations as to where all these things came from. I don't think it matters.

Valerie Martin

Interviewed by Mary A. McCay
and Christine Wiltz
(1994)

Valerie Martin was born in Sedalia, Missouri, grew up in New Orleans, and has taught at several universities, among them the University of New Orleans, Mount Holyoke, and the University of Massachusetts. She is currently living in Rome. Her novels include *Set in Motion, Alexandra, A Recent Martyr, Mary Reilly,* and *The Great Divorce.* She has also published two books of short stories, *Love* and *The Consolation of Nature.* Martin was interviewed on December 27, 1994, at the home of Christine Wiltz, a long-time friend.

NEW ORLEANS REVIEW: I would like to begin by asking you what is most important for you in the act of creating fiction? You often use other writers, historical events, or urban myths to center your writing. Why is that technique important for you?

VALERIE MARTIN: I've spent a long time doing my version of other writers, of writers I liked. The stories in *The Consolation of Nature* are almost entirely the result of my reaction to writers and stories that I liked. There is a Hawthorne story, a Cheever story, and my version of James Joyce's "The Dead," which is called "The Freeze." I thought about these stories, and what it was about them that I admired, and I reworked them, very loosely touching on the original situation. There is some historical stuff, but it surprises me when people think of me as an historical writer. I don't think of my writing that way. It's just that old stories attract me. The only one that I ever had to do a whole lot of research for was *Mary Reilly.* In

The Great Divorce, I used stories that I knew from my childhood. I don't think that it's necessary for me to have an historical component. *A Recent Martyr* moves into the future; *Set in Motion* doesn't really have an historical component. Strictly speaking, *Alexandra* doesn't, but it is a reverse Gothic. In the Gothic novel, a woman is taken away and imprisoned in a big house. In my novel, a man is imprisoned by two women. I thought that was funny, but nobody else did.

NOR: So reactions to your reading are an important element in your fiction?

MARTIN: Yes, when I am thinking about writing, I often read and react to fiction, but when I begin to write, I cannot read fiction; I read nonfiction. When I was working on *The Great Divorce,* I read about veterinary medicine, zoos, nature and about humanity's present situation vis-à-vis nature. When I was writing *Mary Reilly,* I read lots of diaries of working-class people, Victorians. I read essays about Victorian life. I also read Dickens, but that was the only fiction I read.

NOR: It is impossible to read your fiction and not be struck by the abundance of animal life in your stories and novels. What do animals signify for you, and how do they work as a part of your fiction?

MARTIN: I don't think I knew when I started writing how important animals were to me, but when I look back at all my work, I see just how significant animals are to my stories. I think that's caused by two things. The first is that nature is ever-present; we can't get away from nature, especially in New Orleans. When I was a child, I used to love to be outdoors, in my treehouse. I just loved to hear birds and the buzzing world. I didn't even mind the mosquitoes. I just slapped them. Roaches are ever-present. That is one thing I love about New Orleans. You just can't get away from the encumbrance, the flourishing and oozing, of nature. I think that view was, from childhood, an unconscious sensibility that came into my work in a very natural way. Later, I began to understand the awful fate of nature in the contemporary world, and I began to see the contradiction in the idea of wanting to live in human society and wanting to care about nature. Then the animals began to move to the forefront. I noticed it especially in *The Consolation* *of Nature,* which I originally referred to as "Dead Animal Stories." I just wrote a few stories without thinking of putting them together; then I noticed there was a dead animal in each one, and so I began actively seeking dead animal stories, that is, asking people for stories. I asked Chris Wiltz what was the worst thing that happened to her, and she gave me the story that became the title story.

NOR: Was the story about the enormous rat your story, Chris?

NOR: That was my story; I told Valerie that I wasn't going to use it, so she could have it. Now every time Valerie writes a story about a rat, one shows up at my house. It's terrible!

MARTIN: In most of my stories, animals have the metaphorical value they have for everybody, but for me personally, they have a special value because I sense that the loss of them is so imminent and so personally sad. It makes me angry. I was talking to a man in Chicago who put together collections of stories about cats and dogs published by Doubleday, *The Company of Cats* and *The Company of Dogs.* The proceeds of the books go to animal shelters. When I was talking to him about *The Great Divorce,* he said, "What I like about your work is that you are inconsolable." I really do feel that way. The loss of the wild really is unbearable. Fiction is a way of dealing with loss, with loss so great we cannot be consoled. When I was a child I knew this unconsciously, and as I have gotten older, it has moved to the forefront of my notion of subject matter.

NOR: Certainly in *The Great Divorce* the loss of animals is central, and related to that menagerie of wild and domestic, living and dead animals and related to what you just said, you often focus on nature gone awry—the plague in *A Recent Martyr,* the siege of the rat in "The Consolation of Nature," the lost snakes in "The Woman Who Was Never Satisfied," and the strange killing virus attacking the great cats in the zoo in *The Great Divorce.* Yet your characters seem to crave the natural world to escape the ugliness of their lives and their built environment, so nature is really a consolation, isn't it?

MARTIN: Oh, yes. I think it is interesting that you speak of nature gone awry because it is not nature gone awry. A plague is a natural occurrence, and the rat's behavior is perfectly natural. In part that is what I am reacting to—the feeling that we are a part of nature, but we fail to sympathize with or understand the way nature operates.

Also, there is the real pickle that we can't live in nature, but we can't live without it. Unfortunately, what we really want is to be comfortable, and living in the natural world is hard and dangerous. It is one thing to weep for the loss of your pet dog, but to really weep for the extinction of a species, a toad or an owl, that is a different thing. If we could have a choice between owls and a comfortable life without owls, most people would take the comfortable choice, especially if having owls means you have to go without, or chase your dinner down with a knife.

NOR: I have a question about *The Great Divorce* that is related to that. Some people think that the message of the book is that we should go back to nature. Certainly what you are saying belies that. I think that is a very superficial reading, but a lot of people read the book that way. Could you talk about the ways in which that is not the message of the book?

MARTIN: There are several places in the book that practically I come right out and say, "We can't go back to nature." I have a little spiel in the book about how going back to nature today consists of standing on a hill and saying, "I want to build my house here." The popular notion of going back to nature is very superficial, but it is also a part of our desire to find a way to cause less destruction as individuals and also as a species. A lot of people think that the book is about going back to nature. Even my editor thought that's what it was about. I think because there is a sort of recommendation in the book that the wild has something that we need, and people who want to go back to nature think that, too. People want to think that if they could be more wild, more like the Indians, they would not require dishwashers, but in fact that is not the case. The Indians were just as destructive as we are. Given the time and the numbers, they probably would have wiped out the buffalo eventually.

NOR: Do you think that part of our desire to go back to nature has something to do with the fact that at one time we were a part of the wild?

MARTIN: That's the thing the book is about, and that's what puzzles me again and again, so I can't stop writing about it. I keep going back to it, and my new book is about it, too. Why do we have this memory of being at peace with nature when from everything we can discover, it has been a battle from the beginning? Ever since we came down out of the trees, things began to get bad, and it has been bad ever since. Yet we have this idea of a natural paradise. Where does this memory come from? Every civilization seems to have it—the Indians have it, the Chinese have it. Certainly Western culture is rooted in this notion. We were in paradise, and we were thrown out. We have to get back to the garden. It's a crazy thing, a memory of something that never could have been.

NOR: When I was a kid I used to have these feelings, once when I was watching the Mississippi River, getting into the rhythm of the water, and feeling for the first time that I had become one with nature. It's a bit of a cliché, but do you think that feeling makes us long for a romantic notion of nature?

MARTIN: I think it does happen to children all the time, and it happened to me and happens to me even now when I am alone in the woods when no one else is around and everything is silent. Those are wonderful moments. That is part of the romance of the Indian. The Indian is seen as one who can read nature better than we can. He keeps his ears and eyes open in a visceral way, more like an animal. He can tell if it is going to be a cold winter, what animal has just gone by, where the deer are. He has sensitivity to the natural world that we have lost. That sensitivity is a way to get back to nature, and that is a really important feeling. To me those are the happiest moments when I feel I am a part of something. But then I wake up and realize that what I'm part of is the destruction of that "something" I felt a part of.

NOR: And when you get struck with that notion, do the happy moments become rather melancholic?

MARTIN: Yes, they do. That's what romantic poetry is all about—about loss.

NOR: Then why, Valerie, do I find and many others find that your novels and stories end with a burst of joy, or an almost unwarranted exultation, given the facts of the story? How do you account for that almost inexplicable sense of possibility in the world you have created?

MARTIN: I can't. Why do I have happy endings, happy moments? I just can't account for it—in spite of my recognition that there is realistically no way out for us, no way to return to nature, and no way for us to escape nature either. It is not as if there is a real separation. Where can you go where you are not in nature? I can't account for the moments of joy, but I know that people do experience them. The fact that your heart beats, that the planet still moves, that you are still alive. I remember a friend who was stabbed and nearly died. She was staying at my house, and I was taking care of her. I brought a flower into her room one day and then went away. When I came back, she was holding the flower, just looking at it, and she said that the flower had made her day. She couldn't even express how wonderful the flower was for her. I know that is true. Sometimes after great suffering and pain, we see the beauty of life, and that brings us real joy. To me, those moments are worth the pain.

NOR: I would like to speak to you as a writer, about your craft, from a writer's viewpoint. In *A Recent Martyr* you chose a rather difficult point of view in that Emma is your narrator, yet part of the story is the separate relationship between two other characters, Pascal and Claire. Why did you choose such a point of view, but more importantly, how did you make that work?

MARTIN: I think when I started I didn't really quite know what I was up against. I wanted to write a story about somebody who was watching somebody else. In a story of that kind, the subject is always the watcher, the voyeur. This comes with the first-person point of view. Whenever you have a first-person narrator, such as in Melville's "Bartleby, the Scrivener," I always tell my students that the lawyer tries to tell the story of Bartleby, but the story he tells is really about his own terrific moral struggle. Bartleby is, in fact, a resistant, immovable object against which the narrator throws himself again and again, and in the process reveals himself. I wanted to do something like that. I wanted my narrator to be trying to observe another person; she is trying to observe Claire, but the problem is she is also describing her love affair and the triangle that develops, so she ends up having to describe the relationship between Claire and her lover. She hears various things that happen, she has to intuit a bit, and she has to make up the story of what happens between them. In fact, nothing happens between Claire and Pascal, and that just about drives Emma out of her mind. I liked that because it creates a lot of tension and forces Emma to reveal herself, which is, from the first-person point of view, what the writer is up to. I was trying to break the character down, to show how she operated, without having her say, "This is how I operate." I wanted her to reveal her motives without knowing what she was doing. I couldn't have done it any other way. I needed that point of view, and I didn't think it was really that original. I think I have seen other books that have done that sort of thing, but I ran into difficulty, and the book was turned down several times because of the point of view. One editor actually said he would be interested in buying the book if I would change the point of view. I was desperate for a sale, but I wouldn't do it because, to me, that point of view was, in a way, the subject of the book.

NOR: Well, I think you made the right decision because the book is about revelation through imagination.

MARTIN: That is what the book is about, and the narrator does come to amazing revelations not only about her own character but about the nature of the ties that exist between people.

NOR: It is interesting that you had trouble selling the book about a triangle told from a woman's point of view because, in fact, there are countless stories of that sort told from the man's perspective. If it had been Pascal's point of view, you might not have had trouble selling the book. It would have been a very different book, but I wonder if you would have had trouble selling it.

NOR: That's really a good point, Mary.

NOR: Related to that idea of point of view is the way in which characters link up in your fiction. There is the Emma and Claire friendship in *A Recent Martyr,* and there is the relationship between Alexandra and Diana in your early novel, *Alexandra,* and there seems to be the hint that there could be a female friendship in *The Great Divorce* between Camille and Ellen.

MARTIN: Ellen turns her back on Camille. She has the opportunity to help, but she doesn't.

NOR: I'd like you to talk about those female friendships in terms of coping with the world and in terms of how the qualities of those friendships are important to you as a writer.

MARTIN: There is also one in *Set in Motion,* too. There are two women who should be fighting over a man, but they don't fight at all. They accept what he is and how they have been forced to relate to him. Finally, they realize they are going to have to part because of him. Those friendships are really important to me. I don't think enough has been written about friendships between women. I think often those relationships are described as ones that could be smashed by the entrance of a man. I like to write about those that couldn't be. I think that has come up again and again. I also write a lot about mothers and daughters. I guess in a sense *Mary Reilly* is one of my only characters who is a friendless woman. Almost all my other women have a woman they can turn to talk to.

NOR: In "The Consolation of Nature," the mother combs the daughter's hair and closeness is engendered between the two, and then, after the siege with the rat, the daughter wants to have her hair cut and the mother doesn't object. There is a kind of breaking there, too, isn't there?

MARTIN: Yes, but there is also a scene in that story that actually took place between me and my grandfather. The digging in the soil. That story is full of symbols, but the moment when the girl hands her mother the soil and they both experience its warmth is not a breaking but a bonding. The mother is like the earth. It is in the mother's embrace that the child is safe. When my agent first read the story, she told me I should change the last line because the child would realize she's not safe, so I changed the ending from safe to not safe. Then, a few weeks later, I changed it back. I didn't know quite what I meant, but I knew the child was safe, safe in her femaleness.

NOR: Speaking of that story, there is a female friendship here between two writers, Valerie Martin and Chris Wiltz, who support each other and share stories. How does that affect you both as writers?

NOR: She's a lifeline.

MARTIN: I can't do without her. There are daily faxes.

NOR: Are there really daily faxes?

MARTIN: Sometimes, sometimes hourly faxes. When I see her faxes coming through, I love it when they are two pages.

NOR: But you live very far away from Chris and from the subject of much of your writing. Living in Rome, do you feel the strain of being an expatriate for the time being?

MARTIN: A little bit. I keep coming back. I don't know how long it will last. I don't think of myself as an expatriate. When I moved to Massachusetts, the local paper referred to me as an expatriate writer, and I'd only moved out of state.

NOR: You had the audacity to leave New Orleans.

MARTIN: I had the opportunity to take a look at the Old World, and it is worth looking at, especially now. Europe is really interesting right now, but I am not writing very much, so it has been a little difficult.

NOR: When you're in Europe, do you find that your view of the United States changes?

MARTIN: Very much so.

NOR: How does that happen; how does your view change?

MARTIN: I like the United States better. I think the thing I have come to appreciate is how well our government works. We are really the only democracy ever to understand the essential feature of democracy—that you have an election and live with the winner until the next election. Other countries have very little patience with unpopular leaders. They think if someone turns out to be a bad guy, you should just get rid of him.

NOR: That's interesting because that need for instant gratification would seem to be more an American trait. Europeans have been living with problems for so long, you would think there would be more resignation.

MARTIN: They don't have the checks and balances we have that make our government processes move very slowly. In Italy they have created an impossible version of democracy that requires a coalition of people at the top scrapping over every piece of legislation.

NOR: So in a way, as an "expatriate," you are more consciously an American. Are you more consciously a New Orleanian?

MARTIN: I don't think there was ever a time when I wasn't a New Orleanian. I am trying to work on a book that takes place in New England. This is the first time I have tried that; maybe that is why I am not getting very far.

NOR: To go back to living outside the U.S. You are seeing the political structures more clearly, so do you think that politics will figure more prominently in your fiction in the future?

MARTIN: The book I am working on now is about a utopia— how could we live better? What would be a good society? The sad thing about this country is that while it is in some ways a smoothly operating democracy, it is a nightmare. It's a terrifically violent culture full of murderers and people who don't read. The Italians have no government to speak of, but most of them can quote Dante, and none of them have guns.

NOR: So this leads right into your own issues about freedom.

MARTIN: It does. That's why I am interested in utopias.

NOR: That was a question that came up for me while I was reading your fiction. Character after character seeks freedom. The most obvious one is Paul in *The Great Divorce,* who struggles to be free, then doesn't know what to do with his freedom. What constitutes freedom for you? What do you think of when you think of that word?

MARTIN: I agree with Ellen [in *The Great Divorce*]. It is a word that has no meaning. People have come to think it is desirable, that they must have it at all costs, and that they have a right to it, but my observation of what is going on in the world is that we don't. I would like to have a character say that we don't have a right to freedom; all we have left is obligations.

NOR: That sounds very New England. Your seven years in Massachusetts have had some impact on you.

MARTIN: There is something to be said for the way New Englanders view the world.

NOR: Walker Percy once said that he thought we were oppressed by freedom. Do you agree?

MARTIN: I don't think we are oppressed by freedom. We are oppressed by the idea of freedom. To say we are oppressed by freedom implies that we have it, but I don't think we have it. We just have a notion that we should have it. Americans associate freedom with happiness, and they think they have a right to both. It's written into the Declaration of Independence—life, liberty, and the pursuit of happiness. But pursuit is different from actually having it. The founding fathers may have observed that we can't have it, we can only pursue it.

NOR: Speaking of that freedom, with *Mary Reilly* you got freedom. What happened?

MARTIN: I like it. My highest expectations were simply to get a tenure-track job and to stay in it until I retired. I never expected to be liberated from teaching. When I got the chance, I jumped at it. I can write all the time. *Mary Reilly* was the first book that made it possible to devote all my time to my next book, and *The Great Divorce* shows it. The amount of concentration I was able to put into that three-year project shows in the novel. I was never distracted from the book. I never had to pull myself out of my fantasy world and into my students'. I was able to work without having to change gears. I got all three stories in the novel started early, and they worked together from the beginning. I was never distracted from the work at hand.

NOR: Speaking of students, do you think that you can teach students to be good writers or can you only teach them to appreciate good writing?

MARTIN: No, I don't think I can teach them to be good writers. Writing is essentially a gift. The movie *Amadeus*, about Mozart and Salieri, is a good description of teaching writing. You get a student who is obnoxious, but who has a gift. Then you have a hard worker who has no gift. You can't change that. You can only work with what each has. I once had a woman in my class who told me that I ruined reading romance novels for her because she began to realize how bad they were. I guess that is what I can do. I teach young writers to find better books to read. In the last ten years or so, a lot of my students, even graduate students, have been coming into my classes without ever having read any European literature or any early American literature. They have only read books published since the 1950s. So getting them to read old books is, I feel, an obligation and sometimes an eye-opener for them.

NOR: I found that to be the case. I had a student who took a writing workshop from me who told me that many of the books I had the class read she never would have read on her own because they would have intimidated her. This leads me to the question about the difference in the way critics and scholars read and the way writers read.

MARTIN: Well, it is completely different. That is why I think teaching creative writing at a university is, despite what some may say about it, really valuable. Of the people who want to write, most will figure out how anyway. Others may never write, but they also don't know how to read the way writers read. Writers can teach them that. They won't learn how to do that in a literature class. Critics read what's there for meaning. Writers read to find out how it got there, how it works. It's really so much more nuts and bolts kind of reading. A critic may pay attention to diction, but a writer has to look at a sentence over and over to see how it's put together, not what it means. In fact, when I teach writing students a story, I don't ever even fool with the meaning. I talk about point of view and how it operates. We don't even talk so much about the finished product but rather the construction of it. When I read, I read very slowly to see how the story is put together.

NOR: I think reading slowly is a writer's disease. Many writers I speak to tell me they read more and more slowly as they get older.

MARTIN: The other thing is liberating students from the idea that what they write has to mean anything. Of course it will, no matter how you try. Especially if you are a good writer, it will mean something. But starting out to mean something and filling a story full of meanings and clues is a very artificial way of writing. Students read something like *The Old Man and the Sea,* and they want to turn everything into a symbol. It is what young writers often do. As a writer, though, you can't work from outside and shove meaning into the story; it has to grow organically like a plant. I think you can learn that from reading if you read like a writer because, instead of noticing the fish as a symbol, you notice the scales, the size of the tail. It is an actual fish, not a symbolic one. You see how it arrived in the story, rather than how it looks once the story is over.

NOR: Execution rather than explication, as in *The Great Divorce.* When I first read that novel, I was impressed by the seamlessness of the three stories. You have three story lines, yet there is never a wrenching. How did that happen?

MARTIN: I had the notion of the three stories in my head early on and even wrote a proposal for the book—it doesn't look anything like the finished novel, but from the beginning I had the idea for the three stories. I got all three stories underway very quickly. That was my goal in the beginning of the book. The scenes at the beginning of the book are short ones, but they get longer as the novel develops. Once I got all my characters set in the reader's mind, I was able to work on each for a time and then move on to another without any wrenching of the reader's concentration. The actual counterpoint of the stories came naturally. I worked every day until I came to a stopping place. Then the next day, I would move over to another story. They all fit together so naturally. There were three dinner parties, the grand dinner party at the antebellum mansion where Elizabeth met Hermann, followed by the annoying party at Ellen and Paul's house while he is still plotting his break for freedom, and then Camille's cheese sandwich with Eddie in the diner. Later the theme of imprisonment ran through all the stories. Elizabeth was locked up by her husband, Camille was always locked up, and the animals in the zoo are locked up. I wrote the novel very slowly, about four pages a day, and always moved naturally from one story to the next. All that contributed to the seamlessness of the novel.

NOR: As you were writing, did the notion of imprisonment that was organically growing out of the stories become clear to you, or did you see it after the fact?

MARTIN: I saw it as it was happening. In fact, I can remember the day I realized it. *The Great Divorce* was about imprisonment.

NOR: But all your novels are about imprisonment. In fact, another take on freedom is imprisonment, and in all your novels, that theme recurs. You focus on imprisonment in *A Recent Martyr*, in *Set in Motion*, in *Alexandra*, and in *Mary Reilly*. Mary Reilly is imprisoned by the secret of her past, and Dr. Jekyll makes a prison for himself that he cannot escape. The metaphor of imprisonment runs through every part of your work. How do you understand it? Why are you so drawn to it?

MARTIN: I guess I have grown into the metaphor. I have always thought of the body as a prison, and the subject matter of a lot of my books is about that—that imprisonment that we all share. I think that I didn't really understand how complex the notion of freedom and imprisonment was until recently. I think I believed there was a solution to this conundrum of the value of the wild and our need for the wild to be imprisoned. I have come to see that this is an insoluble problem. As a young writer, I admired Camus; I went to his grave recently in France. It is quite a thing to see, very simple, very sad. As a young writer, I identified with outsiders. I was drawn to the notion of people who were anti-social, cut off from the rest of the world in some way. This is a romantic notion, and young writers are often romantics. My early heroines are cut off, and that is fine. It's like the young woman in "Why I Live at the P.O." who is finally driven to live in the P.O. and says, "Here I am and here I'll stay." As I have grown older, I have come to see that the romantic notion of the outsider in love with death doesn't solve a thing. It only makes life worse. We have to find ways to create communities. This is exactly the progression Camus makes. In *The Stranger,* the hero is the outsider, the murderer, but in *The Plague,* there is a sincere argument for the necessity of community. There is no God, but there is a need to hold on to what is good.

NOR: In your fiction, while you do not speak of God, there is certainly a hint of a real spiritual quest hiding behind the murder, death, and chaos of much of what you write.

MARTIN: That's another conflict for me. I really am attracted to the Christian ideal; however, no church has anything to do with that anymore, and maybe never did. While I was a non-Catholic in a Catholic high school, I read stories about the lives of the saints, many of whom did live entirely good lives, devoted to the teachings of Christ as they understood them. St. Francis of Assisi is my latest interest. Of all the saints, he grasped most completely the very simple dictum of Christ, which is simply this, you can't own property and be like Christ. So he resolved to be a beggar. He refused even the idea of community property, which was both his triumph and his ruination. Unfortunately, in spite of my fascination with saints and mysticism, I don't believe that Jesus was God, nor do I believe that there is a God up there directing our lives, determining whether so-and-so has a happy life or not. A lot of people lately are grabbing on to the notion of Gaia, the planet as a self-regulating goddess. It's just like people to do this: there has to be a goddess somewhere regulating things. The revenge of the rainforest is another recent fantasy. Really, it's so absurd and superstitious, it's touching in a way. I would love to believe it, but the rational part of me just rejects that out of hand. I really wish that I could believe in God, but I don't.

NOR: Yet you are perceived of as a Catholic writer. In fact, I understand you were once invited to a conference at Loyola to speak as a Catholic writer. Did you go?

MARTIN: No, I wrote a letter and told them that I was not now and had never been a Catholic. I got a letter from a priest who assured me that my Catholicity was not a problem; the group still wanted me to come and speak. He had read *A Recent Martyr* and was interested in my character, Claire, who may or may not be a saint. I like to think she would be accepted in the church as a saint and a martyr. I had conflicts—time and teaching—and couldn't speak, but I was very interested. There is a lot I like about Catholicism. I think it is possible to be a good person and a Catholic, though not all Catholics are good people. There are things that Catholicism teaches about spirituality and mysticism and about what good is that ring true for me still.

NOR: Is that why you have turned to St. Francis?

MARTIN: Yes, I think he may have been the last good man. I'm trying to fit him into my new novel.

NOR: You are writing about a New England utopia, but how is St. Francis going to fit into that?

MARTIN: I know that's going to be tough. I don't know who my character is yet, whether he is St. Francis or knows about St. Francis. I would like to retell some of the stories that I know about St. Francis because he is a really interesting character, and I am fascinated by his belief that if you were going to be good, you had to give up property. Even the church did not want to do that. They did not want to charter his order in that way. As he was dying, he knew he had lost his life-long battle, that the Franciscans would have community property. There is a story of how, when he learned that some of his monks had built a stone house to live in, he went up on the roof and began to throw down the tiles like Christ throwing the moneylenders out of the temple. He was betrayed in the end; as he was dying, he knew that his order would not follow his rule and live as beggars.

NOR: Is this St. Francis the same man who communed with animals?

MARTIN: Yes, he did. In fact, he catechized the birds, and he spoke of Brother Sun and Sister Moon. The thing I like best about his naming is that he called his body Brother Ass. The communion with the birds is a bit overstated, though. He wasn't a vegetarian. He was definitely a thirteenth-century Italian. He talked with the birds, then he cooked them.

NOR: I would like to ask you some more questions about *Mary Reilly* because it is the book by which you are most well known and when the movie comes out, it will bring you a lot of publicity. What is it that attracted you to the story of Dr. Jekyll?

MARTIN: Well, it is the obvious thing. In the novel, Dr. Jekyll writes that from an early age he found himself, in essence, living a lie. He was split. He wanted to have the respect of society, but he also had anti-social urges that caused him lots of trouble. He was imprisoned by the conflicting sides of his nature. I read a lot of Victorian essays while I was working on the book. Huxley, Darwin, and others, men of science and of letters—Hardy, for example—all understood that we were creating a world in which it would be impossible to live with a clear conscience. Such speculation is all over now. We are living in that world.

NOR: Dr. Jekyll is separating himself from the impulses he was afraid of by creating another person. He was trying to free himself from the responsibility for part of himself.

MARTIN: Yes, he thought that if he could get the bad impulses to go one way and he could go another, he could rest, but of course, he couldn't.

NOR: I would like to ask you a bit about the movie, and I suppose several people have wanted your impressions of the movie. Chris and I have spent a good deal of time casting the movie, and I suppose you had your choices as well. If you could have chosen the cast, did you have people in mind?

MARTIN: Yes, John Malkovich was one, but I did want them to use two actors. A woman who wrote a screenplay for *Mary Reilly,* and not a bad one at that, wanted me to get it into the right hands, and she proposed Donald and Kiefer Sutherland, and I even suggested that to the powers that be, but the idea was overruled. John Malkovich had worked with Stephen Frears, and he did an excellent job in *Dangerous Liaisons*. Many people who worked with Frears in *Liaisons* are in *Mary Reilly*.

NOR: Do you feel that the movie illustrates, because it is visual, some of the concerns that you had when you were writing the book?

MARTIN: A little, but at this point the movie has very little to do with the book. Right now, I am trying to have some impact on the ending of the movie. The book's ending all happens off stage, so I am working on an ending to bring it on stage.

NOR: How does the movie deal with Mary Reilly's psychic longing for a father, for somebody gentle and kind?

MARTIN: It doesn't really. And that is the thing about movies; they aren't the books they are taken from. Everything has to be more explicit. The subtleties of Mary's character are gone. I've actually lost touch with much of what is going on in the movie.

NOR: As long as we are talking about movies, we might as well talk about sex and violence. In your work there is a definite connection between sex and violence. How do sex and violence co-exist in such a way as to create a sense of peril and yet still give the reader a sexy scene?

MARTIN: Well, that just shows how *you* are. Some people don't find those scenes very sexy; they find them offensive.

NOR: Who might those people be?

MARTIN: People with an agenda. I think sex and violence are related, and we don't have to stretch our imaginations to see how they are. I did not make it up. It's not new with me.

NOR: Some of your critics complain because they say that the way you connect sex and violence is rather repugnant and that your novels are demeaning to women.

MARTIN: I was not invited to read in Salem because the woman who scheduled the readers said that she was tired of the woman-as-victim theme, and I could just stay the hell out of Salem. I did eventually read in Salem, the first chapter from *Mary Reilly*, and someone in the audience told me that Mary would not have had kind feelings for her master. She said a working woman would not have had any respect for her master, who obviously doesn't really care for her. It was another instance of my turning women into victims.

NOR: I don't find many of your women to be victims, so the idea of the victimization of women doesn't really come up very often, except when women victimize themselves. There is one scene, however, that I do find particularly violent, but it isn't explicit violence. It is the scene between Paul and Ellen, in *The Great Divorce,* on his last night before he leaves to find his freedom. They have sex all night long, sleeping and waking, weeping and making love. I asked myself, what is he doing? Does he know what he is doing? I find that scene, in many respects, appalling. I think it is beautifully done, but it is truly chilling. Do you agree, Chris?

NOR: That scene is true for me. You are writing about real women. To speak of these women as victims is to not understand what is really going on.

MARTIN: The scene is just a natural response. They have been married for twenty years, and they have always had a good sexual relationship. Ellen thought she could turn her back on this last night and go to sleep, but she can't. I think Paul gets a lot of bad press, but he is not a bad guy. He is weak, he is a romantic, and, in some ways he is me. He wants to make a leap. He wants to make a change. I know that is childish, but I understand it. I did it. I made enough money, and I ran away. Of course, as Paul found out, you can't escape the prison of yourself. Paul just panics.

NOR: Ellen wants a community and Paul wants freedom and in some ways those two ideas are mutually exclusive. Ironically, his mistress is busy making him a little community as fast as she can.

MARTIN: We can't blame Paul for wanting a romantic life. Ellen is absorbed in science. She is in many ways unsympathetic to his need to be the center of his own romantic fantasies. He has been in academia for twenty years, and all his triumphs have been small, small pats—even the slaps are small. He wants something different.

NOR: It seems like he is having a fairly typical response to middle age.

MARTIN: Right. That is why I don't like to have my characters labeled as victims. I like all my characters. They are all trying, given the resources they have, to do the best they can. Even Camille, few as her resources are, makes her own choices. Another point is that I don't take sex that seriously. Nor do I see marriage as sacred in the way that some of my critics seem to. Ultimately those issues aren't important in the light of the big question, which is how are we going to die?

NOR: In *The Great Divorce,* you have Ellen speak of "the concentrated ugliness of contemporary life." Would you comment on that phrase?

MARTIN: It has come to me that the thing that is causing all the violence in America is the architecture. About 100 years ago, people stopped caring about how our cities looked.

NOR: But Ellen isn't just referring to architecture; she is referring to everything.

MARTIN: Yes, the food, the garbage, everything. That is why we want to escape to the country. New Yorkers work all week and then run for the country on the weekends. Melville was right. The ugliness of the cities had begun to drive us mad. Rome is still a beautiful city because of the Romans' resistance to change. They still believe that when people walk in their cities, they should experience beauty. I don't know when people stopped caring what their cities looked like. I don't know how anybody could want to live in most cities anymore.

NOR: I love cities. New York is a city I love. I like Washington, and Boston. Even though I write about nature writers, built environments don't bother me. While I don't find most American cities beautiful, I love parts of Boston, and Washington Square is really graceful.

MARTIN: But the hamburger places, the clown serving burgers, the awful colors, Muzak—they all drive me crazy.

NOR: So, in a way, you write as a hedge against that concentrated ugliness. You create something beautiful.

MARTIN: That's a nice thing to say, but I think my books are depressing.

NOR: I don't find them depressing, partly because of the moments of exultation and joy when people are not defeated, when the little jaguar in *The Great Divorce* survives. Also, you are a beautiful stylist, and that mitigates what might seem a hopeless vision. Who do you look to as being stylists, people whose style you appreciate?

MARTIN: Edith Wharton. Elizabeth Taylor. Although she isn't a great stylist, she's fast and draws a clear picture with quick, sure strokes.

NOR: Do the two of you share tastes in novels, Chris?

NOR: Yes, we are always telling each other about good things we have read. We both loved *Brazzaville Beach* by William Boyd. It is a well-structured, fascinating story, a novel that is a fast read yet full of ideas.

MARTIN: I return again and again to books that taught me what style was—Flaubert, especially, which is odd because I read Flaubert in translation. Tanizaki is another example. I love his work and think of him as a great stylist, but perhaps I only admire the style of his translator. Chris and I both enjoyed a novel of his, *Naomi,* a wonderful story of obsession. I think it was Raymond Carver who observed that writers love stories of obsession because, in many ways, to be a writer you have to be obsessive. You have to be willing to sit down alone day after day, working out the details of your story, struggling to reconcile irreconcilable conflicts and trying to answer big unanswerable questions.

Jack Gilbert

Interviewed by Ralph Adamo
and John Biguenet
(1996)

Jack Gilbert was born in Pittsburgh and lives in San Francisco; he has spent much of his adult life abroad, in Greece, Japan, and Paris among other places. Though he is the recipient of a number of prizes and awards, and twice nominated for the Pulitzer Prize, Gilbert remains oddly under-anthologized and less well known than some of his important contemporaries. His books are *Views of Jeopardy* (Yale Series of Younger Poets Prize winner, 1962), *Monolithos* (Knopf, 1984), *Kochan* (limited edition), and *The Great Fires* (Knopf, 1994).

NEW ORLEANS REVIEW: One of the themes of contemporary poetry is the family. But that subject is rarely addressed in your work?

JACK GILBERT: Well, I understand why people write these domestic poems, but—maybe it's where I grew up—I'm just not interested in it. We had a family life that would be great for a novel. We didn't read books. I never tasted tea until I was in high school. I didn't know there was tea. I'm interested in Dostoevsky. I'm interested in Thomas Mann and things like that. But that's on a large scale. It was havoc in our house. My brothers and sisters would chase each other with butcher knives, and they were always getting pregnant or living with people. It was like Thomas Wolfe. It was very Southern. But the quiet, nuanced kind of life, to me, is deficient in energy and scale. Jane Austen's a wonderful writer, and Edith Wharton's a wonderful writer. Their subject doesn't engage me. I respect it. I enjoy the books, but I go back to Dickens, or something like that. Living in Pittsburgh was like a Dostoevsky novel. It was, and still is, hard for me to live in a nice, clean new city, built after the Second World War in California. It doesn't seem real to me. I finally left Paris because it was like being on vacation, and I went to live in London because that seemed a city to me. Rome seemed like a city to me when I lived there. The middle class has been the source of most of what's important in our civilization, except the vision. The visions usually come from someplace else. The dreams are invented someplace else.

NOR: So your life and your writing are not inseparable?

GILBERT: No. Being seriously in love is much more important to me. I rejoice in Gianna Gelmetti, Linda Gregg, and Michiko Nogami. Those to me are the riches in my life. I love my poetry. I am very serious about my poetry. But it doesn't come first.

NOR: You've said that living your life is essentially your work. There has been a tradition in American literature to make a distinction between published writers who think of themselves as professional writers and ones who think of themselves as amateurs. Do you think of yourself as a professional, not as an amateur? It's clear that you have not been driven to publish.

GILBERT: I consider myself a professional, but not in the sense that I make my living at writing—although I do. It's not a hobby. I work very hard at it, and that makes a difference. I think people who study creativity make a basic mistake. They assume creative work is a kind of play. People do it for pleasure. That makes sense, but I think the amateur is the person for whom writing is still fun. When games become difficult, children lose interest.

NOR: But to you, the difference is not money. It's the intensity of the effort.

GILBERT: It's also a question of having my life. I started out a little famous. I won the Yale prize and a Guggenheim. But then I stopped publishing for seventeen years. I went away to live a life, though I always wrote poems.

NOR: You managed to write even though you traveled all over the earth. Could you write as soon as you moved into a new city?

GILBERT: Well, first thing, I don't like travel.

NOR: But you like arriving?

GILBERT: I don't like arriving either. I like living there. I think, unless you have a lot of money, traveling is hard work.

NOR: So you tended to stay where you were.

GILBERT: I stayed because of what was there.

NOR: When you left a place where you had stayed for a significant period of time, why did you leave?

GILBERT: Usually because I ran out of money.

NOR: Were you typically not earning money while you were in these places? You were there on money you had earned in between journeys?

GILBERT: Well, sometimes yes and sometimes no. One of the times I lived in Rome, I taught conversation to one student a day, one hour each time, six days a week. In other words, I had only one class each day. I put an ad in the paper and when answers came in, I took all the female names and arranged to interview them. Why not? But on the other hand, you can't take advantage of it. Because you can't go to bed with a woman and then charge her for the conversation.

NOR: There's the student-teacher relationship to respect as well.

GILBERT: As a matter of fact, we didn't talk in English. We talked in my terrible Italian. I said to them finally, "I feel like a gigolo. I come here, and we flirt with each other, and I get paid." And they said, "No, you don't understand. This is much more valuable to us. It's impossible for an Italian woman to have a conversation like this with an Italian man in a room alone. Because if you're informal, intimate about a subject, the men will pounce on you." They expected that to happen with me, and they flirted to make it happen, but I couldn't afford it. I couldn't afford to go to bed with them. Some of them were wonderful.

NOR: That would be a strange sort of prostitution. The sex is free, but you've got to pay to talk. Did poems come out of that?

GILBERT: No, but a lot of yearning.

NOR: You lived in San Francisco for several years. Was that after college?

GILBERT: I first came to live in San Francisco in '54. A couple of weeks before Ginsberg got there. It wasn't the Beat Generation yet. In the beginning, the Beat Generation was maybe ten, fourteen people. It wasn't like in the books. The books lump everybody together, but they weren't together. The people that became known as the Beats, largely, were people that didn't have any money and stayed up talking or playing chess most of the night. The people that were painters were as much a part of the group as the poets. The group that was around Jack Spicer didn't hang out with the group that was around Bob Stock. Ferlinghetti and Ginsberg and Snyder and Williams were each approximately a different group. I don't remember Corso being there, except intermittently. He was always going back to New York. Ferlinghetti was and is a very nice man. His first book, *Pictures of the Gone World*, is lovely. He was, in the early days, more normal than the others, with his wife and neighbors, a lovely man and a talented writer who did a lot of good for people in running City Lights. He didn't hang out. He wasn't like that.

NOR: Your name is not associated with the Beats at all in the anthologies. Did you feel as though you were a part of them? Certainly in your work, the elements that we think of as part of Beat poetry are not there, but you were part of the social—

GILBERT: I was there. The Beats were important. I think the Beats and the Haight-Ashbury period were two of the most significant eras of post-war America. They differ in the sense that the Beats really considered themselves artists, but the Haight-Ashbury people usually didn't.

NOR: How else did they differ?

GILBERT: Take the Haight-Ashbury. There have always been alternate traditions, under the official traditions, that periodically surface. When they surface, they have a lot in common. They are politically radical, sexually disreputable, and revolutionary. That's too strong a word, but they go against all the accepted rules in literature and the arts and lifestyles. They tend to be involved with drugs and liquor, morally irresponsible, and religiously heretical.

Their idea of love is not respectable. They don't obey the rules. The Haight-Ashbury tried out all those dreams. That children are pure; if left alone, they will educate themselves. If they are not forced into school and made to sit all day, there will be a golden age. People have for centuries dreamed about sexual liberation. Norman Mailer said the other day that there has been only one golden age of sexuality, and that it lasted only ten years. He meant the Haight-Ashbury, and he was wrong. It only lasted five years. The people actually tried out the secret dreams that have haunted humankind. All failed, but that doesn't matter. The fact is that they tried them. They tried their own version of anarchy, open marriages, and predominance of drugs as a way of enlightenment. One could go down the whole list: no rules for the arts, let the kids educate themselves. The Haight-Ashbury tried all of them. I was teaching at San Francisco State on and off. It was great good luck to see it up so close.

NOR: What were you teaching?

GILBERT: The Advanced Theory of Poetry. Originally, twelve people signed up. But young poets would come from all over the Bay Area. We finally had over seventy people coming every class. There was never a time when less than a third of the students were stoned. I would say that was the last part of '66, '67, and a little bit of '68. I would be working with the class, and people would fall off their chair—WHACK—onto the floor. Nobody paid attention to it. I had a student come up to me once and say, "Do you remember whether I was in class last Tuesday? You probably don't." Then he said, "But it would be nice if you did, because it would get me out of a murder rap." It was a wonderful class. Ron Silliman was in it. It was a very special time.

NOR: You're responsible for the L=A=N=G=U=A=G=E poets!

GILBERT: No. But we had great arguments about it. Ron finally said, "I'm not going to argue with you because if I argue with you I'll lose the argument and I believe what I'm saying."

NOR: Do you remember what you taught in Advanced Theory of Poetry, and does it still seem to you to be true? You said that your approach to teaching poetry was to focus on the process.

GILBERT: Understanding the process is one thing and also scale. I didn't want to talk about cosmetic mechanics. I wanted to talk about the mystery of writing a poem or a novel. I taught novels, playwriting, and such. I worry about the mechanics; I think the mechanics are something you teach, but I would never start out by teaching metrics. If a person doesn't have an ear, he's not going to get an ear. He'll get a bad ear from metrics, if he's so conscious of it. It would be constant, like metronomes. With some students, I was working with the novel. I wanted to give them a sense of strategy in literature and its craft. Pointing out that the first line of a novel is a remarkable event, I brought in twenty-five masterpieces. I asked them what the first line of each was, and they didn't know, except for *Moby Dick*. I'd say to them, "What kind of line is this? What's it trying to do? Is it giving information? Is it setting the scene, the tone, the action?" They wouldn't know, and we'd talk about it. When I read them the beginning of the twenty-fifth, which was *The Sound and the Fury*, I could see a shiver of understanding. The author had thought about that first line. Each first line does something specific, and it does it amazingly well. I teach literature as literature, not as a form of criticism. Almost all the literature classes I've seen are taught by a critic in terms of criticism, in terms of explication. These teachers find the secret of the symbolism, rip its heart out, and discard the work of art. Or, the teachers lecture about how this person was influenced by that one, and what he wrote subsequently. Then they talk about the lineage of literature. That's not about literature. They puzzle out the symbols and meaning. And they don't even know that they're not talking about literature. They'll say it's a good, OK, or a bad book, or this part is funny, but the joy of literature is the joy of an art. That's what I try to teach.

NOR: Do you take the same approach in teaching a workshop?

GILBERT: The same thing in a different way is what I try to teach in a workshop, along with making the students try for something beyond their ability. I tell them, "Fall down. Fall on your face. Fail, but fail because you tried to do something beyond your strength." I don't care about fixing up the poem. Workshops are terrible, in the sense that everybody wants to put a Band-Aid on the poem. Everybody will tell you to take out the fourth or seventh line. I say to them, "No, no, we have to talk about the whole poem." I ask them to tell me what they think about it as a poem, not as something to be repaired. They are confused and say, "Nobody ever asked me to do that. I can do that other thing. I can say, 'This is in passive voice. This is front-loaded rhythm,' but I don't know the things you're talking about." I'll say, "What is the engine of this particular poem? How does that engine differ from another engine?" One of the assignments I give is for the students to steal the engine from a good poem. I ask them to adopt a poem. To carry one book around and read it over. When they finish it, start at the beginning again. So they have their own poet as a place to stand, to look at literature. Don't give me any hubcaps, don't give me any grilles. Steal the engine. That'll teach them something about how to write their poems. I teach them to vary their strategies, to be dissatisfied with the same solution, to avoid doing what many poets do—use the same solution to poetry over and over again, with a new title on each one. I don't understand why poets aren't interested in the poetry of poetry. When I was growing up, kids liked cars. They'd get in somebody's garage and watch one of them take out the carburetor or do stuff with the spark plugs. They loved it; I can't imagine a race car driver who doesn't like to look under the hood. It wouldn't make sense to me.

NOR: So you're talking about looking at a poem the way a carpenter looks at a house?

GILBERT: Except a carpenter doesn't work with magic. That would be like learning all the forms and doing villanelles, sestinas, and such without any feeling about the poem. You can write a villanelle backwards. You just get your two lines sitting side by side at the end. Then fill in a few slots and work backwards.

NOR: Then the poet is more like the architect?

GILBERT: I'd like to think that the poet is—in a way—a magician. He makes something happen that the technique does not account for. But I love the fact that what happens in a poem is caused at the same time. It is a result of the dynamics of craft if it is a poem that's pregnant. Use all the craft in the world; if you're not pregnant with the poem, you're not going to get anywhere that matters to me. I'll understand it's beautiful. Writing within a form is hard. Some poets do it with extraordinary deftness. But I don't understand why. The result is a lovely object, something that's gracefully done. So what? That's like collecting Chinese ivory balls that have seven balls miraculously carved inside the outside ball. It's like treating poetry as though it's learning how to balance brooms on your head.

I think it's clever, but I wouldn't spend my life doing it. Mechanical form doesn't really matter to me. It doesn't put any pressure on my life. It doesn't help me be here; it doesn't help me get there. It's like people who think sexuality is fun. Sure it's fun, but it's a way of getting someplace, not just running to the corner for a little spasm, if you get there in time. It's extraordinary what you can get with poetry, love, sexuality, and perhaps God. I don't understand people in workshops being willing to paint signposts saying, "That Way." The object is to teach students to want to experience poetry as something alive. And to make it for themselves. It's as if they went on vacation and took their daughter's watercolors. They draw and color something badly. The buildings are leaning, the fisherman looks like a dog, the color of the roof runs into the sky's blue, but there is a feeling there and a truth that's not in a photograph. The student can experience the day. Painting it, or writing the poem, slows down the flux of our days. Otherwise it's like trying to see or live our world as we drive past. The country is disappearing right behind us. We try to see it, but it's not easy.

NOR: Things go by too fast.

GILBERT: If you can stop it, you can see it long enough to know what you are seeing. Partially, preliminarily. And then, when you can do that you can, like a child, put it in your mouth to experience it, to feel it. For me, I find it very difficult to have any clear idea of what's happening emotionally at first when I'm writing. Like the first time you go to bed with somebody. The next day you try hard to remember what actually happened. It's like a powerful wind blowing. Everything is wonderfully blurry. But you cannot keep it clear.

NOR: It's a kind of confusion.

GILBERT: Yes. But the second time you are with this woman—if you can go to bed with her the second time—you can pay attention. You're not overwhelmed by your own intensity. You can put it into words; it becomes available to being experienced in particular.

NOR: Your sense of aesthetics and your idea of form—the way you taught them in Advanced Theory of Poetry—have they been pretty consistently the same?

GILBERT: I think the difference is that I don't have theories. Theories make you tell the poem what to be. Imagism is a theory, Black Mountain poetry is a theory, L=A=N=G=U=A=G=E poetry is a theory. I don't work that way. I don't want to write a theoretical kind of poetry. It displaces the primacy of content. For many people, the poetics are the content of the poem. The poem is just an illustration of the theory. I'm not interested in that. It doesn't mean it's bad. But I don't know what it's for in my life. For me, craft is basically a tool for effectuating the poem. I think one of the things that I've spent much of my writing life on is something that is never noticed. I think two reviews have noticed it. I think my books are almost a museum of strategies. In that sense, I think about the nature of poetry a lot. I'm interested in a craft that is connected to the subject matter. Pound says someplace that craft is the means by which the poet says what he wants to say to the reader with the least loss possible. I like craft. I love strategy. If I were a coach for football, I could, like Bill Walsh, be crazy about the method. But the coach's primary concern is winning the game for the joy of it. I think of craft as an old-fashioned courtesan. The poem is my wife, and my obligation is to my wife. But the craft is just for me. Even though nobody notices that I am doing it, it's a special kind of pleasure. It's all there, always there, waiting for me, not busy with the children, just for me.

NOR: You're making a distinction that is a little difficult to grasp, I think, between the craft and the result. I think some people would say that you can't differentiate between the two.

GILBERT: Let me give you an example. Suppose a poet is writing about the Vietnam War, and he is going to write about the atrocity of dropping napalm on children, on mothers—people that don't even know who the U.S. is—without any real excuse for doing it. Now he could do it like Neruda. He could do it as surrealism to communicate the texture and unspecified horror, or he could do it like, say, Robert Bly, with diatribes of accusations. Suppose one could do the same thing with the Holocaust. In both cases, we run into the problem of compassion fatigue. People have heard about the Holocaust so often and the Vietnam War so often it's like smelling the rose four or five times. You can't really smell it anymore. What the artist has to do is to find a way to make the subject fresh. There is no question about the validity of the subject or the horror of it.

We're not talking about that; we know what the aim is. But what if the poet wrote about the Holocaust in a villanelle. I'm not saying that it would work. But it might—for the inappropriateness of watching the elegance as the writer overcomes the obstacles which he accepts in the villanelle or a sestina. If a poet uses that form for the Holocaust or the Vietnam War, it might have a consequence. Its inappropriateness might freshen the reader. You could call it irony. Giving common themes a new freshness is what I am interested in. One of the things I was thinking about when I wrote *The Great Fires* was that the critics never write about short-short poems. Their effect is largely because of what's not there. But something about the brain makes the length of a standard short poem perfect. The brain can hold the idea in the head all at one time, like the breath used to read the poem. We know what a long poem is, the epic, the *Odyssey*. But each age has its own definition of what the epic is. The long, long poem is centered on either narrative or the exposition. But what about the poem between 28 lines and 40 lines in length? What is going to hold the poem together if the poet doesn't use the narrative or the exposition and he doesn't use rhyme, patterning, prettiness, or orderliness. What holds *that* poem together?

NOR: If no one notices what you've accomplished, who is the audience for poetry? How do you feel about giving readings of your poems?

GILBERT: I think it's strange that people read poetry. It's not natural.

NOR: To read poetry is not natural?

GILBERT: That's why the oral tradition revived by the Beats damaged poetry. It's hard to read complex poetry to an audience, so poetry readings became more like entertainments.

NOR: But your reading last night to a fairly wide audience—a university audience, mostly—was an effective reading. It wasn't simply entertainment.

GILBERT: Because my poetry is not founded on decoration. I think that most people's idea of poetry is tropes, similes, and careful descriptions of trees. I don't do that. My poetry derives from early Chinese poetry, the Greek anthology, and the Anglo-Saxon sense of language. It's a plain style. It's not using poetry primarily for color or embellishments. That's what most people think of as poetry. I don't think—despite Shakespeare—that it's the basic quality of poetry in English.

NOR: Borges said that all the great works of English literature were written in German. I think he's talking about the same thing, the language's Anglo-Saxon roots.

GILBERT: There's a different way of thinking. I knew a Wordsworth scholar at Oxford. We used to correspond. He said the difference between American poetry and English poetry is that English is the native tongue of Englishmen. The English feel comfortable in the sentence, the paragraph, and the stanza. He was saying that the English take the language for granted. It's natural to them. But not the Americans. Americans, he said, are always fiddling with the language, making it do things it's not supposed to do, fooling around with it, playing with it. That's why almost every important literary accomplishment in the twentieth century in English has been done in America, he said. It makes a lot of sense.

NOR: Even more than most of the poets of your generation, you have a remarkable consistency of voice from work done in your twenties, maybe—certainly in your thirties—to the work you did over the last ten years. Do you think that's true?

GILBERT: I think so, but it's not completely true. Allen Ginsberg and I used to argue about aesthetics a lot. Every week he had a new idea. Usually hopelessly wrong. One time we were talking about spontaneous poetry, and he said, "Well, you believe what I believe, which is that an artist is a person who makes things." He doesn't *submit* to voices speaking, I said. You hear voices thinking, you write it down, but I am in charge of the poem. You might let the horse run for a while, but you tell it which direction to go, because if you don't, the horse will eat all day. I believe in the horse. I believe in listening to the horse, but I'm riding the horse. And Allen said, "You're afraid to release your poetry from your control. You're afraid. Let me see," he said. "Write some poems that way." So I wrote some poems that way. They're in my first book. They are the only two poems in the book that I wish weren't there. If I ever do a selected poems, those two poems certainly won't be there.

NOR: Speaking of choosing a collection of selected poems, are you going to write a memoir?

GILBERT: People have been asking. I don't know if I'll do it. I'm thinking of writing something to publish posthumously. I'd like to write a book about love with each chapter being a specific woman I've known. A book about the kinds of romantic love. I want to do the book with the picture of each woman. Some of them nude, some of them half nude, some of them not nude. I'd like to do it like a collage. I've always been interested in that moment just before the material becomes a work of art. Something happens then. It crosses a line, and it becomes something apart from reality, something wonderful. I'd like to use bits of letters, their letters, my letters, maybe watercolors I've done in a particular town, the manuscript of a poem and then the printed poem about the woman. Each chapter, a different kind of love. One might be pure physical joy and one might be. . . . But it's hopelessly incorrect. The idea of the nudes is a madness.

NOR: So your life as your loves?

GILBERT: I don't know for other people, but every time I've fallen in love, it's been different, sometimes unrecognizable. I didn't know that I was in love with Michiko for two years. We were together, lived together and all of that. It was like the difference between sunshine and moonshine. Totally different. Splendid, passionate, deep deep, but different, unrelated. Maybe Japanese. There's a muscularity to that kind of Japanese emotion. It doesn't reach out and try to grab things. It's available.

NOR: Whom else would you include in the book?

GILBERT: Pimpaporn Charionpanith.

NOR: I don't suppose we could ask you to spell that.

GILBERT: I met her while I was living in Thailand. She really was spectacularly beautiful, but Michiko was waiting in San Francisco. I almost got married.

NOR: To that woman?

GILBERT: Uh huh.

NOR: Have you gotten back in touch at all?

GILBERT: We were in correspondence for a while, then the mail got messed up. I think she went back to living in the jungle in teak houses. She might've stayed at the university where she was teaching. I always lived my simple life, poor in terms of money, but I had been lecturing for the State Department. I had saved most of the money I'd made in India before I discovered you can't use it outside India. When you leave, it's worthless. We went to the black market and bought up a lot of money for Burma, where I rented a whole three-apartment boat in Kashmir, a pleasure barge. I don't spend money like that. It impressed me! A perfect life. A lovely time that doesn't matter to anybody but me. Finessed death.

NOR: We come back to your comment about your work being to live your life.

GILBERT: There's a joke about competitive people who want to be more famous than others that says, "Whoever has the most toys at the end is the winner." I'd like to not have any toys left at all. The unforgivable crime to me, apart from butchering people or something like that, is not to live your life. My life comes before any literary product. I'll be damned if I'm going to trade my life for turning out an art product. I understand that for other people that's what the good life is, writing. But I'm not going to do that. I have a friend who has published fourteen books. He's a good writer. He goes into his study every day, and he writes all day. He has lunch and goes back and writes some more, turns on the TV, watches the evening news. And goes to bed. I'm dying. I've been dying since I was sixteen. When I go before God, and he says, what did you do with that life, I'm not going to tell him I wrote twelve books. I'll tell him what it was like with Pimpaporn, living on a pleasure barge in Kashmir.

Sheila Heti

Interviewed by Ari Braverman
(2013)

Sheila Heti's third book, *How Should a Person Be?*, is about Sheila. The character is a Toronto-based writer grappling with a play she can't seem to finish, stuck in a marriage that stifles her. Enter Margaux, a peroxide-blonde painter who "looked at the same time like a little girl, a sexy woman, and a man." What follows is the story of a friendship between two people who happen to be artists, who happen to be women. Through their conversations and their adventures—things like taking a trip to the ice cream parlor, sharing studio space, traveling to Art Basel in Miami, buying the same yellow dress—Sheila arrives at her own answer to the titular question.

The book is mystifying and exciting in a quiet, internal way. This comes from the piece's main conceit: characters that are named (and modeled) after real-life counterparts. Heti includes transcripts of real conversations and email threads between herself and her real-life best friend, Margaux Williamson. She jettisons the traditional idea of narrative for an episodic structure that mirrors what she has called "the messiness of life." Instead of alienating the reader, these personal fragments make the book accessible. Sheila's experiences are specific, but her thoughts and feelings are familiar. Because she communicates through a pantomime of the personal, Heti forces the reader to contend with questions of love, identity, and authenticity on an intimate, uncomfortable level.

The Heti I'd read about in other articles seemed like all the things a writer should be: self-assured but humble, articulate, and accomplished. In the photos I Googled, it even looked as if she had impeccable taste. My image of her was all I could think about when

I dialed her number. But when she answered, she immediately put me at ease. I could hear birds in the yard outside her Toronto home. She asked me about myself and laughed a lot. I realized, yes, the individual on the end of the line is the originator of books, ideas, and the writer Sheila Heti, but she's also a person. As Heti said in our interview, "No one is an exception." Everyone is a self, and everyone is a character.

NEW ORLEANS REVIEW: What do you think is the difference between memoir and autobiographical fiction?

SHEILA HETI: I think memoir is about one's identity. I'm not so interested in identity. I'm more interested in the self. I feel very palpably that my identity and my self are really different things—and for me the self is the interesting part. That's the part that could be God. It could be all humans. It could be nothingness. It could be anything. Identity is really clear—what it is. I have no questions about what my identity is—I'm a thirty-six-year-old woman living in Toronto. But the self seems very different. It's not something you can catch. It's always shifting and it encompasses more than just one self, more than just *your* self.

NOR: Why did it feel important to you to write a piece like this, with so much of the narrative structure and characterization drawn from your own experience?

HETI: I just think there's something so strange about the idea that a person writes alone. You don't raise yourself, you don't kill the food you eat, you don't educate yourself. Everything we do is bound up in everything other people do. I think about *Crime and Punishment.* We think of that book as something Dostoyevsky did on his own, and it's true, he did—and a very simple story of a writer working alone was my inherited idea of the artist. But over my life, I've seen that it's wrong. Artists get ideas from other people, suggestions from other people, and encouragement. As though Flaubert came up with his ideas by himself and not through conversation with everybody he knew and from being in the world, from reading the newspaper. That's just the way everything works. I wanted the structure of my novel to be honest about that aspect of how art is made—and how this book in fact was made.

NOR: Did you think about future readers as you were writing the book?

HETI: I was never wondering, "Is somebody I don't know going to have a problem with this?" My main audience at the time was Margaux, and I knew what she thought of the book because she would tell me! I remember giving her this huge, 600-page draft to read a couple years into writing it. I was so excited. She took it on vacation with her and I couldn't wait for her to get back. I remember the day I gave it to her. I felt like I was giving her a ring; I felt so lit up and excited for her reaction! And she didn't like it. She was really disappointed. She had all sorts of problems with it. At that point, I felt I had to make the next draft a draft she would like, which is different from making a book some abstract audience would like. I love Margaux. I wrote the book as a gesture of love. And such a book would also not be different from a book that I would love, because we had the same aesthetic goals at the time.

NOR: What were those goals?

HETI: So many things. To make something without using resources in a wasteful way. To try and understand each other's ideas about art and life more completely. For instance, I had this very Platonic view of the world. Margaux didn't feel that way.

NOR: It's interesting to hear you say you have a Platonic idea of the world because the book is so much about destroying that.

HETI: Exactly. When I was writing this book, I was going against my instinct to try and make some Platonic form. I'm more confused now because I've learned about the value of going against your instincts. All my life, I thought the way to live was to follow your instincts, but now probably the most personally transformative project I've worked on came out of going *against* my instincts. The discomfort with writing this book and the discomfort of—at times—our friendship turned out to be very good for our lives and our work. But surely there are times where you go against your instincts and it's not beneficial. It's horrible, it's painful, and it doesn't lead to anything good. How can you tell which one you're doing? I think you can't tell until the experience ends. Margaux doesn't think you can learn lessons from one experience and apply it to other experiences, because every experience is different. But that's all I ever want to do! You just want to know: Is this a good rule to follow? Is this the way to go forward? But it doesn't work that way.

NOR: The form of your book reflects that difficulty. Of course, it has an internal logic and of course there is a narrative, but on the surface it rambles.

HETI: It was a search. Formally, I wasn't trying to write a novel for a very long time. I was just writing. For years, I wasn't thinking, "I'm going to write a great book" or "I'm going to write a bad book." I was trying to understand different things, and I was trying to understand them by writing them down. When I wrote the sex chapters, for example, I wasn't imagining I was going to publish them. I just wrote them. So I had been writing this way for a number of years, and then the first draft took form in one night.

Ticknor, the novel before *How Should a Person Be?*, was formally very tight, and after that I didn't feel the need to prove to myself that I could make something tight. And *Ticknor* had been a reaction against *The Middle Stories*, because after I published that, people kept implying that I was going to write these short fairy tales or whatever forever. I always feel a lot of contempt for what people think about me, and I said, "I'm never going to write like that ever again. This will be the exact opposite. You don't know me!" I think a lot of negative emotion goes into why I make some artistic choices. "You don't know me." That's a really weird motivation for a book!

NOR: Do you feel that motivation now?

HETI: Not so much. But people keep sending me these autobiographical novels to review! And it's not correct—I was never interested in this as a genre or thinking about this genre. I just like good writing. Maybe a certain book happens to be good writing, maybe it doesn't. But the autobiographical genre doesn't interest me in itself. I mean, it doesn't have to be "autobiographical" to talk about life. All novels are basically saying, "This experience is also human," or "This life is no less of a life."

NOR: People talk about how books like this one run the risk of being really self-indulgent and maudlin. How does a writer avoid all that?

HETI: I think it has to do with the writer's motivations. And also, there's something to be said for this: some people are just very good writers. For instance, I'm working on a book right now with some other women, and we're getting in surveys with people's answers to a questionnaire we've sent out. Lena Dunham was one of the people we asked to fill out the survey, and her survey is just so fucking good. It's so smart, it's so funny, it's so interesting, and you just want to read it for a hundred pages. She's just a really good writer. I'm talking about her right now because people had a lot of jealousy, asking, "Why her? Why her? Is it because she lives in New York?" After reading these surveys, I wanted to say to the people who were saying that, "You don't know what your HBO show would be like." Maybe it would be great. But on the other hand, you read her survey and it's like, "No. She's a really fucking talented writer."

You can say that Wayne Gretzky is a really talented hockey player, and the same goes in art. Talent is real—like height is real. I think it comes down to how a person's mind works. Does their mind work in a way that's beneficial to writing literature? Are they stupid in the right ways? Are they smart in the right ways? Are they ignorant in the right ways? Talent is probably just a combination of helpful stupidities and helpful intelligences and helpful dispositions.

NOR: It's interesting to hear you talk about talent as this luck-of-the draw combination of characteristics. It makes me think about authenticity. There's not authentic talent, like there's not some authentic narrative arc. Would you tell me about your idea of authenticity?

HETI: Authenticity doesn't make any sense as something to *strive* for. Because the question is, authentic to what? Authentic to your feelings, your instincts, your moral code? All of these things are constantly in conflict. That's the human condition, negotiating the fact that these things often point in different directions. You can't be authentic, because even if you are, say, authentic to your instincts, you're maybe being inauthentic to your moral code. Is that why Jesus is such an example of goodness—because his morality and his instincts and his feelings and all that stuff all pointed in the same direction? I think that kind of simplicity is what makes him a beautiful character, because that's a fantasy, and that's the fantasy of being a truly good and great and transcendent person. But modern literature really is the story of inner conflict, and it's the conflict, I think, of never achieving authenticity. Because no one lines up that simply.

Andy Warhol is interesting because "Andy Warhol" was a construction, an artistic act. The real man was not what he gave us. I think the culture right now understands that the self can be an artistic act, a creative act, a deliberate act. And maybe it's not immoral because maybe there is no "true self" that's being betrayed. The hippies—they were all about "being real." When was the last time somebody said to you "Be real, man?" Every era is wrong in its own way, but that's kind of fun! Maybe I'm wrong about authenticity, but it's fun to be wrong in the way your era is wrong.

NOR: Why do you think so many people responded to this book?

HETI: When I was writing this book, I was thinking deeply about what was happening in the mainstream of culture. I was thinking about Paris Hilton, I was thinking about reality TV. So for probably the first time in my life I was in sync with what other people were thinking about while I was writing my book, so it makes sense that when the book came out it was in the same place that other people were. Before this book, I was terrified of putting pop culture into my brain. If it wasn't for Margaux, I might never have done that.

Also, I wanted this book to be accessible. I remember I was working at a hair salon and this older woman, a client, said to me, "I've read your books but they went completely over my head." That made me really sad. I didn't want my books to go over this lovely person's head. So I was trying to write a book that you wouldn't have to be a certain kind of person to read. Because no one's an exceptional case. The things that happen to one person happen to other people, more or less. That's just faith in "the human experience." You have friendships, you have something you try and apply yourself to, you have sex, you experience being in a body moving strangely through time.

I wanted the book to feel like it was moving around in your life or that you were moving around inside it. I didn't want it to be a static story on the page that you would visualize in your imagination and afterwards think, "What a great story that was." I wanted it to feel like part of your life. I wanted it to be an encounter rather than a narrative. I had that in my mind from the beginning. I was thinking a lot about the sculptor Richard Serra. He had this line about wanting to take sculpture off the pedestal. He creates these huge site-specific projects—one of the ones I kept thinking about was in Manhattan, called "Tilted Arc." A few office buildings faced each other around a very large courtyard. Serra spent a long time watching the paths people took when crossing from one building to another, until he finally found the one main route that people used. It traced this sort of arc, and he put up a gigantic steel-curving wall so people could no longer walk along that path. People were so mad at it! They pissed on it and they wrote on it. They defaced it. He really hated that they did that, but on the other hand he deserved it. He was interrupting their lives. He was making it hard to walk. That's the kind of novel I was trying to write. Not a sculpture on a pedestal but something else. I wanted to make it hard to walk—hard for someone to walk down the same path they use every lunch hour.

Susan Bernofsky

Interviewed by Clark Allen
(2013)

Susan Bernofsky hails from Louisiana and is an alumna of the New Orleans Center for the Creative Arts. Now living in New York, she is a German-language translator, teaches at the Columbia University School of the Arts, and serves as chair of the translation committee at the PEN American Center.

Room 220 caught up with her to chat about *In Translation: Translators on Their Work and What It Means*, the recent compendium of essays on translation which she edited with Esther Allen. She also discussed her new translation of a grisly nineteenth-century German horror story, Robert Walser, Yoko Tawada, Donald Duck, and the rumor of a novel of her own in the works, said to be set here in New Orleans.

NEW ORLEANS REVIEW: I'd read a number of books of which you had been the translator, but it wasn't until I picked up the third or fourth when I noticed I'd been consistently seeing your name on all of them. The first essay in your book *In Translation* talks about the translator's attempt at invisibility and the ethical decisions that come along with that. I was wondering if you agreed that was a goal, and whether invisibility is a positive or negative thing.

SUSAN BERNOFSKY: I think there are a lot of different sides to this question. On the one hand, as a translator, you are the conduit to the book, and you don't want to distract the reader from the book by your own intervention. People usually notice the translator only if they're bad, but then people who have their eyes on translations will notice good translations—if the prose is particularly elegant, they may note that certain turns of phrase may be the translator's doing. Sometimes you want to be noticed, but not by everyone. Say I translated two different authors and it's not immediately obvious that they're both translated by me, then to me that's good because it means that I've succeeded in creating a distinct voice for each one.

Usually referring to the translator as invisible in the context of discussion is a reference to the traditional under-appreciation of translators and the lack of understanding about what we do. Most people seem to think that the translator's work is something mechanical, like feeding a piece of writing into a machine and having it come out the other end in a different language. It's only when you look at a book with more than one translation side by side with others that you are confronted with the fact that the same book translated by two different people can really be two quite different books.

NOR: Is there a way to simply put your role? Something it's comparable to, like an actor interpreting a script?

BERNOFSKY: I think that's a good metaphor for it—an actor interpreting a script or a musician with a score. The notes are written, but they can be played so many different ways. There really is no such thing as a neutral translation. Every translation is an intervention and an interpretation to some extent of the original. There really is no way for translators to keep themselves out of the process, so the goal is to be in the process in a way that's productive and leads to the creation of a better work in English. You don't want random intervention, but some intervention is inevitable. You've got to be really aware of what you are doing and what is showing up in the text as you work.

NOR: Some time ago, I read your article on the translations of Donald Duck comics in Germany and some of the fairly drastic changes made possible by subtleties in translation. Have there ever been moments like that where you wanted to change something in a way where you thought you may have been stretching your bounds?

BERNOFSKY: Definitely. I did a translation of Hesse's *Siddhartha*. There is a scene in which Siddhartha despairs and wants to drown himself where I worked in an Ophelia reference. It's a really subtle thing, though, so if you don't know it, it isn't going to stick out at you.

In my new Kafka, which is coming out in January [*The Metamorphosis*, Norton], I built in some intertextualities with Arthur Miller's *Death of a Salesman* because I think that is a work which has very important resonance with the Kafka story in the English-speaking tradition. I wanted this work that I was reshaping to interact with the Arthur Miller work. For example, I used the word "drummer" to describe Gregor Samsa's profession, which is the same profession as Willy Loman's profession—they're both travelling salesmen. The word "drummer," which means travelling salesman, was quite commonly used even just a few years ago but has now been pretty much forgotten.

NOR: In regard to labor-intensive translation work, I'm curious about your translation of Yoko Tawada's book—

BERNOFSKY: Oh, I love her work so much! She has a new novel about polar bears that I want to translate. Really! Baby polar bears! I hope I get to do it. It was inspired by the story of Knut, the baby polar bear who was everyone's darling at the zoo in Berlin and then died tragically young. She wrote the story of his life and his mother's life and his grandmother's life, in which his grandmother is a novelist living in the Soviet Union where, as a polar bear, she's an ethnic minority. It was written in Japanese, and then she translated it to German herself. Now the question is: Which version should be translated into English, the Japanese version or the German?

But I digress. You were going to ask something.

NOR: I was going to ask that you elaborate on the work you've done with her books. I saw that you'd written an essay on her writing, but I've only seen it in German, which I can't read. I wanted to know what you might have to say about her, as she is kind of an anomaly—your thoughts on translating a multi-lingual author and any specific differences or difficulties that come with it.

BERNOFSKY: One tricky part is to avoid making the language too fancy in English. Tawada uses a very specific German style, and she actively plays on the fact that German is not her first language. She investigates language, and she uses words often in a slightly different way than a native speaker might, but not wrong. It's a very specific voice, and it's very difficult to capture it in translation. I think hers is a case where the translations feel a little bit more comfortable and conversational in English than her voice does in German. The interesting feeling of her voice in German is so amazing, though, like if you put a pidgin slant on English. Not that she's writing pidgin, but it's difficult to translate directly without making it sound like pidgin, so I don't do it that way. Usually, the drafts come out sounding much more literary and then I have to kind of reel it back in and figure out more straightforward vocabulary words, etc.

NOR: How do you deal with specific explanations of cultural ideas or traditions that may not exist in the language you're translating to? Not being a native New Orleanian, I sometimes find myself explaining different facets of living here to friends living back West as if it were another country. I can only imagine that is more complicated when the reader is expected to be totally foreign to the original author.

BERNOFSKY: I'm a big fan of the "stealth gloss," which means you build a tiny little explanation into the translation and don't have to use a footnote. I try to avoid footnotes—if at all possible, I'll put a tiny little tweak into the text that makes it clear what things are. I've actually got an example right here from a book I translated, *The Black Spider* by Jeremias Gotthelf, which just came out from *The New York Review of Books*. It's a horror story, and in this scene people are preparing for a baptismal party prior to the horror. This is Switzerland in the nineteenth century, and the Godmother is arriving, who everyone has been waiting for. Here's the sentence:

> She came covered in perspiration, and laden with gifts like the *neujahr kleines kind*, that child of Burmese legend sent to bring treats to every boy and girl on New Year's Day. In one hand she gripped the black strings of a large bag with a decorative pattern of flowers, containing a nice big *kipferl* wrapped in a fine white cloth, a gift for the new mother.

A "*kipferl*" had been described a couple of pages before as a kind of local bread, but the explanation of the bread was in the original. When "*neujahr kleines kind*" is used, which literally means "New Year's little child," I just inserted that same sort of explanation and wrote in "that child of Burmese legend sent to bring treats to every boy and girl on New Year's Day." I don't think it sticks out too much, but this is an old text describing even older customs, so I try to smuggle in explanations for the readers whenever possible.

I don't really footnote, but I'll put something in a translator's note if the former isn't an option.

NOR: I've read an older translation of that same story from 1975 in a small compendium called *Three Eerie Tales From 19th Century Germany*. It was a really great story but lousy with footnotes. I can't remember the translator or much other information about it now, but since we're talking about it, I'm wondering if you'd heard of it or read it.

BERNOFSKY: I had read an older translation of the story, but I don't think the one you're speaking of. I believe there are two earlier translations out there, and the one I read I remember being sort of stiff and formal. It's a fairy tale, a folk legend, so I didn't want it to be stiff or formal. I absolutely didn't look at the other when I worked on it because when you're doing a retranslation you need to be finding a voice for yourself. Thinking about other people's voices with respect to the text is just a distraction. The first time I did a retranslation was with *Siddhartha*, and I didn't look at any others until I had finished revising my version. Then, when I was struggling with those last few really messy spots, I checked to see if any of the previous translators had better solutions for them. Invariably, the previous translators had also found those spots difficult.

NOR: I recall reading in Haruki Murakami's essay on translating *The Great Gatsby* into Japanese that translations require an updating on a semi-regular basis. I was curious to hear your thoughts on that.

BERNOFSKY: I disagree. I feel that there are some translations that are so beautiful and perfect that they don't need to be touched, ever. Here's a fun fact: you know how *Siddhartha*, in this country, is typically a book that teenagers read because it's all about finding your place and so on? In Germany, teenagers do not read this book because it feels to them, stylistically, way too antiquated. It doesn't appeal to them there, whereas in translation it appeals to English-speaking youth to this day. In a way, the translation, being more modern, has made it possible for the book to still be read by that age group.

NOR: Could you explain a bit about your role with PEN?

BERNOFSKY: My official role is that I am the chair of the translation committee. There is more than one PEN, but this is the largest branch—the PEN American Center, which is based in New York. There's also one in California and another in the Midwest, which I think is semi-active. The PEN Translation Committee is basically all volunteer labor, people who are members and translators who do advocacy work, trying to make people more aware of literary works in translation. We award prizes for literary translation. There's a section on the PEN.org website with information for translators. We have a model contract. We're right now working on an FAQ to go along with the model contract on the website, as well. We put on panels and various conferences, and there is also something called the PEN Translation Fund, which was made possible by a very generous donation by one literary translator, Michael Henry Heim, who passed away a year ago. It's been around for eleven years now. He had received a large inheritance that he didn't need, and so he donated it to create a fund for translators that could be set up in such a way that you don't need to be well-published or particularly established to get a grant. New people who may have never translated a book before but have an interesting project could have just as much chance of getting one. There are about ten or eleven of them given out each year, at an average of about 3,000 dollars. It's a really wonderful way to support new translators who are trying to find publishers for their projects. We've been able to place quite a few new works with publishers this way.

NOR: I've heard rumors that you'd been working on fiction of your own, possibly a novel set in New Orleans. Is there any truth to this?

BERNOFSKY: I do have a novel in progress, and it is partially set in New Orleans and partially in Poland, but right now it's kind of on the back burner because I'm also working on a biography of Robert Walser. I've been between these books for a few years, back and forth, kind of working on one, kind of working on the other, also translating books and teaching, and nothing was getting done that way. I've decided to focus on the biography because it's a more finite project, so the novel isn't really actively in progress right now, but I hope it will be in a couple of years.

Francine Prose

Interviewed by Ari Braverman
(2014)

I was late telephoning Francine Prose. Thrilled by (and not a little nervous about) our impending conversation, I forgot that New York operates one full hour ahead of New Orleans. Thus, I returned home from the store to a missed call from a 212 area code. *Francine Prose had called—and left a message!* I was mortified as I dialed her number. But, even after a crazy spring of interviews and reviews, she sounded genuinely glad to hear from me. As we talked about her new book, *Lovers at the Chameleon Club, Paris 1932,* I was struck time and again by the range of her grace and empathy, characteristics that inform every facet of her work.

The book, inspired by a real-life photograph of Violette Morris—an accomplished French athlete turned Nazi collaborator—is a multilayered portrait of Paris before and during the Occupation. Each of the book's many narrators has a different perspective on what happened to Lou Villars (Prose's fictional Morris), how and why she becomes the brutal figure she does. Ultimately, *Lovers at the Chameleon Club* is an excursion through the middle territory between history and remembrance, good and evil, love and betrayal, and a reminder of the importance of art in history's dangerous moments.

NEW ORLEANS REVIEW: Tell me about your initial reaction to the photograph that started it all, "Lesbian Couple at Le Monocle, 1932" by Brassaï.

FRANCINE PROSE: I'm a huge fan of Brassaï's and I know his work—I have about five of his broadside books, so I've known the photograph for a long time. It's very beautiful. But it was only when I found out in the wall text at a museum show that the woman in the tuxedo had worked for the Gestapo that I became even more interested, because I knew nothing about the people in the photograph. When I did some research, I found out she had led this very complicated life. She had, in fact, been a spy and a professional athlete, and she was assassinated by the French resistance. That's really where the book started.

That club, which I called the Chameleon Club, really existed. It was called Le Monocle, and there are all these Brassaï photos of it. Recently, I was reading a biography about Jane Bowles, and she went there in the 1950s. It was still around! That was amazing to me.

NOR: What was it about Violette Morris—someone who's not necessarily a huge historical figure but who does exist in history—that drew you to her?

PROSE: Partly it was just her story, but there's also something about the photograph, something about her, that gives off the aura of something disturbing. I can't describe it any more than that. And the longer you look at it, the more her lover looks to be in some sort of drug haze. At first, she just seems to be a pretty girl, but if you look a little closer, there's more than that going on. There's a lot about the photo that not only draws you in, but also sets you on edge. And I think it's meant to.

NOR: There's something grotesque about it.

PROSE: I mean, Morris's ring, her fashion choices. She's not just your normal cross-dresser. There's something else going on there.

NOR: Is this the first piece you've written that's relied so heavily on looking at photographs?

PROSE: I've written a lot about photography. I've written a lot of catalogue essays for photography books. I wrote a long piece about Diane Arbus. I'm very interested in photography. I look at it all the time and I write about it quite a lot, but typically nonfiction. The thing about photography, everybody knows, is that it just captures a moment. With writing, you need to expand that moment to do anything with it.

I looked at the Brassaï books over and over and over, but I used films, too. There are a lot of film clips on YouTube from that time that you can see that really helped. Images are like portals. They help you imagine your way back into that time. Little kids, when they look at a picture, imagine they can get inside it—at least I can remember imagining that. In a way, writing provides some of that, too. You look at the picture and suddenly you're in the picture. That's sort of what this process was like.

NOR: There are many different narrators in this piece, so the story doesn't progress along a typical narrative track. Did you find that writing about a photograph lent itself to writing the book as a constellation of perspectives, as opposed to a linear structure?

PROSE: It wasn't planned. When I realized the book wasn't going to be nonfiction, I had to find another way to do it. I started with what's at the beginning of the novel, the photographer writing home to his parents in Hungary—Brassaï wrote many letters that were like the ones in my novel. I realized that for obvious reasons he couldn't tell the whole story, that in fact there was no one who could tell the whole story, because each person only knew a part of it. The minute that happened I realized I needed to use a number of different narrators. The question, then, had to do with how I was going to do their voices. Again, it wasn't planned, but it wound up that except for Yvonne the nightclub owner, all the narratives come from written documents of a certain kind. There's the Henry Miller character, the two women who are writing their opposing memoirs. There are a lot of books that have multiple narrators, but I couldn't think of another novel in which the narrators are all writing something, so I was kind of on my own.

Writing that way made the process a great deal easier. The "biographer" of Lou, for example, isn't the greatest writer in the world. She has these lapses into writing quite badly. So far, I've been really fortunate—the novel has gotten a lot of really wonderful, intelligent reviews. But the few that have been not so intelligent don't seem to notice that I wrote those sections that way on purpose. It's not that I didn't know that Natalie, Lou's biographer in the novel, was given to hyperbole and purple writing. I meant to do that! I meant it to be a bogus biography written by a neurotic who can't seem to stop talking about herself.

NOR: Writing memoir-as-history seems to be very popular right now. What do you think about that? Your book trades on some of those tropes but is very clearly a work of fiction.

PROSE: Many of those books are works of fiction and don't declare themselves works of fiction. There have always been books like that. The book I drew on a lot was this awful French "biography" of Violette Morris that was written, I think, in the 1970s. The biographer didn't bother telling you what was true and what was invented. I was thinking about all the biographies that tell you what the character was thinking when the biographer could have had no way of knowing. But more than that, there's so much bad writing in these books. I was very conscious of that, too. I didn't want to do too much of it because it's off-putting, but I wanted it to be clear that I was introducing an element of parody.

NOR: Your characters make a lot of social commentary, particularly about Paris' climate of economic depression and fear of immigration. Was that an intentional correlation to our current cultural climate?

PROSE: Yes. While researching the book, I read all these books about Paris between the wars. I found this paragraph listing all these problems: fear of immigration, heavy taxation, fear that you can't raise your kids to lead a better life than you did, economic problems, and so on. I read it to my friend over the phone and she asked, "Is that about the present moment?" I said, "No. Actually, it's about the 1930s in Paris." Which is very scary to me, because similar things could have been written about Germany in the 1920s and 1930s. I thought a lot about the rise of fascism, what leads people to be vulnerable to totalitarianism. It's a novel, not a historical book, but all those things were in my mind as I was writing. There's no moment in history that's not a dangerous moment.

NOR: As I was reading the book, I had a strange feeling that was like, "God, I hope this novel isn't prophetic!" And then I had to dial myself back because this is a book about things that have already happened!

PROSE: I had the same feeling myself. Absolutely.

NOR: How did you deal with writing about queer identities in a text that's contemporary but also set in the 1930s?

PROSE: The one thing I really don't want to be misunderstood—although there have been some slight indications that it's not clear enough—is that Lou's cross-dressing and gender identity are not causative factors in her becoming a fascist. She was denied the ability to be the person she actually wanted to be. The only things she wants, which are to be loved and to be an athlete, are taken away from her. Then she goes someplace where, after being treated horribly, she's treated like a star. Regardless of one's sexual orientation, that's very seductive. Resentment makes people vulnerable to totalitarianism. The Germans, for example, were told they had been stabbed in the back.

NOR: Has there been any criticism of making the "villain" of the book a homosexual person?

PROSE: No, but I'm sort of nervous about it. My German editor said, oddly, that he wasn't concerned about the reaction of the German readership to the book but that he was concerned about the reaction of the gay community in Germany to the book. I said, "Really?!" The thing is, as we all know, sexual preference and one's moral nature are not connected. Within the gay community, the straight community, this community, that community, the range of saintly to demonic is the same. Just because you're one way or another doesn't give you a leg up on morality, one way or the other.

Also, the book has been described as talking about a period of decadence, but I don't myself particularly see cross-dressing as decadent. I was confused about what that means. I just see Lou as a figure who was born at the wrong time.

NOR: Speaking of the timeframe, I wanted to know about your decision to end the book in the 2000s, particularly with a video still of that hand from *Carrie*.

PROSE: People like Lou or like Hitler—you think they're safely under the ground and then they just pop up again. We can't rid ourselves of that. Somehow it seems to be part of the species. Just when you think it's over, it turns out not to be over. I wanted to bring it into the present because, unfortunately, it exists in the present. Carrie, if you look at her story, is just a normal girl—except that she has some telekinetic powers—who's tormented until she becomes a mass murderer. It's a story that just keeps happening.

Harold Jaffe

Interviewed by Robin Andreasen
(2014)

Known for his "docufictions" that push the boundaries between documentary and fiction, Harold Jaffe has written twenty-seven books, and his works have been translated into fifteen languages. Jaffe is editor of *Fiction International*, a journal of innovative literature and social activism.

NEW ORLEANS REVIEW: Your work in crisis art or docufiction, including incisive discussions of serial killers, prisoners, artists (the piece on Van Gogh in *Anti-Twitter* still haunts me), suggests that it is primarily through dialogue and engagement with the most abject, the spectral in William Spanos' terms, that the right questions can be asked of power dynamics and moral obligation. The stakes are high in every piece you write. Rather than an abject subject, you take on the most "auratic" of subjects, Shakespeare. Is this book a sort of interrogation of the free-floating assumptions of "canonicity" and race embodied in a work like *Othello Blues* spanning 500 years?

HAROLD JAFFE: From serial killers to Shakespeare seems a leap, but *15 Serial Killers* includes texts both on the remarkable-in-his-way Dr. Kevorkian and the detestable "tragic" villain Dr. Kissinger, who can also double as a fool, which may lessen the gap.

Academic desocialized reductions of Iago, such as the oft-repeated "motiveless malignity" summary of his characterization, are predictable. It was my combined interest in the vulnerable Moorish general and the consummate hater Iago which fueled me. That I was in the process of reconstituting Shakespeare meant little. "Icons" are always more elastic than we think; that they are addressed and thereby modified, not blindly venerated, is as it should be.

I think of the elderly French self-described Dadaist who twice urinated in a replica of Duchamp's famous 1917 urinal in exhibitions in Nîmes and Paris. The old pisser insisted that Duchamp would have been pleased at the intervention, and I think he is right.

To respond to your question precisely, yes, taking on "canonicity" was a factor, but my dual interest in Iago's complex hate and the long, unjust punishment of Africans was the primary motive.

NOR: Is it possible for a member of an educated elite to adequately speak to the woes and ideals of a racial and economic underclass without appropriating, thus commercializing through reification, the very racial struggles he/she seeks to diagnose and declaim?

JAFFE: No and yes. For example, Brecht, Neruda, and despite his ambivalence over Algeria, Camus, were able to "speak" to the underclass, whereas Whitman (not among the educated elite, as such), who envisioned his *Leaves of Grass* as another bible, accessible even to the semi-literate, mostly failed.

The underclass will read a book to the best of their capacities, as they consult the Koran, the Bible, or Buddhist sutras; but they must be convinced that the book will help them navigate a problematic world. Now, with books obsolescent, at least in the "First World," it is a moot point.

NOR: In your dystopian future, America is alien yet all too familiar as you ask us to consider our cultural logic. Why this radical change in setting? Why is it important that you set the book in the future? Is this simply to give you flexibility as a storyteller through fabulation, to use Robert Scholes' term?

JAFFE: Odd happenstance. The original volume of *Othello Blues* was published in 1996 in a limited edition. Then, the narrative details were much closer to my declared "twenty minutes into the future." Revising the novel nearly twenty years later presented problems; technology had intervened crucially. And several of the other projected details had one way or another been realized. So I was faced with an anomalous narrative, part futurist, part present, part outmoded (if my virtual exclusion of technology counts as outmoded). After thinking about it and making numerous small changes, I decided that the hybrid quality which combines past, present, and near future (without technology) might have its own peculiar purchase, and I decided to go ahead rather than try to homogenize the text as technically closer to the near future.

Dealing with technology means getting it right, which means up to the nanosecond precision. Moreover, techno-futurism forces writing into predetermined tropes and rhythms. I didn't want that. And setting the novel in the future naturally gave me more flexibility.

NOR: *Othello Blues* stays grounded in African-American experience through the experience of the blues. I am reminded of Baldwin's seminal work "Sonny's Blues." How would you describe the way in which the blues speaks to the American experience in a counter-cultural fashion?

JAFFE: There was a period in the early to mid-1960s, featuring Stokely Carmichael and the Black Power movement, where blues music was reviled as a passive acceptance of victimization. Many other humans, black and non-black, maintained that blues was more complex than that, and I agree. Not in "Sonny's Blues" but in *The Fire Next Time,* Baldwin compares black vernacular to coded communication, such as black prison inmates exchanging messages by tapping at their cell walls, coded so that it could not be readily penetrated by the "Man."

Blues is coded. Of course it could be co-opted, as, say, breakdancing has been co-opted, but as I hear it, Delta and later Chicago blues are derived from a history of black African grief and loving which cannot be duplicated, not even by Iago whose "black" vernacular is more extreme than any black characterization in the novel.

Regarding Iago, it was only after I ruminated about how I'd inscribed him that I realized that deplorable as he was, in a dialectical sense he was close to admirable, in perhaps the way that I meant Charles Manson, in *15 Serial Killers* and *Jesus Coyote,* to be both deplorable and close to admirable.

As I often have cause to remark, this is not a triage system: one can despise a characterization like Iago or Manson for inflicting cruelty on the innocent without addressing the entire complexity of the man. The "admirable" part of Manson is his funky defiance, his insistence on staying alive while thrusting his raunchy ass into the face of institutional law and what is miscalled justice. I think too that his chaotic-seeming discourse about the out-of-joint-world has a point, for those who attend to it without patronization.

With Iago, I wanted to suggest his deeper disgust with a world festering in its own corruption. That he addresses his deep disgust by displacing it, that is, by mimicking official culture's victimization of the innocent, is, to me, beside the point.

NOR: Do you think that your fiction provides the sort of "counter-memory" Toni Morrison calls for—as the Dickinsonian dictum runs, tell the truth but tell it slant? Often, your work asks us to revisit key cultural moments and figures in order to find what the official record cannot or will not say, giving your reader the dread of the abomination, the rough contours of some forgotten theater of cruelty. In *Othello Blues*, we see familiar names, but they are constantly displaced, much like your vision of Iago. The displacement is the chief virtue of liars, who break our ties to the known and give us false harbor. In Morrison's sense, we must engage in counter-memory to reclaim a lost and spectral history. Is such a reclamation possible through the art of fiction?

JAFFE: Institutional memory lies by definition. Street rebellions by the poor are labeled riots. And longer-term rebellions, such as mounted by the Black Panthers, the Young Lords, the American Indian Movement, and the 1968 student uprisings have been blithely transformed into the violent play aspect of Woodstock Nation—our counter-cultural circus.

When official culture finally conveys a portion of truth about social activism, as in the 2014 French-American film (*The Activist*) about the 1973 Wounded Knee uprising, it comes 40 years too late, when contemporary tragedy has become a kind of archeology. Movie viewers are prompted to feel virtuous as they watch the U.S. government violently abort the Native American uprising, but 40 years later the Pine Ridge reservation is still foundering in South Dakota, and the brave Oglala Sioux Leonard Peltier is still in prison for life despite the recantation of witnesses.

To what extent fiction or even nonfictional discourse can "reclaim" the institutionally disappeared history is a grievous question. The short answer is it cannot. Even if planet earth were not seemingly in its death throes, writing itself would be useless without collective social action.

It is true that Sartre's influence was crucial in France's decolonization of Algeria, but that was in 1961 when thinking and writing, especially in France, were sometimes efficacious. In any case, France had decolonized Morocco and Tunisia and was about ready to give up on Algeria.

I've often cited Antonio Gramsci's self-appraisal—that he was a "pessimist of the intellect, but an optimist of the will." Now it is nearly impossible to will yourself to optimism. As best I can, I try to write in the Buddhist sense of "right vocation," without any expectations.

In the late 1950s, Frantz Fanon, the Martinican psychiatrist, writer and social activist, was making a speech in French-controlled northwest Africa about the necessity for a pan-African movement when he broke down and wept. A sympathetic listener remarked that after hearing a series of *proforma* platitudes from African heads of state to suddenly be confronted with this brilliant analyst who dared to show his heart in such an inhospitable setting was shocking. I sometimes feel that that is all we have left—to dare to weep in anguish no matter what the setting.

Anguish need not mean fear. John Berger writes of the Palestinians' "despair without fear." Their Semitic cousins, the Jews who fought back in the Warsaw Uprising, seemed also to possess despair without fear. Nonetheless, fear is eminently justified, especially in these dark days.

NOR: Your connection of Iago the puppet master and Manson, whose cult status and personal charisma built his distorted "family," is intriguing. Iago as military Machiavellian and Manson as cult guru seem like opposed types in some ways. Shakespeare's Iago refuses his foes even an explanation, whereas Manson gave nothing but grandiose justification. To ask the broad question that every age wrestles with in futility, what do you see as the nature of evil in our increasingly complex, relativistic, global system?

JAFFE: My tendency, with Rousseau, is to believe that "evil" is generated and enforced by culture. We are finite and dependent on official culture to supply our basic needs. Most university students these days accrue large debts so they are scarcely in position to contest the culture, to think and feel broadly, to move laterally, as they should while in college. The more time spent learning, the more money they owe. And what they learn is often limited to algorithmic templates, which run counter to intuition, dissent, necessary disruption.

Most humans are similarly enchained; it is much easier for them to be complicit than to rebel with the likelihood of losing what relative civilities they possess.

NOR: As I write this, I spent the day listening to grim news of the Israeli/Palestinian conflict, culminating with footage of a university reduced to rubble. In what ways besides art and our work as teachers do you believe dissent and resistance are alive and well, our cultural "funky defiance" (the Duchamp urination story is priceless, by the way)? How are we empowered to resist the excesses of power in the twenty-first century?

JAFFE: That holocausted European Jewry has devolved into Israel is one of those fateful ironies that pains the heart. That Israel has "verminized" their Semitic cousins in ways that recall their own denigration by the Third Reich is both inexplicable and, given the circumstances, not entirely unexpected.

The Dutch were not genocided, but an Afrikaans in a black culture is not at all like an Amsterdammer. Notice, though, how even "liberal" Western Europe is moving toward despotism, which they attribute to impoverished, immigrating black and brown-skinned Muslims whom they have demonized.

When I speak of official culture, I mean to include the vast problems of over-population, rapidly diminishing resources, and omnivorous capitalism, with its republican guard of corrupt government, media, and maniacal technology.

John Kenneth Galbraith, the progressive Canadian economist who served under several Democratic presidents, was asked what it would take for Americans to finally recognize their servitude and act autonomously on their own behalf. His provisional response was that a concatenation of three large-scale human tragedies might prod humans into waking up and directly addressing their institutional slave-keepers. But Galbraith's response came long before electronic media virused the globe.

Consider: Global warming proceeding more rapidly than scientists could imagine; the endless-seeming tragedy of Fukushima murdering people and animals and poisoning the Pacific Ocean; and devastating wars with the ongoing threat of nuclear weapons all over the world. Still, electronic media informs us that all is as it should be, even as carnivals of frenzied "entertainment" metastasize to confirm the institutional lie.

Edward Snowden is indispensable, and he seems to have the courage of a martyr, but because of his privileged proximity to top-secret data, his is a special instance.

What are the rest of us to do? Locate the seams in the culture, penetrate them purposefully, subvert collectively. Where that is not possible, screw up the courage to weep.

Yuri Herrera

Interviewed by Elizabeth Sulis Kim
(2018)

Yuri Herrera is a Mexican author, political scientist, and professor of Spanish and Portuguese at Tulane University in New Orleans. He has written several short novels, three of which have been translated into English by Lisa Dillman: *Transmigration of Bodies (Las transmigración de los Cuerpos)*, *Signs Preceding the End of the World (Señales que precederán al fin del mundo)*, and *Kingdom Cons (Trabajos del Reino)*. His debut novel, *Kingdom Cons*, won the 2003 Premio Binacional de Novela/Border of Words.

NEW ORLEANS REVIEW: What kind of things did you write about as a child?

YURI HERRERA: Mostly horror tales, I don't know why. I remember one about a giant bird that would go around the city picking up people as if they were worms.

NOR: What made you want to study politics?

HERRERA: I didn't want to study literature. I had this prejudice that if you wanted to do literature, that was incompatible with literary criticism. Now I know that is not always true: you will write if you want to write; it doesn't matter what else you do in life. And I am glad I studied political science, which helped me to develop a critical gaze on power and how it reflects on the bodies of individuals.

NOR: Do you think studying politics gave you something to say?

HERRERA: Yes, I studied political science at UNAM [National Autonomous University of Mexico] when a lot of changes were happening in the world: the fall of the Berlin Wall, fraud in the Mexican elections when for the first time in decades the PRI lost, the defeat of the Sandinista revolution after enduring almost a decade of terror sponsored by the Reagan administration. The political science department was a great place to discuss what was going on in the world. Beyond that, UNAM is one of the most fascinating universities. It is truly diverse, and the political debates never stop. My period there helped me to become conscious of the political implications of every word you choose to include in your text.

NOR: While your language is accessible, you have created a patois of your own, employing in your work invented or recontextualized words such as "*jarchar*," translated into English as "to verse."

HERRERA: I like to build the text with words that at first look like strange objects that seem out of place because in that way both the "strange" word and the environment where it is placed are transformed. In the case of "*jarcha*," it is a medieval word that names the part of certain poems that were written in Arabic characters but was already resembling something like what would be the Spanish language; it was the "exit" of this kind of poem, so I used it as a sort of synonym for exit, exiting, underscoring that this kind of moving from one place to the other is not just a displacement but is a whole transformation, just like what happens to the characters in the book.

NOR: What was it like living in El Paso, Texas, when you were working on your master's degree? To what extent were stories about border crossing and drug trafficking unavoidable subjects in a border town?

HERRERA: My time living on the Ciudad-Juárez-El Paso border was probably the most intellectually intense in my life. The border is a laboratory for new linguistic forms, political practices, identities. It is a place, or a sum of places, that is challenging all the time. And of course, the different kinds of violence that you see there (all interacting and feeding one another: the institutional violence, the organized crime violence) are part of "normal" life, even if you decide not to look directly at it.

NOR: You are known for deliberately abstaining from using certain words. What value is there to be found in silence?

HERRERA: Silence allows readers to make the text their own. Silences in texts are what make them ergonomical: it is how you bring into play the reader's expectations and obsessions.

NOR: Can you provide an example from your work that illustrates how "silence allows readers to make the text their own"?

HERRERA: I try to not use words that are heavily codified; for instance, in *Kingdom Cons* you will not find the words "border" or "trafficking" because the way these words are used in the mainstream media turns them into simplifications. In the same way, I prefer not to use very often the actual names of places, so that the place happening in the mind of the reader is not limited by the preexisting clichés about such places.

NOR: Do you think it's harder to retain silence in a culture that increasingly demands explicit answers and loudness?

HERRERA: Yes, silence has become hard to find, but precisely because of that it has become even more important in art. It avoids the superficiality of pre-packaged discourses and invites introspection. Silence is the opposite of selfies and short-lived breaking news.

NOR: What kind of research do you do before writing your books?

HERRERA: It depends on the project, but beyond the specific archival needs that a project might demand, what I always do is a sort of linguistic research, which means to reflect on the words I am planning to use or not use in the text, to consider their connotations. This kind of research is done not by reading dictionaries but by writing small drafts of scenes or images that will show you how these words work.

NOR: Can you explain what you mean by "I like to say that style isn't surface; style is a form of knowledge"?

HERRERA: I mean that with every decision you make, you are stating something about the world, something that you know about emotions, sensations, time. It is not as if "reality" is something with certain words attached to it and the only job of the writer is to put them on paper. On the contrary, writing is about underscoring certain aspects of the world that appear to be new.

NOR: *Signs Preceding the End of the World* brings to mind recent discussions of Trump's wall, though the book was published before his presidency. What, if anything, has changed for Mexicans living in the U.S. since the election?

HERRERA: Xenophobia has a long history in the United States, and Mexican workers have suffered many atrocities throughout the decades. What has changed recently is the way in which racists and xenophobes feel that their actions are legitimate. The insults uttered by Trump have made hate acceptable, and this has been taken as the cue to be intolerant or violent by agents of certain institutions and by vigilantes that justify terrorizing migrants by calling themselves patriots.

NOR: You portray the crossing of borders as somewhat otherworldly. Is this intentional?

HERRERA: I don't know if that's the word I would choose; what I can say is that for many people the crossing of a border and the starting of a new life after crossing it implies facing challenges that were inconceivable before.

NOR: How does it feel to return to Mexico now?

HERRERA: I go back very often, sometimes just for a few days, but that allows me to not lose touch with friends, colleagues, and with the particularities of our language. It is always a combination of joy and rage, joy for coming back home and rage for the unspeakable things that criminals (and not only the ones publicly acknowledged as such, but also the ones in the financial and political spheres) have done to the country.

NOR: And what are your thoughts on New Orleans?

HERRERA: It is a terrible place where extraordinary things happen on a daily basis. New Orleans is a portent of ideas and affection, so much more because it happens amid a constant tragedy that outsiders decide to simplify or not to see. I would love to write about the city one day, but even after several years here, I still feel I am just scratching the surface. I am willing to wait until I understand more before I try to do it.

Viet Thanh Nguyen

Interviewed by Elizabeth Sulis Kim
(2018)

Viet Thanh Nguyen, the Vietnamese-American author and Professor of English and American Studies and Ethnicity at the University of Southern California, was a recipient of a MacArthur "Genius" Grant in 2017. His works include *The Sympathizer*, which was awarded the Pulitzer Prize for fiction in 2016; the short-story collection *The Refugees*; and *Nothing Ever Dies: Vietnam and the Memory of War*. His most recent book is *The Displaced: Refugee Writers on Refugee Lives*. This interview was conducted in English by phone on April 20, 2018.

NEW ORLEANS REVIEW: Why did you start writing?

VIET THANH NGUYEN: As a child, I think I just wanted to be a writer because I derived pleasure from it; it was fun. My first memory of it was writing an illustrated book when I was eight years old. In college I started paying attention to the art of writing and thinking about writing as something that was important. I wanted to tell stories about what it meant to be Vietnamese—and Vietnamese-American—that dealt with the Vietnam War. And at that time in college, in the late 1980s, early 1990s, there weren't that many stories written by people like me about those kind of issues—so I felt I was becoming a part of traditions—of minority writing and colonial writing—that dealt with similar issues. So those are the two things that have driven me I think: one, this conviction that writing can be important for social and political reasons, and the other, that writing can be important for artistic reasons and for the pleasure that a writer can derive from the act of writing itself.

NOR: So do you see writing as a form of activism?

NGUYEN: Writing can be a form of activism—it certainly seems to me that my writing is. But most American writers probably do not think of their writing as a kind of activism. And it shouldn't have to be—I don't think we can impose that on writers—but it can be. I think for many writers, the ones I admire—it is. And it depends on the writing I engage in—the op-ed or nonfiction, the academic work. But when it comes to fiction, which is what most people talk about, I do think the simple act of writing about people or events or cultures that are not often talked about constitutes already a basic kind of activism, one that can be elevated to something much more sophisticated.

NOR: A common theme in your fiction is duality. To what extent are *The Refugees* and *The Sympathizer* autobiographical?

NGUYEN: I think that my writing is mostly not autobiographical. I've written only one explicitly autobiographical short story, "War Years" in *The Refugees*. I think that's because I was so uncomfortable with talking about myself; that's something I've become more comfortable with recently, so you'll see more of my autobiography in op-eds or in my nonfiction book, *Nothing Ever Dies*. For the most part, the way that the personal part of me is expressed in fiction is more through thematic issues. The narrator of *The Sympathizer*, for example, is not me, for the most part, but his worldview is mine, just greatly exaggerated. We know from the very beginning that he's "a man of two faces and a man of two minds," and that's pretty much me. I think ever since I became conscious of myself as someone who's not just an American but also someone who's Vietnamese—and who's seen that way by other people—I was aware that I had a sort of duality. I was a little bit uncomfortable around generic Americans, and I was a little bit uncomfortable around Vietnamese people. And that sense of duality I think is universal—I think many of us have felt at some time out of place. The difference I think is that when you are a minority, however you choose to define that, the sense of duality is perpetual. You usually feel that way, and when you don't feel that way, you feel at home; it feels incredible. But if you're part of a majority and you usually feel at home, you only occasionally feel that sense of duality.

NOR: Has your work in any way been influenced by Vietnamese art, literature, or culture in general?

NGUYEN: I grew up as an American reading English literature—basically Anglophone, American and European literature in translation. I actually had almost no exposure to Vietnamese literature. I had to actively seek it out in college. And really the kind of Vietnamese culture that I was exposed to growing up was music, for example. And so I think it was actually more the music and poetry that was popular in the Vietnamese community—because poetry was actually important there—that influenced me most. And you know, the sentiments were more romantic, melancholic; these are the emotions I associate with Vietnamese refugee culture, as expressed in poetry and music. The literature itself, which I managed to get to in college, was what was available in translation, and it was mostly about the war. So it wasn't that influential on me. My major influences still remain the European, American and post-colonial traditions, but what I've gotten out of Vietnamese literature is the emphasis on centering experiences—the memory, the history and the suffering of Vietnamese people—which is mostly what Vietnamese literature that I've read is about.

NOR: So exposing yourself to Vietnamese literature was a personal choice?

NGUYEN: It had to be a choice. The literature I was most exposed to that was Vietnamese was the Vietnamese version of the Bible. I'm not a devout Catholic, but my parents are, and they raised me that way. Their idea of teaching me the Vietnamese language was to send me to Vietnamese Bible school. So to actively seek out Vietnamese literature meant going in a different direction from that. I will say that the one Vietnamese book that had a big formal influence on me was *The Sorrow of War*, by Bảo Ninh, which is the best-known novel about the Vietnamese war experience, in this case told by a North Vietnamese veteran. It's a great novel; it's a great war novel period. Its formal innovations—which deal with how to talk about war, how to talk about trauma, how to talk about memory—all those things were actually quite inspirational for me as I tried to think about how *The Sympathizer* would deal with those same issues.

NOR: Would you go so far as to say *The Sorrow of War* was the book which inspired you to write *The Sympathizer*?

NGUYEN: That novel didn't inspire me to write *The Sympathizer*. It came out in the late 1980s, I think, and I probably read it by the early 1990s. No, it didn't inspire me. But it was part of a body of war literature that came out of Vietnam that framed my understanding of the war. The closest American comparison, for example, would be Tim O'Brien. O'Brien and all those other American writers of the war were part of my reading. *The Sympathizer*, to the extent it was inspired by any of those books, is my response to them. So *The Sympathizer* is responding to Bảo Ninh—and it's responding to Tim O'Brien—but its inspiration is actually just that general sense of rage or anger at the erasure of Vietnamese experiences, for the most part, in the Western imagination, and also this desire to tell an entertaining story. The more direct inspirations would be people like John le Carré and Graham Greene. Greene, for example, is probably the one writer who embodies all these things I'm talking about—both in terms of inspiring me, because I admire his writing in general, but also infuriating me, because I think *The Quiet American*, one of the earliest examples of Anglo literature about Vietnam, is also pretty enraging when you read it. So I'm both reacting to and inspired by people like Greene.

NOR: You often speak of anger. Is that something you've always felt, or did it rub off on you from your family or the Vietnamese community?

NGUYEN: My parents were never angry about the past and what had happened to them. I think they were stoic; the suffering they stoically endured was very influential on me. I think my anger does emerge from my response to that—out of my response to what had happened to them—and the silences that came out of it. And from that experience of being a Vietnamese refugee. Growing up in the United States, I eventually realized that I was also a Vietnamese-American, or an Asian-American, and that realization came with a lot of anger because even growing up in a relatively multicultural, liberal place like California, that history was erased. All through college, I heard about the things that had happened to Asian immigrants and Asian-Americans since the nineteenth-century, and that was enraging. But a lot of those things had been actively suppressed from American history. And then certainly, growing up in the Vietnamese refugee community, even if my parents weren't angry, at least not explicitly, there were a lot of angry Vietnamese refugees, who either said so or who expressed their rage in inarticulate ways: through violence, through all the kinds of things that traumatized people engage in. I don't think I was angry when I was young. I got angry the moment I stepped onto the college campus at Berkeley. That's where the anger was unleashed. It was there inside of me, without my being able to articulate or understand it. Trying to give words to it in college was what really allowed the anger to take shape—and eventually be realized in the form of a novel.

NOR: You were four when you left Vietnam. Do you remember anything of the country?

NGUYEN: No, just fragments. It's the images I can recall—whether they actually happened or not, I'm not sure. I think real memory, in the sense of narrative memory, begins when I reach the refugee camp in the United States and I'm taken away from my parents at four years of age to live with a white American sponsor family in Pennsylvania. That's really where my memories begin.

NOR: How did your family end up in California?

NGUYEN: My family was sent by the American government to Fort Indiantown Gap, one of four refugee camps set up to receive Vietnamese refugees. So we settled outside of that fort in Pennsylvania and remained there for three years. In 1978 my parents found California a much more attractive place—which is true—and so we moved to San Jose in northern California, near San Francisco. My parents had a good friend who had gone there first and reported that there were economic opportunities and good weather, so we followed. I lived in San Jose from 1978-1988, and I think that decade was the formative decade for me, in terms of turning me into the angry person I am, hoping to become a writer.

NOR: What were your parents doing in San Jose at the time?

NGUYEN: They opened perhaps the second Vietnamese grocery store in San Jose. It was a very hard existence—all the stereotypes about refugee shopkeepers struggling to achieve the American dream were there for my parents—that's what I would witness growing up. I remember, when I was 10 or 11, walking down the street to my parents' store, seeing a sign in another store window that said, "Another American, driven out of business by the Vietnamese." So that was an early indicator to me that we were not completely welcome in this city—or this country. That was all a part of what would eventually turn me into a writer.

NOR: Did that inspire you to pursue ethnic studies alongside English literature as a double major?

NGUYEN: I started off as an English major because I wanted to have a lot of time to read, and I didn't know what else to do with my life. I thought it would be fun to study literature, but I didn't think I could make a living out of it. My parents were working 12-14 hours days in the grocery store, so there was really no way I could go home and say to them, "Hey, I want to spend the rest of my life studying the Romantic poets"—even though I enjoyed that. So when I went to Berkeley, I discovered something called Ethnic Studies, the study of racial ethnic minorities in the United States. And that just lit a fuse, because part of that major was also studying literature written by people of color in this country. Finally I could connect all the dots. Finally I could connect my love for literature and my unadulterated enjoyment in reading books and writing—which seemed to me to have no practical purpose—with the social and political importance of literature for minorities and for people of color in the United States, and also for colonized peoples elsewhere. I could see that actually the study of literature, the writing of literature, was not just beautiful and pleasurable; it was also meaningful in the political sense. And that's what allowed me to dare to become an academic who could study these things but also a writer who could write about these things—and to think that my writing was not simply something for me personally for my own enjoyment but also something for a collective good.

NOR: You emphasize your love of reading. Which books, genres and authors did you grow up with and which stayed with you?

NGUYEN: There's a lot. When I was a kid, what got me going were some of the classics, you know, like *Curious George* and *Tintin*, both of which I find problematic talking about today. Nevertheless, they were powerful for me, and I reread them now with my son. And then going through elementary school and high school, it was a lot of fantasy, a lot of science fiction—writers like Frank Herbert and Robert Heinlein, Anne McCaffrey. When I got to college, it was more writers of the minority and post-colonial tradition, people like Toni Morrison, Ralph Ellison, and Maxine Hong Kingston. They still remain important figures for me. And then when it came to preparing to do stuff like writing *The Sympathizer*, I read Joseph Heller. I would read authors that I really thought I needed to read like Louis-Ferdinand Céline—he remained an important inspiration for that book. The last major writer who totally made it possible for me to write this book is a Portuguese writer named António Lobo Antunes, author of *The Land at the End of the World*. The experimentalism, density and sheer, harsh beauty of his language really triggered the voice of *The Sympathizer*.

NOR: How did you come to write *The Sympathizer?*

NGUYEN: I'd just finished a draft of *The Refugees*, and my agent said he liked the collection of short stories, but in order to sell it to one of the major publishing houses in New York, I'd have to write a novel—and that we'd tried to sell both. So I said fine. I'd always wanted to write a novel, and that was my inspiration. I was very pragmatic, and I knew right away that I wanted to write a spy novel—a genre spy novel. I wanted it to be entertaining—I'd read a lot of spy novels—I like them a lot as a genre. But also spy novels are deeply political and deeply historical, usually. And I wanted to deal with those kinds of political and historical issues, so that's how I wrote *The Sympathizer*. And of course, after I'd finished writing *The Sympathizer*, my agent sold the novel but didn't sell the short-story collection. So that plan didn't quite work out.

NOR: You've said in various interviews that you find writing hard—is that the craft of writing or coming up with ideas?

NGUYEN: I found writing *The Refugees* to be very, very hard—partly because I didn't know what I was doing. Everything was hard; writing a sentence was hard, how to construct a story, how to edit, how to revise, how to end. It was all difficult. And of course, besides the act of writing, there's the difficulty of publishing and the feeling of writing in isolation without recognition or hope. It's all very difficult. *The Sympathizer*, ironically, even though it's a much more difficult book to read than *The Refugees*, was much easier to write. So *The Refugees* took seventeen years, and *The Sympathizer*, which is twice as long, took a little over two years. The difficult part of writing *The Sympathizer* was probably not the technical stuff but the moments when I talked to an agent and I started to worry whether the book would sell or not. That was the most difficult part.

NOR: How were *The Sympathizer* and *The Refugees* received in Vietnam?

NGUYEN: *The Sympathizer*, when it came out, was very well received, and Vietnamese people had heard about it and were intrigued. But it's a literary novel. It didn't have that much of an impact, I think, until it won the Pulitzer Prize. Then all Vietnamese people, here in the United States but also in Vietnam, suddenly started paying attention. It's ironic that it took an American literary prize for the Vietnamese people to suddenly feel a huge amount of pride in that accomplishment, and that's basically what the reaction has amounted to. The difficulty, obviously, is that *The Sympathizer* is an unequivocally controversial novel in that it sets out to be critical of just about everybody—except the Pulitzer Prize committee—it's critical of the South Vietnamese, for example, it's critical of Vietnamese communists. In Vietnam there is still very active censorship and suppression of writers. So it was a real surprise to me when I was able to sell all three of my recent books to Vietnamese publishing houses—because all three are, to one degree or another, pretty critical. So the first test case was *The Refugees,* which just got published in Vietnamese. In Vietnam it's a censored edition, with an entire short story removed from it, which happens to be "War Years," the only autobiographical short story I've written. So there's a separate overseas, Vietnamese-language edition, which is uncensored, where all the stories will appear. And I agreed to that censorship in Vietnam because I felt the short-story collection could still stand on its own, and I really wanted it to reach a Vietnamese audience there—and overseas as well. The translation of *The Sympathizer* has been finished, but it is now being reviewed by the appropriate government officials for approval for publication. That's a much more serious task—they would basically have to remove the entire last quarter of the novel to remove any negative allusion to communism—and that can't happen. So I don't know what will happen with the publication of that book in Vietnam.

NOR: Have you returned to the country since you left as a four-year-old in 1975?

NGUYEN: I returned in 2002—that was my first return. Between then and 2012, I visited about five or six times for about a year altogether so that I could study formal Vietnamese, travel the country, do research for my nonfiction book, *Nothing Ever Dies: Vietnam and the Memory of War*, and write. I was actually writing *The Sympathizer* on my last trip in 2012. Now I just want to wait and see if *The Sympathizer* will get published there and what the official government reaction will be. Because I don't want to show up in the country and get turned back at the airport and sent home. That has happened before.

NOR: One final question. What kind of projects do you have lined up for the near future?

NGUYEN: I just published a book called *The Displaced*, by refugee writers about refugee lives, that continues the work that is important to me in terms of advocating for refugees. In this case, not just in some kind of editorial way but in collecting seventeen writers who are also refugees and having them talk about very specific kinds of human experience that their communities have been through. And then the big writing project for me personally is the sequel to *The Sympathizer,* which I'm hopefully halfway through right now.

Luisa Valenzuela

Interviewed by Elizabeth Sulis Kim
(2018)

The Argentine writer Luisa Valenzuela has published more than thirty books, among which are novels, short-story collections, flash fiction, and essays. Widely translated, Valenzuela is the recipient of a number of awards, including a Fulbright and a Guggenheim. She has taught at New York University and Columbia University. In 2015 she became president of PEN Argentina. This interview was conducted in English between May 24 and June 14, 2018, in a series of phone calls and emails as well as during a visit to the author's home in Buenos Aires.

NEW ORLEANS REVIEW: What changes have you witnessed in Argentina in your lifetime?

LUISA VALENZUELA: Far too many. This is a roller coaster country, with good moments and very upsetting times like the current one, though the civic-military dictatorship was worse. But we have an incredible, almost miraculous capacity for recovery, which I hope will at some point still save us.

NOR: What can you remember of the civic-military dictatorship?

VALENZUELA: So many memories, all indelible. And they are coming back because the current elected government has decided to call upon the military to reinforce internal security, which is only threatened by the peaceful marches of people intensely worried about the astronomical cost of living. Or by women marching against male violence—a woman is killed every 32 hours in this country—and demanding legal abortion. But all I can tell you about those fateful times you may read in my books, *Cambio de armas* (*Other Weapons*), *Cola de lagartija* (*The Lizard's Tail*), and even *Novela negra con argentinos* (*Black Novel with Argentines*). It is hard to elude writing about those terrible times.

NOR: So it gave you much to write about. Do you think hard times fuel creativity?

VALENZUELA: Let me separate this question in two. No, I don't think that hard times necessarily fuel creativity. Often it silences you. Freud knew that very well. I had this ongoing discussion with Joseph Brodsky at the New York Institute for the Humanities; he used to affirm that censorship is good for literature but bad for the writer. But at home it could be seriously bad not only for the writer (who finally takes responsibility for his or her words) but also for everyone around us, even innocent people who appeared in our phone books.

And, on the other hand, I did write a lot during those terrible times. But I was one of the very few, and it all started before the military takeover. The Triple A (Argentine Anticommunist Association) under the leadership of José López Rega, Minister of Social Well-being (*Bienestar Social*), triggered the most irrational state terrorism, which inspired my book of spontaneous short stories, *Aquí pasan cosas raras* (*Strange Things Happen Here*). Things were already cooking then. *Como en la Guerra* (*He Who Searches*) was published, taking a risk under the dictatorship, but was written before that. Premonition? Of sorts. Horror was already in the air, ever since the late 1960s, as you may read in my novel *Cuidado con el tigre* (*Beware of the Tiger*), written in 1966 but which I dared publish only in 2011.

NOR: Growing up in the household you did, was there any way you could have not become a writer?

VALENZUELA: There were practically all the ways not to. It was an overdose of writers around me, beginning with my mother, Luisa Mercedes Levinson, and all her friends and colleagues. I was a voracious reader and from a very early age attended their talks, but I wanted to become anything—mathematician, explorer—other than a writer.

NOR: So did you attempt to pursue an alternative career?

VALENZUELA: Oh yes, I wanted to be an explorer, an adventurer, or study a variety of subjects such as mathematics and physics that really attracted me. I was, and still am, omnivorous and knowledge excites me to such an extent that it makes a choice impossible. Wanting to be everywhere and learn everything, journalism seemed the best, or perhaps easiest, option. There were no real schools of journalism then, so I went head-first into the practice. Of course, I had a rich background of lectures and readings and so on.

NOR: Were you encouraged by your mother to write?

VALENZUELA: My mother was a well-known writer at the time, so she knew what kind of life being a writer meant and did not encourage me at all. At least, not to write literature. She sent me to a private British school saying she wanted me to do sports and not become a "greasy intellectual." Journalism, though, was okay; she considered it a minor form, and in a way, she was right. But I did not enjoy it and ended up writing fiction in spite of her. And married a Frenchman, went to live in France at twenty, and in a way left all that behind and wrote my first novel, *Hay que sonreír* (*Clara*), while there.

NOR: Did you see much of Jorge Luis Borges, Julio Cortázar, and other literary figures growing up? What impression have they left on you?

VALENZUELA: I did see Borges often, and so many other intellectuals of great value, fiction writers, essayists and publishers and poets. My mother had some sort of informal literary salon, and they gathered often at our home, so since my early teens, even before, I would listen, fascinated by their debates and talks, but I found them excessively passive. That was not for me, just food for the mind. At one point, Borges ("Georgie," at the time) and my mother wrote a short story together, "*La hermana de Eloísa*" ("The Sister of Eloisa"). It was meant to be an obnoxious story, and they both laughed so much that probably I thought story writing was joyful. Which it is, because even if you deal with the darkest of subject matters, the immersion in language is always elating. Cortázar, on the other hand, whom I admire deeply, I met much later in my life.

NOR: Do you think seeing writers from a young age gave you a different perspective on what makes a good writer? There's a growing tendency, for example, to associate the writer with a certain charisma, eloquence and wit, but I know you've said Borges was shy and didn't necessarily stand out from the crowd.

VALENZUELA: Charisma has nothing to do with the equation. What I learned then was to be natural and even irreverent around writers. No respect as such, only for their talent, in a casual manner. And yes, Borges was very shy and ironic and somewhat self-absorbed. His colleagues admired his writing, of course, but said he was a writer for writers, that the common reader would never understand him.

NOR: What do you think about the American writing scene that encourages open mics, participation in writing workshops and other activities that might cause anxiety in the quiet or timorous writer?

VALENZUELA: It's not only an American scene nowadays. Here in Argentina there are many private and public workshops, lectures, readings and other activities that may or may not cause anxiety in a writer. Writers have to earn a living, and it's not easy to do so with our books, so all these other literary activities help a lot. Of course, there are many shy writers who do not like to speak in public. And there are others who love it, even to excess. But writing is a solitary job, so one needs at some point to be secluded. You do have to go out at times, though, and perhaps promote a new book—that means a launch party, getting in touch with your public in lectures at universities and in places where you can have a dialogue with readers.

NOR: Which other Argentine and Latin American writers do you appreciate? Or writers from farther afield?

VALENZUELA: Oh, the list is vast, a movable feast if we may say so. Cortázar is the one who is closest to my way of understanding the act of writing. And nearer to my heart. I admire Carlos Fuentes on the opposite extreme of the equation. That is why I wrote a book on both of them, *Entrecruzamientos: Cortázar/Fuentes* (*Crossings: Cortázar/Fuentes*). It is astonishing to discover how much they connect in their so different personalities. But if you ask me for a list, it can go from Clarice Lispector to Haruki Murakami, with innumerable names on the way.

NOR: You mentioned you started out as a journalist—you worked for *Radio Belgrano*, *El Hogar*, and later for *La Nación* and *Crisis* magazine, among others. Do you think journalism is that different from fiction? Did you enjoy telling other people's stories?

VALENZUELA: Already at eighteen, I wrote my first short story, "City of the Unknown," which still exists in translation. But from the very beginning, I knew that journalism and fiction travel on very different rails. And I wasn't necessarily telling other people's stories for the papers but doing full-fledged journalism, in the streets, on journeys, and of course interviews, but that's a different matter. And later as a columnist, offering opinion and analysis of the news, the sort of journalism that forces you to be very close to facts.

NOR: To what extent is journalism, as your mother believed, a minor form in comparison to fiction?

VALENZUELA: My mother believed strongly in intuition. She thought intuition was the way of accessing profound poetic thinking. She would often repeat that I was too intelligent to be a good writer; she thought intelligence wasn't something that had to be at work when creating literature. I don't agree; I think you need a blend of intelligence and intuition. But in journalism you cannot allow a flight of fantasy. And probably my mother was thinking of journalism as simple reporting. A reporter has to be very factual. Of course, New Journalism relies on intuition, and we have something called Performative Journalism, and great nonfiction books are published—the Truman Capote kind of journalism. On the shadowy side of this story, I remember the case, many years ago, of a very bright journalist who was kicked out of *The New Yorker* when he cheerfully admitted that he sometimes changed the locations where his interviews took place to give them a more interesting background. Reality in excess was the old-fashioned way of seeing journalism; it killed whatever poetic insight you could have.

NOR: What about telling your own story, as in *Dark Desires and the Others*, where you recount your own experience of living in New York for a decade? What was that like?

VALENZUELA: Again, it was a different matter because I didn't sit down to write about my New York experience but simply was talked into using my diaries of the time, which were extremely personal and emotional, not at all factual in the sense of telling my comings and goings.

NOR: How is it different to be a woman in New York compared to being a woman in Argentina, where there is still a culture of machismo?

VALENZUELA: The difference is that machismo here is out in the open, whereas it is subtle and undercover in the States. There I learned a lot about those nuances.

NOR: And how does Argentine feminism differ in its objectives and its methods to its American counterpart?

VALENZUELA: Well, feminism in the States was overpowering during the 1980s, while it was quite isolated here. But now the scale has flipped, and it is important to point out that finally, here in Argentina, women's struggles are intense and out in the open and that force is taking over the streets in a very courageous and powerful way, as you might have well experienced.

NOR: Yes. At present Argentine women are marching for their right to legal abortions—through the referendum tomorrow. Do you think that it will happen here?

VALENZUELA: I think they will vote for the law. By a very narrow margin, but they will. I think the government, even if shamelessly rightist, is interested in getting this law passed as it is a distraction from the current horrible economic situation they've got the country in. What is absolutely fantastic here is the power of the women's movement—the fight is very intense at this point. But we do have a history of courageous and combative women; think of the mothers and the *abuelas* of *Plaza de Mayo*. And now the young people are really joining in the demands; it is moving and very heartwarming. I hope that the senators will vote in favor because of all the lives lost from women doing illegal and very unsafe abortions. So what kind of life are they defending, those against legal abortion who call themselves pro-lifers? We should be defending the lives of women in general, including those who cannot afford a child. I am president of PEN Argentina, and PEN defends all liberties for women, the essence of freedom of expression.

NOR: I'm asking for many comparisons, but what differences do you notice between the Latin American and North American literary worlds?

VALENZUELA: We have a completely different approach to the act of writing, and we are intense about reading between the lines. It was fascinating to compare both approaches while teaching creative writing in English.

NOR: You taught creative writing at New York University. Do you think creative writing can be taught?

VALENZUELA: At Columbia, I just taught Latin American Literature for Beginners. Only NYU finally tempted me to try something I thought was out of my reach when it offered me the Berg Chair for a semester, by the end of which they decided to keep me on. So I can now say that writing cannot be taught, no, but stimulated, yes.

NOR: How do you recognize emerging talent in creative writing classes?

VALENZUELA: Oh, it is not hard to discover those who have a real, deep feeling for language, not just a talent for telling stories.

NOR: Where do your ideas for stories come from?

VALENZUELA: Good question. That is a mystery that keeps you going, from one surprise to the next. Which is my way of writing, without a prepared plot or anything.

NOR: Where and when do you write?

VALENZUELA: Anywhere, anytime, when I manage the connection with that creative part of the self which we ignore.

NOR: Do you enjoy rereading your own work?

VALENZUELA: Yes, when I am forced to; otherwise I don't. But when perchance I do, I usually find that I was a much better writer at that time.

NOR: Do you still feel you have a lot to say?

VALENZUELA: I never felt I had anything to say. Just the curiosity to explore. . . .

Sister Helen Prejean

Interviewed by Mark Yakich
(2018)

Anti-death penalty advocate and author of *Dead Man Walking*, Sister Helen Prejean is the rock star of nuns. At least that is how I think of her. We met years ago through a personal connection and have been close friends ever since. When I first asked her about doing an interview for a book about writing and resistance, she answered: "Bring it on!" If you haven't seen Helen give a talk (she's on the road nonstop September through May), you might not quite fathom how in character her response was. This interview took place in her home, a modest apartment, in Mid-City in New Orleans. We sat in our usual chairs. She'd recently gotten over a bad case of pneumonia, which included a week in the hospital, but that didn't prevent each of us from enjoying a Dixie beer.

NEW ORLEANS REVIEW: When we first met, I quickly realized you weren't anything like what I was expecting from a typical nun. How has that helped you, and how has that hindered you over the years?

SISTER HELEN PREJEAN: Partly it's helped because no one expects a nun to have been to the death house—to know how politics and the criminal justice system work. It helps, too, when people say things like, "Hey, this is a nun who's been in the fire."

But it's also worked against me. When the book *Dead Man Walking* was coming out in 1993, there was the hurdle of how my being a nun was going to play out with a story about a murderer. Eighty percent of the population on average was for the death penalty—in Louisiana that was probably 90 percent. A lot of people likely expected me to be that classic nun—only all into Jesus and forgive your enemies stuff—and that I was going to be unable to dive into the horror of the crime and the victim's family.

I had this great editor, Jason Epstein at Random House, who really helped me shape my story. The first thing he did was show me that it took too long in the first draft to acknowledge the terrible crimes that Pat Sonnier and his brother Eddie had done—killing two innocent teenage kids. Jason said, "Helen, they'll say this is a nun full of platitudes—'Jesus said to forgive'—and can't really stand in the horror of this crime, and acknowledge it, and be outraged by it. And if you don't put that in the first ten pages, nobody's going to read this book."

The other thing was that I made a big mistake in not reaching out for a long time to the victims' families. I figured they were so upset and angry and would especially think that anybody against the death penalty is an enemy. And Jason, again, said, "Well, it was cowardice, wasn't it? You were scared of them? Scared of the rejection, scared of the anger?" I said, "Yes." He said, "Put that in your book. Acknowledge your mistakes, and people will stay with you in the telling of the story because you're showing your humanness. If you try to always spin things to come out good, they're going to sense your dishonesty, and they're not going to read your book."

NOR: It makes me think of a piece of advice I once heard—that there should always be someone the reader can root for in a narrative. It circumvents the perennial question of having "likeable" characters. Do you think at a certain point in *Dead Man Walking* that the reader is rooting for you?

PREJEAN: I've never thought of the rooting question. What is this, a pig thing?

NOR: It's helped me—when I feel like a character is too goody-goody or too unreliable—because as long as you're rooting for the character, you want to see them get over whatever challenge they're facing.

PREJEAN: That's very interesting. Tim Robbins remarked once that I was "the nun who was in over her head," and that is just what people thought, and rightly so, when they saw me getting into this. I knew nothing about the courts, the criminal justice system, how politics work—nothing.

NOR: The reader wants to see if you're going to make it.

PREJEAN: True. And I didn't have a clue what was going to happen as I got into it.

NOR: This year is the 25th anniversary of the publication of *Dead Man Walking*. What's the state of capital punishment?

PREJEAN: The pattern of the death penalty is imminently clear, that the guidelines the Supreme Court set in the Gregg v. Georgia decision of 1976 are not holding. The guidelines are so mercurial and impossible— that the death penalty is supposed to be reserved for "the worst of the worst." But guess what, if you leave it up to individual prosecutors to be the determiners of what "the worst of the worst" means, it's no big surprise that the Deep South states that practiced slavery are the states with the highest rates for seeking the death penalty. There are six or seven counties of rabid prosecutors responsible for close to 50 percent of all people on death row in the U.S. You have someone like Bob Macy in Oklahoma, for example, who single-handedly was responsible for sending 54 people to death row.

The prosecutor has two key decisions to make: first, to go for the death penalty or not; and second, if they go for the death penalty, will they allow the person to plea bargain and accept a life without parole sentencing in exchange for a guilty plea.

NOR: Most of the prosecutors don't allow for a plea bargain?

PREJEAN: Some do, some don't. It's arbitrary.

Denny LeBoeuf, one of the great human rights lawyers and a good friend of mine, represents people in Guantanamo. She heads up the ACLU John Adams Project, which puts millions of dollars into the defending of people accused and targeted from 9/11. She says the death penalty rests on the premise that we can entrust the government and the courts to set up criteria in some kind of predictable, reasonable, and lawful way to select and punish with death the "worst of the worst"—and do this according to norms of the Constitution. And nobody really knows what that meant.

NOR: So there are two trials—one for the guilty or not guilty determination, and the other for sentencing?

PREJEAN: Bifurcated trial, yes. Which is partly why the death penalty will always be more expensive than any other kind of trial. The sentencing trial can take double or triple the time because everything is open in looking into the life of the defendant, and what might be a mitigating circumstance.

The status of the victim also comes into play. Almost everybody wants the death penalty if you kill a policeman, but then not if you kill a fireman. Not if you kill a public health official. Not if you kill a teacher. So you begin to have this hierarchy or this meritocracy: what is the status of some victims, that their killing would automatically make their killer eligible for the death penalty, but not others? And you begin to realize how unrealistic this is. Or, for example, if someone kills a child. But you've got to define child, because when you have a law you always have to have a cutting-off point. So you can have parents come in before the judicial committee and say, "Our son was killed! He was killed, our son, he was the light of our eyes." But he was 14 years old, and the law says that a child is 12 years old or younger. They respond, "But doesn't his death call for the ultimate penalty?" And you begin to see how arbitrary the whole thing is, and you can't apply it—or you make a mess of applying it.

This is nothing to say for the biggest mistake: the huge number of innocent people we've wrongfully convicted, put on death row, and then exonerated—162 and counting.

NOR: And that's what your second book is about?

PREJEAN: *The Death of Innocents*, yes. That book is about how someone could be innocent and still be thrown into the death machine. For it, I had to learn a lot about the appeal courts. The reason, for instance, most people are on death row is because they didn't get a really good, top-notch lawyer. If you don't have a lawyer who raises a formal objection to so many things, you are in trouble.

Dobie Gillis Williams, a black man accused of killing a white woman in her bathroom in a small Louisiana town, had an all-white jury. And there was no formal objection from his lawyer. When the case went up for appeal at the state level and then the federal, the thinking was that Dobie and his lawyer had discussed having an all-white jury—that it was okay and fair—therefore it was no longer an issue. Without that initial presence on the record—of a formal objection—well, that means the appeals court can't hear that issue in the case.

NOR: Many states have, in fact, pulled back on the death penalty?

PREJEAN: The number of executions and death sentences is going down year by year. In 1998, for example, the number of death sentences handed down was 295. In 2017, that number was down to 39.

NOR: Do you see the Supreme Court changing the law of the land?

PREJEAN: It comes down to the individual justices, and all of them except Justice Clarence Thomas come from privilege. As Justice Thurgood Marshall, the first black justice, pointed out, your life experiences have a lot to do with the way you interpret words. You have privileged white people, who went to privileged schools, interpreting words such as "equal justice under law" whereas those from humbler backgrounds, like Marshall, have an entirely different take on what those words mean. We now have Justice Neil Gorsuch, who will probably be pro-death penalty right down the line. He will use conservative interpretation of the Constitution to argue the death penalty is in there, the people want it, the Constitution allows it, and only state legislatures can change it and not the courts—that's called judicial activism. Justice Antonin Scalia always argued that the only way to change the death penalty is through state legislatures, that is how we got the amendments to the Constitution, that is the way to change everything. But they cannot see in those words, by sentencing human beings to death—conscious, imaginative beings— that the death penalty is a form of cruelty. They do not acknowledge the cruelty of it because they're blocked from feeling the pain of the condemned. All they can see is a legal argument. If you murder, you die. They don't have any experience that can help them interpret those words differently—to see what it means to predetermine, step-by-step, killing an alive human being who anticipates death and dies a thousand times before they die.

NOR: It's the life experience of these justices that is crucial to their interpretation.

PREJEAN: Yes. Look at us—as writers we bring our life experience to the way we interpret words and articulate them. As well, people bring their life experience to the way they read. When you're reading a book, what flashes in your imagination? What connections are made?

NOR: One sees what one wants to see.

PREJEAN: Not just "want to see," but what you've had some experience in. Or not. Sometimes you draw a blank. Words just leave you cold.

NOR: What you have a bent to see, then.

PREJEAN: Yes. It's almost like electrical connections with things way deeper than just a rationalized approach. Anybody who has experienced any form of abuse is going to be alert to words where somebody is dominating or using their power over somebody else. It can be very painful to read; we avoid reading some things that will evoke pain. So you have people who are very cushioned, from privileged experience, interpreting words, really that could set your soul on fire. And that is the anemic, protectionist interpretation of law that we have often gotten from privileged individuals. But we have to add that no matter what a justice's past is, he or she can grow and develop through the debate that happens in the court.

Still, there is a clear pattern that when white people are killed, the death penalty is often sought. And yet when people of color are killed, it's seldom sought. But you have these legalistic arguments that say it's not up to a court to assess sociological patterning and statistics—

NOR: You can't talk about the patterning and the facets of institutions that oppress?

PREJEAN: Nope, you can't look at patterns—only individuals and their intentions.

NOR: That seems like the definition of anemic and narrow.

PREJEAN: And that's what racism and prejudice does. You actually have people like Scalia who, when the first Affirmative Action cases came in, asked why we owed something to people of color just because of slavery. "Slavery's long over" is what he argued. That classic argument.

NOR: Like what Kanye West said recently about African-American slaves: "They chose it! 400 years of slavery and they let it go on." What's it take to make a statement like "they chose it"?

PREJEAN: Scalia said things like, "My family is Italian, we came as immigrants but we overcame. My father became a professor. What we did, they can do."

NOR: The pull-yourself-up-by-your-bootstraps mentality.

PREJEAN: That's the sure sign of people speaking out of privilege. The capacity for compassion is limited. And the law codifies the prejudice and so does its application. Isn't it odd that the worst of the worst almost always is when you kill a white person?

NOR: You're not supposed to look at the pattern.

PREJEAN: That's what real intelligence is—seeing patterns.

NOR: And synthesizing them.

PREJEAN: Then, if one is a moral being, asking oneself, "What does knowing this ask of me?" Like the response to widening inequality between rich and poor by the Poor People's Campaign right now in the U.S.

A lot of people think intelligence is what you get on quiz programs—knowing trivia. But it's really about seeing the pattern in things. That's when you come into the spirit. There's the spirit of the law, and there's the legality of it, the empirical. It's the same thing for teaching. Are you going to teach for testing, in order to see how the scores come statistically, and how your students ranked high or low? Or are you going to teach because you love the way teaching can open up creativity in others and unleash potential for change in the world? The bind that teachers are being put in all the time between spirit and the law, and the empirical justification of what they do and how their students score. It's in everything. Do you become a writer because you desire to become famous and make a lot of money? Or do you become a writer because there's something you discovered, this spark, this flash, that you want to share with other human beings knowing that they can enter into the words too?

NOR: That brings us to your forthcoming book, *River of Fire*, which you've described to me as your spiritual awakening that led you to Louisiana's death row. But it also makes me think of your journey as a writer. You've mentioned your daily journal to me a number of times. Did your writing grow out of that? How exactly did your writing evolve?

PREJEAN: My journaling was triggered by an exhibit about John F. Kennedy here in New Orleans. They displayed postcards he had sent home as a boy from camp. For some reason those postcards fired up my soul. I got one of those three-ring binders—the blue horse binders—and started writing a journal.

NOR: So it wasn't something you did as kid?

PREJEAN: No, I never did much writing as a kid. I'm a talker.

NOR: What year did you begin it?

PREJEAN: 1963. The journal really began just as a way of clarifying my soul. I talk about it in *River*.

NOR: You've titled the book *River of Fire*. Why fire?

PREJEAN: They killed a man with fire one night. This line begins the book.

NOR: The electrocution of Pat Sonnier?

PREJEAN: Right, they pumped electricity into his body until he was dead. His killing was a legal act because he had killed. No religious leaders protested the killing that night. No people from churches were raising their voice. But I was there. I saw it with my own eyes. And what I saw set my soul on fire, a fire that burns in me still.

River of Fire is the account of how I came to be in the killing chamber that night, and the spiritual currents that brought me there. In the early morning hours of April 5th, 1984, I came out of that execution chamber and couldn't believe all of this had happened. That the government had actually killed a citizen in the United States of America. After the execution, they put a coat around me—I felt chilled to the bone—put me in the car to take me home, and we had to stop the car because I had to throw up. I had never witnessed a scripted, legal death. What I saw was a premeditated killing disguised as an act of justice.

NOR: You were a witness.

PREJEAN: It became clear to me, that night, that I had to tell the story. But I didn't know what I was going to do exactly. I didn't know I was going to write a book. At first I resisted writing a book. I'm from Louisiana; we talk. So the first thing I did was start talking to anybody who would listen—one of the first times was to captive students in sociology at Loyola University.

NOR: Really?

PREJEAN: Giving talks in schools, community centers, churches—it's where and how I learned to hone the story. I began to realize, and this was before the book, that I had to be able to really stand in outrage and talk about the victim's family. That's been a whole growth process. If you don't stand with the victim's family, then everything you're trying to say about human rights, where you want to take people at the end of the journey, won't work.

NOR: When and where did you first publish something about your experience?

PREJEAN: I began to write op-eds—one for the Pacific News Journal, a syndicate based in San Francisco. Then I got an invitation, from a Mr. Charles Singer in California, who had seen my writing, and he said, "You should do a book. I can get it published for you." So I went, *Wow, maybe I ought to write a book.*

This brings Jason DeParle into the story. Have I ever spoken to you about him?

NOR: I don't think so.

PREJEAN: Jason DeParle is a close friend. He had done his undergraduate in English and then he went to the Poynter Institute in St. Augustine in Florida, a six-week course in journalistic writing. After an internship at the *New Republic*, he had two offers for a job: one was with *The Washington Post* and one was with the *Times-Picayune* in New Orleans. And his mentor said, "Jason, go South and do honest work." And he did.

So he comes to the *Times-Picayune*—this is in the 1980s when I'm at Hope House in an inner-city project, St. Thomas—and of course the first beat they give a rookie reporter is the crime beat. Executions are just beginning again, and Jason meets me. When Jason later left for *The New York Times*, he covered the stories here of the death penalty. Some have called him the conscience of *The New York Times*, because his whole mission has been to put human faces to policies. For I don't know how many years, for example, he followed three single women and chronicled the story of their lives, going from welfare to work.

Anyway, when I got this offer from this man, Singer, in California, I called up Jason. You know, I've never told this story before—

NOR: I don't remember you ever mentioning this.

PREJEAN: —about Jason's role. He told me that if I wanted to get a book published, I should go through New York. Jason had a connection to Bill McKibben, who had written *The End of Nature*, and he had me send my writing to him, hoping that if he liked my work he'd recommend me to his agent.

NOR: What did you have to send him at this point, just op-eds?

PREJEAN: I had done a few, including one on Pope John Paul II's visit to New Orleans for the *Picayune*. I remember a special punch at the end of my op-ed. You know how everyone shouts *Viva il Papa!* to the Pope? Well, I had the Pope respond *Viva le mamme!*— a prophecy still a long way from fulfillment in my patriarchal Catholic church. It was Jim Amos, editor-in-chief at the *Picayune*, who first told me I have a distinctive voice. I didn't know what a writer's "voice" was.

In any case, I sent my writing to Bill McKibben. I still remember what he said in his letter in reply, "I have not seen such quiet writing since Orwell."

NOR: Quiet writing?

PREJEAN: I understand now a bit better what that meant. I wasn't punching the writing with adverbs or adjectives, or trying to make it sensational, with drum-rolls of building up the emotions. I was just taking people there with simple Anglo-Saxon words—the Hemingway pared-downed formula.

Bill put me in touch with his agent, Gloria Loomis, and I sent her the stuff I'd sent him. And she said to me, "Yes."

You hear of people's huge challenges trying to get literary agents—for me, it happened right away. But I think I was part of something bigger. Executions in the U.S. are hidden from the public, just 12 witnesses behind prison walls. No one was ever going to see the government killings up close unless eyewitnesses would bring people inside the killing chamber.

NOR: The agent recognized the need for a witness to bring the public close?

PREJEAN: She saw the writing and said that I was bringing readers into both sides of the suffering—to the condemned and his family as well as to the grief of the murder victims' families. And that is really a summary of the book, going back and forth to both sides. Gloria told me, "I want you to write three chapters which don't have to be in order, a table of contents, and a two-page proposal. I have a publisher in mind."

That took me nine months to do, because we were doing long marches. In May 1990, we were doing a march from death row in Florida to The Martin Luther King, Jr. Center in Atlanta where we entered the city carrying 90 coffins—the number of people who had been executed thus far. It was the only way the media would give us any coverage. Lord, we were on the road for two weeks. I was so tired at the end of that march I fainted, and I thought there's gotta be another way.

I finally got the materials to Gloria. She walked right down the street and put them into Jason Epstein's hands at Random House. He wrote me a letter asking if I'd come up to New York to talk about the possibility of publishing a book.

Mama said to me, "Honey, you can't go to New York without a suit." So, my good Southern mama gets me a nice suit to wear to meet my New York editor. She was on the phone big-time to all her friends. [*Laughter.*]

NOR: What year was that?

PREJEAN: It was '90. I had no comprehension of Random House, thought it was a little bitty publishing company. And then I'm in the elevator at Random House, going to Epstein's office on the eleventh floor, and all these different floors are coming up—children's books, adult fiction—and I realize the whole building is Random House!

I meet Jason and we sit at this table overlooking the Hudson River, absolutely beautiful. And we talk about writing and the death penalty, and I come out of there thinking that was the best dang-gone conversation I've ever had with anybody about the death penalty.

Later, Jason DeParle told me that any writer in North America would kneel on crushed glass—

NOR: —to even have a telephone conversation with Jason Epstein.

PREJEAN: Yes. And for two years we worked on the book. He had a very inquiring mind and really wanted to dig into the death penalty. He was a very hands-on editor, who taught me so much about writing. For example, I talked about going into the death house—that my fingertips were cold and I had a cold band around my stomach that was tightening. He said, "Choose the stomach or the fingertips? Don't say both, give one impression that you're scared, then move on." I still remember his little metaphor: If you're walking along a path and a pebble falls on your head, you'll remember it. If pebbles keep hitting you on the head, you'll soon feel nothing." One impression, and move on.

I gobbled it all up. He said afterwards, in an interview, "I never had a writer who did everything I told her to do!"

When it was time for the book to come out, he stood in front of all the sales and marketing people, held up the book and said, "See this book? It may very well change how we think about capital punishment, like Rachel Carson's *Silent Spring* changed how we think about the environment."

They got me out on this book tour where I'm in Los Angeles at six in the morning doing a radio interview. *The Today Show*. All of it. And NPR covered everything, letting me tell the whole story. Twice. People were talking about pulling over to the side of the road to listen—once people get in the current of this story, they see the many fascinating elements in it.

My little boat began to ride this very big wave. And my spiritual task has been to be faithful to what I've seen and the people I have accompanied to their deaths (six of them), to tell the story in as pure a way as I can. It's not about me, it's about getting this reality close to the people. And that night, outside the execution chamber, I was thinking as much about the American people as I was about anything, and that people have good hearts. That people are not wedded to killing criminals. They just have been made to be afraid; they don't have any information about how it's done. And most never think much about it at all.

NOR: *Dead Man Walking* wasn't about you, but *River of Fire* is all about you. What made you turn the limelight on yourself?

PREJEAN: What makes you think the light is lime?

NOR: Maybe it should be yellow!

PREJEAN: But seriously . . . over the years people wanted to know what led me to the death chamber.

Susan Sarandon always said that when you look at a film the one who undergoes the most change is the hero of that film. Before we started filming *Dead Man Walking,* she said to Sean Penn, "This film is going to make your career. You're the one who's undergoing the most change—not me—it's going to be you."

You see how a book honestly written can transform a reader. I take the reader with me through every step. Meeting with people on death row, who have done unspeakable crimes, I get to witness the goodness in them, the humanness in them. They're more than the worst thing they have ever done. That's a shining miracle of life that a lot of people don't get to see because they don't really have any experience. They just write people off, "Oh, this person's a killer, a murderer. These people are evil to the very core."

On the one side, I got brought right into the secret of what life is about, that every human being has in them a spark, this transcendence to be more than we've ever been. And then I watched people go to their deaths with great courage that I don't know I could muster.

On the other side, I've been able over the years to meet victims' families, who have been thrown into this crucible of suffering nobody can imagine, and some of them come out whole. I have had the incredible experience of being with these people who get out from under what could have been a life of hatred and anger, and being consumed for the rest of their lives, but in this miracle of grace, they crawl out and they're transformed. They remain and even increase in their capacity to love other human beings, and to trust life and give themselves over to it. I'm on my knees in front of these people. I get to be the storyteller for them, and hold them up. All of this has been part of my experience. *River of Fire* came because more and more people asked me, "How'd you get into this? I mean, you was a nun?" And the media in the beginning would ask me all the time, "What's a nun doing on death row?"

NOR: Right, the dissonance between "nun" and "death row."

PREJEAN: They'd say, "Shouldn't you be with children, teaching in a classroom?"

NOR: That's where you begin the story of *River of Fire,* as a teacher in a classroom?

PREJEAN: It begins with joining the convent in the late 1950s, before the Second Vatican Council.

Then, it moves to how Vatican II changed things. It was the first time the windows of the church opened to the modern world—acknowledging that there are good things happening in science, good things happening in technology, good things happening in people. Pope John XXIII who opened the council said that the United Nations' Universal Declaration of Human Rights was going to be the road that all of us can take into the future. Human rights gives us a path to stand on with people. A lot of times the conversation is, for instance, "Well, you're a nun, you have faith. But a lot of people don't have your faith. So what?" But then we're able to talk about human rights. One of my first teachers on the death penalty was right here in New Orleans—Bill Quigley, who's been at Loyola for years. Then I met Denny LaBoeuf, then folks at the ACLU and Amnesty International. And it was a whole other way of approaching the world, that inalienable dignity of human life. The church back then had a compromised stance on the death penalty, upholding the right of the state to take human life.

NOR: What's the church's stance now?

PREJEAN: Last year, Pope Francis made a clear declaration that the death penalty is against the Gospel of Jesus. But you can't just have top leadership making statements and think all the soil gets tilled. It's a whole journey of conversion that has to happen in the people.

NOR: How do nuns fit in exactly?

PREJEAN: Nuns have always been like free agents for the Gospel within the church. Of course, you want to get along with your bishop and give him respect. But unlike diocesan priests, most religious orders of women are not directly under a bishop's authority but under Papal authority in Rome. (We like it that way.) In the past, there were some bad scenes in which some bishops interfered drastically with the internal life of women's congregations.

The first religious orders were cloistered places. Families sometimes would send women into the nunnery, because they figured they couldn't get them married or something. To be a nun was to be behind nunnery walls where you'd pray for the world. This is based on a concept that the world is full of sin, and you will do penance for the world, and you will pray for the world but you will be separated from the world.

When I entered the Sisters of St. Joseph before Vatican II, it was an entirely different world than today's. We were in habits, and lay people couldn't set foot into the convent. We couldn't have meals with people, even with the teachers we taught with at a school; nuns had a separate dining room. When Vatican II came, our sisters studied those documents and within an incredibly short time, we had changed our constitution—no more blind obedience to a superior.

What became most important was that each individual, in consultation with the community, could sort out where the spirit leads her. Which is what gave me the freedom to get into my death penalty mission. I had that freedom within the sisterhood to do it—and they supported me. People have always seemed intrigued by a nun's life. That's in part what led me to write *River*.

NOR: I read an interview you once gave where someone asked, "Sister Helen, you've written a bestseller, been nominated for the Nobel Peace Prize, have had a movie made about you . . . what do you regard as your biggest accomplishment?"

PREJEAN: Those words, like achievement or accomplishment, have no meaning for me. I don't even know how to answer that question.

NOR: I know how you answered it.

PREJEAN: How?

NOR: You said, *Being with people. Just to be there.*

PREJEAN: Yes, just being present. I mean it's the secret of life right now, to really be able to be present, and let the moment flower, and be what it's going to be.

NOR: Like we're having a moment now.

PREJEAN: Right.

NOR: Do you also find that "moment" while you're writing?

PREJEAN: Absolutely when I'm writing.

NOR: You have to be super present.

PREJEAN: Presence is an elusive thing. There's a lot said in the spiritual life about the presence of God. You start exploring presence, though, and all of a sudden you fall into a hole, into mystery.

NOR: What does in "the presence of God" mean to you?

PREJEAN: St. John says, "Where there's love, there's God." And so what's love? Well, that openness that there's a commitment. Like now. We're going to have this afternoon; we give ourselves over to it and see what flowers from it. It's a hopefulness, that you're going to be with somebody you love, and if you're really with somebody you love . . . it's going to produce something good, you're going to write something good that's going to refer to something bigger than both of us. And you trust that.

NOR: When you're gone someday, do you trust that others will continue the work you do?

PREJEAN: There are plenty of people in the United States doing this work right now. Lawyers, activists, citizens—all awake to injustice. I don't ever have concerns about how things go on. You do your bit. You do it fully. You turn it over. That's in the *Bhagavad Gita*: *You do a thing not seeking its fruit.* You do it for its own integrity and because it's the right thing to do, what you've got to do. And you leave the fruit up to whatever it's going to be. It was the same thing with publishing a book; I didn't have a clue. I just put the story out there.

NOR: And the new book—*River of Fire*—the title is a bit of a paradox, the tension between water and fire. When I looked up the phrase, I found a biblical passage from Daniel's description of heaven.

PREJEAN: You're kidding! Look at you, quoting scripture to me. [*Laughter.*]
    Let me see the paper there.
    [*Reading aloud.*] "Until thrones were set up, and the ancient of days took His seat; His vesture was like white snow and the hair of His head like pure wool."
    I know that part.
    "His throne was ablaze with flames, its wheels were a burning fire. A river of fire was flowing and coming out from before Him; thousands upon thousands were attending Him, myriads upon

myriads were standing before Him; the court sat, and the books were opened."

I'll be danged.

NOR: It's the ending that strikes me: "and the books were opened." In the beginning was the word, and the word was God. Now, this is literally a bookend. At the end of time, there are going to be *books*.

PREJEAN: "And the books were opened."

NOR: So beware, when the book comes out next year . . . someone will find that bible excerpt.

PREJEAN: Well, people dig into all kinds of stuff.

NOR: They're gonna dig.

PREJEAN: Downright helpful, Mr. Yakich. Didn't realize I had a biblical scholar on my hands.

NOR: I try.

PREJEAN: Naw. Don't try. I don't believe in try. You do it or you don't, and you let the chips fall where they will.

ACKNOWLEDGMENTS

Headnotes for each interview remain in their original form at the time of publication in *New Orleans Review*.

* * *

Ernest J. Gaines interview reprinted by permission of the Writers Forum of The College at Brockport and *New Orleans Review*. Video of the interview is available at digitalcommons.brockport.edu/writers_videos/32.

Joseph Heller interview reprinted by permission of John Mosier and *New Orleans Review*.

Christopher Isherwood interview reprinted by permission of Sarah Smith, Marcus Smith, and *New Orleans Review*.

Anaïs Nin interview reprinted by permission of Jeffrey Bailey and *New Orleans Review*.

Lina Wertmüller interview reprinted by permission of Paulist Press and *New Orleans Review*.

Bertrand Tavernier interview reprinted by permission of John Mosier and *New Orleans Review*.

Eudora Welty interview reprinted by permission of Jeanne Rolfe Nostrandt and *New Orleans Review*.

James Tate interview reprinted by permission of Connie Bellamy and *New Orleans Review*.

Jorge Luis Borges interview reprinted by permission of John Biguenet and *New Orleans Review*.

Catharine Stimpson interview reprinted by permission of Mark Lussier and *New Orleans Review*.

Carolyn Heilbrun interview reprinted by permission of Mark Lussier and *New Orleans Review*.

Armando Valladares interview reprinted by permission of William Marling and *New Orleans Review*.

James Baldwin interview reprinted by permission of David C. Estes and *New Orleans Review*.

John Ashbery interview reprinted by permission of Paul Munn and
    New Orleans Review. The poem "At North Farm" reprinted with
    permission of the Georges Borchardt Agency.

Valerie Martin interview reprinted by permission of Mary McCay,
    Christine Wiltz, and *New Orleans Review*.

Jack Gilbert interview reprinted by permission of Ralph Adamo, John
    Biguenet, and *New Orleans Review*.

Sheila Heti interview reprinted by permission of Ari Braverman,
    Room 220, and *New Orleans Review*.

Susan Bernofsky interview reprinted by permission of Clark Allen,
    Room 220, and *New Orleans Review*.

Francine Prose interview reprinted by permission of Ari Braverman,
    Room 220, and *New Orleans Review*.

Harold Jaffe interview reprinted by permission of Robin Andreasen and
    New Orleans Review.

Yuri Herrera interview reprinted by permission of Elizabeth Sulis Kim
    and *New Orleans Review*.

Viet Thanh Nguyen interview reprinted by permission of Elizabeth Sulis
    Kim and *New Orleans Review*.

Luisa Valenzuela interview reprinted by permission of Elizabeth Sulis Kim
    and *New Orleans Review*.

Sister Helen Prejean interview reprinted by permission of Mark Yakich
    and *New Orleans Review*.

INDEX